Sensing *the* Future

How to Tap Into Your Intuition and Read Signs From the Universe to Predict What's to Come

Trish MacGregor

renowned astrologer and author of *The Biggest Book of Horoscopes Ever*

Rob MacGregor

author of *Psychic Power* and *Jewel in the Lotus: Meditation for Busy Minds*

First published in 2017 by
Page Street Publishing Co.
27 Congress Street, Suite 105
Salem, MA 01970
www.pagestreetpublishing.com

Distributed by Macmillan, sales in Canada by The Canadian Manda Group.

20 19 18 17 1 2 3 4

ISBN-13: 978-1-62414-334-2
ISBN-10: 1-62414-334-2

Library of Congress Control Number: 2016941507

Cover and book design by Page Street Publishing Co.

Printed and bound in the United States

For Megan, with much love always.

We would also like to thank:

All of you who allowed us to use your stories; Al Zuckerman, agent extraordinaire; and Will Kiester and his terrific staff at Page Street.

Contents

Introduction: Your Greatest Ally

Does precognition mean the future is determined in advance? Does it mean free will is impossible? Does it lead to paradoxes whereby knowledge of the future changes the present, which in turn can change the future?

—Rupert Sheldrake

A few years ago, we were driving on a narrow mountain road in the Andes, outside of Quito, Ecuador. A wall of rock rose on our left and a cliff plunged several hundred feet on our immediate right. There wasn't any guardrail. Just ahead, a sharp turn was visible. As Rob tapped on the brakes, we both experienced a powerful feeling that we should stop. It was an illogical thing to do on this narrow road, but the feeling was nearly overwhelming. Rob slammed on the brakes and seconds later, a car barreled around the curve, swerving well into our lane. If he hadn't taken the action he did, we would have been in the car's path and possibly plummeted into the abyss.

This is how precognition usually works. The warning signal was involuntary, unexpected and thrust suddenly into our awareness. We had motored around numerous curves on this road without stopping. But in this instance, we somehow had pierced the veil of time and glimpsed the future. By taking the action we did, we *changed* the future.

As self-employed writers for more than 30 years, we have found precognition to be an invaluable tool in many facets of our profession. We started out as freelance magazine writers and, early on, paid close attention to our hunches and impulses about which magazines to query. One night, Rob dreamed of writing on red paper. So, when we noticed that *OMNI Magazine* featured a section called "Anti-Matter" that dealt with things that go bump in the night, the paranormal and UFOs, not only did that subject matter interest us, but the "Anti-Matter" section had been published on red paper! We sent the editor a query and subsequently received numerous assignments for articles that were featured in the "Anti-Matter" section. As a result, a new world of experiences and contacts opened up for us.

Precognition grabbed us and wouldn't let go.

Once we came to accept how it benefited our professional lives, we started paying attention to subtle hunches that foretold events to come. We saw these premonitions as a facet of synchronicity or meaningful coincidence, when similar internal and external events came together in a way we found meaningful and couldn't be explained by cause and effect. For example, you think of someone you haven't seen since high school and, a couple of hours later, that person sends you a friend request on Facebook. That's synchronicity *and* precognition.

Over the years, precognitive dreams and hunches have led us to the sources we needed, to agents, editors and publishing houses, and to a vast spectrum of opportunities as writers. They have guided us in our personal lives as well. It's our hope that *Sensing the Future* not only entertains you, but that it opens you to the possibility that precognition may be your greatest ally. It's invisible yet tangible, sometimes bewildering or confusing, but your best interest lies at the heart of it, and it's as close to you as your own skin. By becoming aware of your own innate precognitive abilities and developing them, you can hurl open new doors that enrich your life.

What Is Precognition?

Precognition is the least understood of psychic experiences, but also occurs the most frequently. The greatest misconceptions about precognition are that it isn't really possible or it's an ability that's accessible only to talented psychics. Yet we all experience it—perhaps as a sense of foreboding, a premonition, an impulse or urge to do something that seems unreasonable or maybe even irrational. But we often dismiss such feelings as random and meaningless. As a result, we fail to benefit from an insight or miss an opportunity.

It may be that precognition was more prevalent when we lived in caves or tribes and needed to know where the largest herd would be, where the nearest enemy would be located or what areas would be safest. But even in today's world of instantaneous information and technological wonders, precognition is an inner GPS that guides us in particular directions, toward certain people and experiences. Like any ally, it can offer needed reassurance.

Precognition occurs most frequently in dreams, when our conscious mind can't hurl up defenses and barriers to information about the future and our unconscious mind is open. When we sleep, we are closer to what Michael Talbot, author of *The Holographic Universe: The Revolutionary Theory of Reality*, called the "primal ocean, in which past, present and future are one." In dreams, precognition may be couched in symbolism or it may be so simple and direct that there's no mistaking what it means.

The Symbolic and the Simple

A writer friend dreamed that he was in his car, driving up a steep hill, when the brakes on the vehicle suddenly failed. His car started rolling downhill, picking up speed, a situation that in real life would be terrifying. But at no time in the dream was he frightened. The car finally stopped at the foot of the hill; the car hadn't been damaged and he wasn't hurt. Then, he woke up.

He understood the symbolism. The car represented him. At the time, he was experiencing financial difficulties, was blocked on his next book and was besieged by creditors. He suspected that things were going to get worse—the rapid descent downhill—and that his best recourse was to trust that he wouldn't be injured.

His home eventually went into foreclosure and he was forced to move in with his parents. Even though the process was difficult and challenging, he held hope that the situation would work out and improve. And it did. Within a few years, he overcame his block and went on to write a *New York Times* bestselling novel.

By contrast, Trish had a simple precognitive dream. After returning from a writers' conference, she dreamed that she was still at the conference and someone handed her a telephone message: "Your mother has just passed away."

At the time, her mother was in an Alzheimer's facility. The dream was so vivid that she knew her mother's death was imminent. Her mother died a few weeks later.

These examples illustrate how precognition can be of important personal benefit. During the chaos the writer experienced when he lost his home and was forced to move in with his parents, he kept believing in the dream, that he would come out okay in the end. Trish's precog about her mother's death enabled her and her family to prepare themselves emotionally for her mother's death.

Sensing the Future through Creativity

Although precognitive experiences often serve as warnings, they sometimes relate to creative acts that can have tremendous emotional momentum behind them. When our daughter was eight, her third-grade class was assigned a Thanksgiving project: create an object from clay that symbolizes something for which you're grateful. The objects were to be presented the day that school got out for the holiday and parents were invited to attend.

Megan created a brownish red dog from her lump of clay. At the time, we had three cats, but no dog and no plans to get one. We were puzzled when she got up with the clay dog in her hands and announced that she was grateful for the golden retriever she *was going to get*. Precognitive gratitude! The sculpture looked like a golden retriever. When we asked her about it later, she insisted that a retriever would be hers.

A couple of weeks later, shortly before Christmas, a family friend asked whether we would adopt a dog that needed a home. We said we would try out the dog for a week and picked up Jessie, a red-toned golden retriever. She immediately got along famously with our cats, settled in front of Rob's desk, made herself at home in Megan's room and started her new life with us.

In creating the clay dog, Megan was expressing a powerful desire that she may not have known she had. After all, prior to her sculpting project, she had never mentioned wanting a dog. Did that desire resonate within such a deep part of herself that it eventually materialized full-blown into her life, as the reality she had glimpsed?

Throughout history, numerous examples exist of how writers, artists, moviemakers and others in creative professions depicted inventions and details about future events that they realistically had no way of knowing. In 1865, Jules Verne wrote *From the Earth to the Moon.* The novel describes the details of the space capsule that in 1969 sent astronauts to the moon, the number of astronauts on the mission, how long the voyage would last and even its splashdown in the ocean. He also predicted light-propelled spacecraft now known as solar sails. How could a man living in the time of the Civil War do this with such accuracy?

Leonardo da Vinci, who lived in the 15th century, was a master precog. Many of his inventions are used today, more than 500 years later: the parachute; the anemometer, which measures the velocity of wind; the precursor to the armored car; a self-propelled cart that could move without being pushed—that is, the car! He also designed scuba gear, a revolving bridge and a flying machine.

Are we, through our creative endeavors, able to dive into the archetypal well of ideas where time does not exist?

Physicist David Bohm believed there is a deeper order in reality, the enfolded or implicate order, a kind of primal soup that births everything in the universe—consciousness, space, even time. He referred to our external reality as the explicate or unfolded order. Is it possible that during intense creative periods, when our right brain is jammed into overdrive, we're able to tap into that primal soup? Perhaps precognition is where the implicate and the explicate, the inner and the outer, collide.

This collision certainly does seem to have occurred in Steven Spielberg's 2002 movie *Minority Report*, about a future where "precogs" detect crimes before they happen. The movie, starring Tom Cruise, is set in 2054, a time when criminals are arrested *before* they commit their crimes, thanks to three precogs working for PreCrime, a specialized police division. Spielberg set out to make the movie as technologically futuristic in appearance as possible so that it wouldn't quickly look outdated like other science-fiction movies, such as *Blade Runner*, which today resembles the world of the 1980s rather than the future.

Many of the technological advancements seen in the film are already in existence or in the developmental stage, suggesting that Spielberg had real-life "precog" advisers working for him. An article published in 2012 in *WIRED* describes the uncanny way that tech advisers for that film accurately foresaw the future. Among them:

- *Iris recognition scans as an ID are seen repeatedly in the movie. By mid-2015, a few hundred million people in several countries were enrolled in iris recognition systems that are used for passport-free automated border crossings.*

- *The highways and even the outer walls of skyscrapers in the world of 2054 are dominated by self-driving cars in a system called "individual mass transit." The vehicles are voice-activated and run using magnetic levitation, a technology that lets vehicles float inches above a surface. In the real world, the self-driving vehicles have already been designed and are expected to be on the road, at least on highways, by 2017 to 2020, well ahead of 2054. Google already has a driverless vehicle with no steering wheel or pedals that in 2015 was prowling the streets of San Francisco.*

- *In the movie, eight-legged bots scramble about a flophouse, their sensors—including iris scanners—track residents and relay that information to authorities. Pure fiction or the distant future? Think again. The US military, aided by British Aerospace, is developing a fleet of insect robots made specifically for reconnaissance missions. The goal is to equip soldiers with an extra pair of eyes in urban environments and other potentially hostile areas.*

- *In the movie, three precogs lie in a shallow pool of water, their brains linked to police computers that display their visions of crimes to come. Equipped with the precrime data, the cops will be able to swoop down and arrest the bad guys before they break the law. So much for constitutional rights. Revelations of massive spying programs on US citizens aside, predictive policing is already underway in a few police departments. Police in Chicago and Los Angeles use an algorithm that analyzes crime data and allows them to predict crime trends and locations. No precrime arrests are made, but hot spots receive more attention by cops on patrol. While investigators occasionally use psychics to help solve crimes, no departments have publicized any program where precogs look for future criminal activity. But then, 2054 is still a ways off.*

Tuning In

Precognition can't be taught, but we can create internal climates that are more conducive to it happening. Meditation, deep relaxation, yoga, hypnosis, shamanic journeys and spiritual retreats help open up our consciousness to these experiences. But unless we acknowledge that precognition is possible and recognize it when it occurs, we may just dismiss that crazy dream or that weird feeling as meaningless. And we do so at our own peril.

When Dr. Ian Stevenson, now deceased, was a professor of psychiatry at the University of Virginia Medical School, he researched paranormal experiences connected to the sinking of the *Titanic*. Writing about his findings in 1960, in the *Journal of the American Society for Psychical Research*, he found nineteen documented cases of passengers who had premonitions about the voyage. Some of the nineteen heeded the premonition and survived. Others didn't heed it and drowned.

If the *Titanic* had occurred in the 21st century with our 24/7 news coverage, would more people have tuned in on the disaster before it happened? Undoubtedly. Look what occurred during the recent tragic bombings in Paris, where more than 100 people were killed. People being held hostage inside the Bataclan theater were tweeting for help. It was news all over the world.

So, yes, you can bet that the launch of the *Titanic* would be covered extensively, would feature interviews with passengers, the ship's captain and the people who built the unsinkable ship. It would make headlines on websites, photos of the ship would be plastered everywhere, passengers would be tweeting and texting about it and posting pictures on Facebook. Wikipedia would have an entry about it. *Awareness* about the impending voyage would be so heightened that its sinking would be considered a mass event.

Mass events, such as the 9/11 attacks, the bombings in Paris and at the Boston Marathon, are so dramatic that many people tune into them in advance. In the aftermath of 9/11, dozens of people reported dreams that seemed to relate to the upcoming disaster. Scientists consider such dreams as anecdotal evidence, not proof of precognition. They require proof through laboratory experiments. However, ignoring instances of precognition that occur outside of the lab overlooks important examples.

Take the computer-related documentation of precognition connected to the shooting of congresswoman Gabriel Giffords (D-AZ) during a speech in Tucson in January 2011. The deranged shooter killed six and injured fourteen, but Gifford survived. The incident and the issue of gun control attracted widespread attention in the days that followed.

On January 4, four days *before* the tragic event, the number of hits on Gifford's Wikipedia page spiked as people looked up information about her. Meanwhile, Raul Grijalva, a fellow Democratic congressman from Arizona, experienced no bump on his page. According to economist J. Bradford Delong of the University of California, Berkeley, "By Friday, January 7, more than three times as many people were looking at Gabrielle Gifford's Wikipedia page than had done so in a normal day in the previous month and a half."

Was the upcoming violent event on our collective unconscious radar days before it happened? The computer data suggests that might have been the case. If Gifford or someone on her staff had noticed the spike in visits, would she have canceled her speech in Tucson? Probably not, if there was no emotional reaction to the shift.

So, even though we all have precognitive abilities individually and collectively, it doesn't matter unless we're paying attention. If the precognition is dire, then recognition is vital in order for us to take some sort of action that might change what we've seen. Granted, most of us won't be shot by deranged ideologues or board ships that will sink or planes that will crash. But we might miss opportunities that would otherwise enrich our lives—the perfect job or career, meeting the right romantic partner, finding the ideal home or winning the lottery.

Precognition and Synchronicity

Recently, a friend remarked that the Internet seems to act like a huge synchronicity machine. You might be listening to a particular song, for instance, and then when you open Facebook, someone has posted the words of that song. That's both synchronicity and precognition, and the immediacy is facilitated by social media. We are connected to one another as never before and this interconnected world is one of sound bites and brief visuals, where everything is instantaneous, in your face, happening *now.*

Douglas Rushkoff, in his book *Present Shock: When Everything Happens Now*, calls this phenomenon "presentism." His title is a strange twist on Alvin Toffler's 1970 *Future Shock,* and takes an in-depth look at what happens "when we try to make sense of the world entirely in the present tense. Without a timeline through which to parse causes and effects, we instead attempt to draw connections from one thing to another in the frozen moment, even when such connections are forced or imaginary."

One thing is certain: The shift to an omniscient *now* has triggered a growing collective awareness that the underlying reality—David Bohm's implicate or enfolded order—gives birth to our external lives and to both space and time. In this marvelous, confusing *now*, synchronicity and its jeweled facets engage us, grab us and whisper, *pay attention in your now—and see the past, the future, the you that you were, are and might be.*

And one way we do that is by drawing upon those jeweled facets—telepathy, clairvoyance, psychokinesis and precognition. In fact, if we're all living more in the now than at any point in history, then the future is closer to us than ever before and much more accessible. Dip into it, listen to it, engage with it and use what you learn to sculpt the life that you desire.

In the chapters ahead, you'll discover more about precognition, how you can recognize and develop your own skills and how you can put them to use to live a happier, more productive, abundant and creative life.

We Are All Precogs

Any precog will tell you that if you have the will to develop your precognitive abilities, you can do it. It's just as natural as the human brain, and just as powerful and mysterious.

—Ari Lakakis, *Earth Unchained* blog

Researchers say the ability to glimpse the future is a common talent, but when we experience it, our left brain often interferes and hurls up arguments that contradict what we're glimpsing. These left-brain objections and arguments are usually rooted in our cultural mass beliefs, which prove to be powerful and persuasive. We are so conditioned to thinking that precognition is impossible that our natural precognitive abilities to sense future events have gone dormant.

Children, however, aren't fully embedded in society's mind-set. They tend to heed precognitive nudges that adults might ignore. That was the case in the dramatic story recorded by David Adams in his book *Test Your Own Super Mind: Your Hidden Powers and How to Use Them*, in which a child's premonition saved the life of his mother and sister, and possibly his own life as well.

In 1972, Margaret Woellner was at home with her two children in Witzenhausen, Germany, when the incident occurred. At the time, her daughter, Ulrike, was three years old and her son, Joachim, was ten. The boy was playing outside when a voice inside his head urged him to get his mother and sister out of the house immediately or it would be too late. The voice was so insistent that Joachim rushed into the house, where his mother was making lunch and his sister was playing on the floor nearby.

Margaret recalls that Joachim's expression was "a mask of horror." He shouted, "Mother, get out of here! Something terrible is going to happen!"

She didn't know what was going on, but sensed something was terribly wrong, so she scooped up Ulrike and fled outside. Just seconds later, a deafening explosion rocked the house, followed by a ball of fire that quickly engulfed the entire structure. The kitchen, where minutes earlier Margaret had been standing, was reduced to a blackened, smoldering crater. Nobody could have survived the blast and fire.

The explanation for the blast was a leaking gas pipe, but how did Joachim know that he should warn his mother? When questioned, he said: "I just had a strange idea. It was as if there was a voice inside me saying, 'Go and fetch your mother and sister, otherwise it will be too late.'"

Joachim's story illustrates that when our need and desire are great, a window between now and the future may hurl open. What we do with the information depends on our particular beliefs. Michael Talbot, writing about people who sense the future, noted: "Like the superhuman strengths individuals display during life-threatening emergencies, they only spill over into our conscious minds during times of crisis—when someone near to us is about to die, when our children or some other loved one is in danger, and so on."

Younger children might even confuse the future and past, as Mary T reported in a post at Mike Perry's blog, *67 Not Out*: "Jake was home from nursery as he hadn't been feeling too well. I was doing some housework and he said to me, 'Mummy, tell me about the car crash we were in. It was when a red car crashed into us and I was in the front seat.'"

She told him they'd never had a car accident, and he said no more about it and went back to playing with his Legos. Later that day, Mary remembered that she needed some bread. So, she strapped Jake into his car seat in the front passenger position and headed to a local shop. They had gone only a few blocks when a car came out of a side road and collided with Mary's car. Nobody was hurt. "Later I realized that the other car in the collision was red. It was as if Jake had known about the crash four hours before it happened."

Ingo Swann, who died in 2013, was a talented and well-known psychic researcher who became convinced that everyone has the ability to see the future. He was probably best known for being the co-creator—along with Russell Targ and Hal Puthoff—of the remote viewing (clairvoyance) project at Stanford Research Institute (SRI) in the 1970s. That project eventually became the US government's Stargate project that involved psychic spying.

Swann also wrote several books about remote viewing and psychic phenomena, including *Your Nostradamus Factor: Accessing Your Innate Ability to See into the Future.* The premise is that any of us can see the future—something that Swann didn't understand until April 1988, when he was invited to give a series of lectures on psychic (psi) research in Dermold, then in West Germany. He was billed as the famous American superpsychic who had astonished scientists since his first formal laboratory experiments at SRI in 1970.

Other speakers were there, too, some of them practicing psychics who were doing readings. The irony was that Swann didn't do individual readings. Despite all his research into prophecy and prediction, he didn't provide any general predictions about the future, either. He knew that many predictions turned out to be wrong and felt he had a scientific reputation to protect.

After he gave the keynote address, he asked for questions from the audience of several hundred people. The room was utterly silent. Finally, an elderly woman asked Swann to give the group at least one prediction. Irritated about being put in this position, he frantically sought a diplomatic way to get out of the situation.

As his irritation escalated into anger, he heard a rushing sound around him and had a sense that his body was getting larger: "Then there was a clarity of some unfamiliar kind, which was somehow like liquid, and in this liquidness what seemed like a thousand pictures flashed through my consciousness. I had the distinct, lightning-like impression that most of the people in the audience *already knew the future* at some 'place' deep within them. And I knew their conscious minds were disconnected from this deep place."

He felt he knew what they knew collectively and an aspect of this "hidden knowledge" exploded into his consciousness. He blurted, "Okay, you want a prediction? Here's a prediction. The Berlin Wall will come down in eighteen to twenty-four months." The translator repeated the prediction twice. After an initial silence, the people in the audience began rising to their feet, clapping, and then the crowd, Swann wrote, "became unglued." People burst into tears, hugged one another, and some people even rushed to the podium and hugged him.

Swan couldn't understand why he'd blurted it. After all, at the time he gave this prediction, it looked as if the Berlin Wall would be standing well into the 21st century. He felt his colleagues would believe he had lost his marbles.

However, nineteen months later, the Berlin Wall came down practically overnight. Swann felt vindicated: "I had one of the most rewarding experiences of my life . . . watching my prediction come true on real-time television right before my eyes."

As he watched the wall coming down, he wondered whether he could foresee other things. By the end of 1990, he had discovered the answer was yes. And that answer was one of the reasons he wrote *Your Nostradamus Factor*, telling us that we can do the same.

If everyone is a precog, as Swann insisted, then why can't we win the lottery every week? A valid question. Apparently, our unconscious mind, part of the implicate order—the hidden reality and the source of precognitive experiences—isn't as concerned about winning the lottery as our conscious self is. So, when we say that everyone is a precog, it doesn't mean that everyone *controls* the process. In fact, precognitions are usually spontaneous and involuntary.

When Rob mentioned to Trish the sad fact that neither of them could foresee the right lotto numbers, she asked him whether he'd read her latest blog post. He hadn't and to his surprise found that it was about that very subject. She explained in the post that she'd bought a Powerball ticket for $2, a long-shot chance at winning $154 million. As she came home, she called out the randomly generated numbers on the ticket. Rob looked up from what he was doing and asked, "What was the Powerball number?" When she answered 23, he said, "Oh, a good number. What do you win if you only get the Powerball number?"

She thought it was odd that he was only interested in that number. When she looked up the winning numbers the next day, she found that the Powerball pick was 23, the only one of her six numbers that matched. She won $4. Rob had picked out the one winning number, an example of a lottery precog, however paltry the winnings!

But if you pick all the right numbers and win the lottery, does it make you a precog? Well, maybe. You might just be a lucky guesser who beat the enormous odds. However, if you dreamed of those numbers or saw them in a vision, then won with them, that definitely would qualify as precognition.

A Common Talent

Since the early part of the 20th century when the scientific study of precognition began in earnest, researchers have had no difficulty gathering anecdotal evidence. While such evidence isn't considered to be scientific proof, it supports results of laboratory experiments that suggest we are all precogs.

In 1934, during a radio interview on BBC, Dame Edith Lyttelton, president of the British Society for Psychical Research, invited listeners to send her accounts of their precognitive experiences. She received so many responses that even after weeding out stories that lacked corroborative evidence, she still had enough to write a book, *Some Cases of Prediction.* Similarly, Louisa Rhine, wife of renowned parapsychologist J. B. Rhine, gathered thousands of cases of paranormal experiences—many of them instances of sensing the future—before publishing *Hidden Channels of the Mind* in 1962.

Carl Jung considered synchronicity—or meaningful coincidence—an umbrella phenomenon that included paranormal experiences such as telepathy, clairvoyance, psychokinesis and precognition. In other words, a vision or inkling of a future event that comes to pass is both a precog and synchronicity.

A straightforward example of a precognition happened to Rob in April 2015. He was supposed to be interviewed by a reporter from the *Tallahassee Democrat* for an article that would publicize an upcoming writers' conference where he would be the keynote speaker. He'd forgotten all about the planned interview when it occurred to him that the deadline might be near for getting an article published in time for the conference. Within seconds, an e-mail arrived from the reporter, who was ready to move ahead.

Rob's experience was a precognition in the sense that he thought about the interview moments before receiving updated information about it. However, the timing between his thought and the e-mail was so close that it could be considered a telepathic experience. Either way, it also fit as a synchronicity—similar inner and outer events coming together in a way that is meaningful to the individual and can't be explained by cause and effect.

Everyday Precog Dramas

Ben Goertzel, a scientist involved in artificial intelligence research, has an interest in parapsychology and wrote a lengthy analysis of a well-known precognition experiment by Daryl Bern that we touch on later in the chapter. In his article, he mentions that he doesn't believe that he has any particularly strong psychic abilities himself, but in his daily life he has witnessed some rather striking examples of psi phenomena involving others.

"For instance, one day a few years ago, a friend and I were walking in the forest with her beloved dog, and the dog ran far away from us, exploring the woods and chasing animals. Then, all of the sudden, my friend said, 'She [the dog] is looking at a turtle. I can see it right now as if it were in front of me.'

"I was understandably skeptical: 'Yeah, right. How could you know?' Turtles were not that commonly seen in those woods."

Goertzel was about to call the dog, but his friend stopped him. Instead, they quietly looked for the dog, and found her about 100 feet (30.5 m) away in the woods, staring intently at a turtle resting by a stream. "Strange and striking—and, like so many other real-life anecdotes of psi phenomena, damnably hard to replicate in a lab," Goertzel concluded.

When Rob read the story, he was reminded of a precognition he'd experienced a couple of weeks earlier that also involved a turtle in a wooded area. He and two friends were mountain biking along a narrow trail in a county park in South Florida when Rob suddenly knew, without knowing why, that there would be a land turtle on the trail. About five minutes later, the lead rider suddenly stopped and nearly toppled over. On the trail in front of him was a land turtle. When Rob mentioned his precog, his friends weren't impressed. One of them said there were undoubtedly lots of tortoises in the park. Maybe so. But there was only one on the trail where they were riding and it was only minutes ahead of Rob's premonition.

Precrime Precog

In Spielberg's *Minority Report*, the precogs were psychic crime-stoppers who caught the bad guys before they acted. If there are any precogs today performing precrime skills in such laboratory conditions, it's a well-kept secret. But outside of the lab, in real life, uncontrolled precog experiences happen, even with crime-stopping results.

When Connie Cannon, a retired nurse, lived in Georgia in the 1970s, she was involved in Wicca and progressed through the degrees of magical skills at the House of Ravenwood, her Wiccan coven.

> *"One night I bolted upright in bed, wide awake. In the dresser mirror across from the end of the bed, an image began to play out. I saw Ravenwood, an old two-story Victorian home with a front porch and lots of trees and shrubs in the front. In the mirror, I saw a short, bulky man with shoulder-length hair, wearing a red plaid shirt, walking up the sidewalk toward the porch. He carried a pistol that he held down alongside his leg, and I knew he was planning to kill our high priestess, Lady Sintana. I glanced at the clock. It was exactly 3:30 a.m. Psychically, I knew it was going to occur the next night."*

She drove to Ravenwood the next morning and told Lady Sintana details of her waking vision. The Atlanta police were called and Connie repeated the story to the officer who arrived. He didn't laugh. In fact, he took the information seriously enough so that an officer was posted that night on the front porch in a spot where he couldn't be detected. At the request of authorities, Lady Sintana stayed elsewhere that night.

"At exactly 3:30 a.m., a short, stocky man in a red plaid shirt walked up the sidewalk toward the porch. They snagged him, and he did have the pistol I'd seen—a .38. They learned he was a religious fanatic who considered Wicca to be satanic and was intent on 'killing the witch.'" After that, the Atlanta police occasionally used Connie on an on-call basis. In Lady Sintana's case, she was in a position to help prevent a murder; "In most instances, I just get the visions but can't do anything, even if I understand the message."

No doubt Connie moved up a notch in the Wiccan degree system after that incident. She recalls one other instance when her precog abilities might have saved a life. It happened during a reading for a woman named Rosie. In Connie's words:

"I wanted no information from her, which is just my way of working, and went into my alpha state. My spiritual helpers instructed me to tell Rosie that her husband of 25 years, who was healthy, would sustain a stroke in May. He would be admitted to a nursing home and would die by the last day of June. Afterward, her life would be much lighter and brighter."

Connie silently argued with her guides about predicting the man's death; she never predicted death. But they insisted it was necessary for her to tell Rosie, so she did. That night, Rosie told Connie that she couldn't tolerate her life with Jack any longer, but the reading had calmed her.

Weeks later, Rosie called again and told her that Jack had suffered a stroke. On June 30, a few minutes before midnight, he died. "Rosie's life improved afterward, and I was grateful I'd been the messenger. These events happen rarely, but I'm deeply honored that I was able to help."

In the Laboratory

According to mainstream science, time flows in just one direction—from the past to the future by way of the present. We can remember the past and we can attempt to predict the future based on past events. But we can't *perceive* the future. However, some scientists, aware of the astonishing anecdotal evidence, have attempted to duplicate precognition in laboratory settings.

In spite of strong skepticism in the scientific community, paranormal research over the decades repeatedly has shown that the ability to perceive future events is widespread. Experiments in the 1930s to test precognitive abilities were similar to those for telepathy and involved guessing cards. But in the precognitive studies, the subject would guess the order in which cards would appear *before* they were shuffled. On average, subjects did better than would be expected by chance. To avoid human error, cards were soon shuffled by a machine. In later experiments, the cards were replaced with automated tests on computers with symbols generated randomly.

Dean Radin, in *The Conscious Universe*, points out that between 1935 and 1987, 50,000 subjects were tested for precognition in a total of nearly 2 million individual trials. Precognitive effects were replicated by dozens of different investigators and studies were reported in 113 scientific articles. The combined results of these studies produced odds against chance of 10^{24} to 1.

In spite of the positive, scientifically obtained results, most scientists don't accept the reality of precognition or other paranormal abilities. "Many scientists are so convinced that paranormal functioning does not exist that no amount of evidence, no matter how substantiated or credible, will ever persuade them that it does," wrote Michael Talbot in *Beyond the Quantum*. He cited an incident that Hal Puthoff and Russell Targ experienced when they submitted an article on remote viewing. One of the responses they received from an alleged expert consulted by the editor of the periodical pretty much summed up the scientific take on the paranormal: "This is the kind of thing that I would not believe in even if it existed."

Instead, mainstream science refers to the study of such phenomena as pseudoscience. In his book, *Why People Believe Weird Things: Pseudoscience, Superstition, and Other Confusions of Our Time*, arch-skeptic Michael Shermer defines pseudoscience as "claims presented so that they appear [to be] scientific even though they lack supporting evidence and plausibility."

Even J. B. Rhine, who spent decades in parapsychological research at Duke University, initially dismissed precognition as impossible. However, when lab results repeatedly showed otherwise, he became convinced that science needed to change so as to accommodate the phenomenon.

Meanwhile, a National Science Foundation study in 2003 found that 60 percent of Americans believed that some individuals possess psychic abilities. In spite of the reticence of mainstream science, a small community of scientists, who often have difficulty obtaining funds for their research, continue to study precognition and related subjects.

Feeling the "Erotic" Future

In 2011, one of those scientists, Daryl Bern, a professor at Cornell and formerly at Harvard, published a controversial study, "Feeling the Future," in the *Journal of Personality and Social Psychology*. His experiments involved 1,000 Cornell students viewing erotic photos and found statistically significant results confirming that many people can glimpse the future.

Among the nine experiments he conducted was one that provided students with a computer monitor showing a pair of curtains, side by side. The students were directed to select the curtain that hid an erotic photo. The idea was that such stimuli normally produces certain human responses. The question was whether the response could be obtained before the stimulus occurred. In essence, the students were asked to "feel" the future—the curtain hiding a photo of explicit sexual activity.

The answer was a resounding yes. Across all 100 sessions, participants correctly identified the future position of the erotic pictures more frequently than the 50 percent hit rate expected by chance. The results were 53.1 percent, considered statistically significant.

One reviewer of Bern's experiment, writing at h+ Magazine, asked why, if precognition exists and we are all precogs to varying degrees, weren't the results of the experiments higher? Why didn't some subjects hit 95 or 100 percent accuracy? Ben Goertzel, a scientist mentioned earlier in the chapter, responded to his own query: "Of course, outside the lab, people have reported many apparent cases of extremely dramatic psi effects. But the long history of parapsychology lab research, going back far before Bern to Rhine's ESP work in the 1930s, shows that when you bring psi into the lab, it tends to become more of a systematic statistical biasing factor than a source of individual mind-blowing 'miracle' events."

Interestingly, when students were asked to find nonerotic photos, their accuracy dropped to about 50 percent, what would be expected by chance. Laboratory studies of paranormal phenomena have also shown that subjects are less successful when they are not told the ongoing results of their efforts.

Skeptics often point out that parapsychology experiments in laboratory settings that get positive results are difficult to replicate. However, scientists and researchers like Dean Radin, in their books on the subject, cite a multitude of studies finding the same results. Those studies, though, often aren't exact replications of other experiments, which scientists find so important.

In the aftermath of the Bern study, other scientists attempted to replicate Bern's "Feeling the Future" experiments. If you Google the subject, you'll find numerous articles exclaiming how those scientists were unsuccessful. In 2013, the skeptical group CSICOP reveled in the supposed lack of replication. In response, Dean Radin responded that the "CSICOP article on Bern's psi experiments is a fine example of how that org is more about propaganda than science." He went on to point out that "80-some replications of the 'Bern effect' show a highly significant overall effect." In 2014, the *Daily Grail* listed eight successful replications of Bern's study.

Regarding scientists who consider positive results of precog experiments as mere anomalies, there's an apt quote in the novel *Mental Radio*, by Upton Sinclair: "It is foolish to be convinced without evidence, but it is equally foolish to refuse to be convinced by real evidence."

Major Turning Points

Precognitions often occur when our life is in flux, undergoing momentous shifts and turning points. They can act as guidance or confirmation and provide insight about possible directions we might take. The death of a parent certainly qualifies as a major turning point.

Three months after sculptor Lauren Raines's mother passed away, she felt that her life was changing significantly—both internally and externally. "I'm no longer a caretaker, and see that role slipping away from me gradually, like a skin peeling off. What's underneath feels rather brittle and hypersensitive."

This feeling stayed with her when she traveled several times to California from her home in Arizona for guest artist appearances at a renaissance fair held in Santa Fe Dam in Los Angeles, a magnificent park with an impressive view of the mountains that ring the city.

> *"On the other side of the park, from the fair, is a nature walk. It has beautiful indigenous plants and a sandy area with a stone circle. I walked into the circle, made some offerings, and created a circle and cross with some stones in the center that represented the four directions—a kind of prayer, a way of centering myself.*
>
> *"The next day, my booth was set up and opened onto a sandy path. In the heat and the hum of voices passing by, it can get rather hypnotic, unless I'm working with a customer. As I sat in the back of the booth, I noticed a man with a carved staff of some kind in front of my booth. He used his staff to create a circle with a cross in it in the sand. I watched him do it, then he walked off and disappeared in the crowd. It was the exact symbol I had created the previous day! It's also the symbol of the four directions and a Native American motif called 'Spider Woman's Cross.'"*

Lauren wrote about her observations on her blog, Threads of the Spiderwoman, and explains that this particular motif occurs on prehistoric Mississippian amulets, in Pueblo pottery and is woven into Navajo

(Dine) rugs as a sacred motif representing Grandmother Spider Woman; "It is a ubiquitous symbol of balance, wholeness, unity. It's also a symbol I've explored in my own humble way in my sculptures because I feel Spider Woman is very important for our time."

Lauren's precognition of the exact symbol the man with the stick would draw in front of her booth the next day was a powerful affirmation for her that she was on the right track with her art. But even more important is that the symbol itself is about wholeness and unity, the very thing she felt had been lacking since her mother passed away. For her, it also became a symbol of healing.

Your Precog IQ

The theme of this chapter, of course, is that everyone is a precog. But, like with any skill, there are different degrees. They range from those who don't know they're precogs to those who experience involuntary precognitions to practitioners capable of programming precognitive experiences through dreams, meditation or other alternative states of consciousness.

Here are a few keys to judging your own abilities and understanding your potential for expanding your innate skills:

- *Do you have a longtime interest in mysteries of the unknown and the so-called paranormal phenomena? Or is it a more recent interest, or simply a curiosity, possibly stimulated by events in your life? Are you surrounded by those who disbelieve in psychic abilities or lack interest in exploring matters outside the everyday world? Or do you associate with one or more people, possibly a group, to investigate matters of the unknown?*
- *Do you experience synchronicities that often happen during times of stress and high drama, travel or significant points of change in your life, such as marriage, divorce or death of a loved one? These meaningful coincidences link you with a deeper part of yourself or a deeper reality that exists outside time and space.*
- *Do you have vivid dreams that you remember when you wake up? Do you record your dreams, talk about them, interpret them? Do you ever come "awake" in a dream where you can consciously manipulate the events? Lucid dreams sometimes contain hints of things to come.*
- *Do you sometimes anticipate what someone is going to say or do, even though you have no conscious reason to know what the person is planning? Do you know when the phone is about to ring or who is calling when it does ring?*
- *Do you pay attention to signs and symbols that appear in your dreams and daily life? Do you ever pose a question and then watch for the first unusual thing to appear in the outer world? Likewise, do you look for answers by interpreting stray bits of conversation around you that you overhear from strangers or on the radio or television?*
- *Do you sense how people feel, even though their appearance doesn't give away their true feelings? Do you have a sense of empathy and compassion related to the trials others are facing?*

Testing Your Precog Ability

As of July 2015, there were 1.6 million available apps for Google Play (Android) and 1.5 million apps for iOS users. Not surprisingly, among these apps are those that test for psychic ability. One of the best we've found is ESP Trainer, developed under a NASA program by Russell Targ at Stanford Research Institute. The app is free and the premise is simple. It shows four colored squares and randomly generates a photograph or image hidden in one of the squares. Your task is to choose the square that contains the image. There are 24 trials in each run. When you succeed, you hear a chime and the image is revealed.

At the top is a score indicator that keeps track of the correct choices. After correct hits of 6, 8, 10, 12 and 14, words of encouragement appear. After six correct hits, you see: *a good beginning.* After eight correct hits: *ESP ability present.* After ten correct hits: *useful in Vegas.* After twelve and fourteen correct hits: *outstanding ESP ability.* In other words, you receive positive reinforcement.

The website—espresearch.com—refers to the app as a test for clairvoyance, but it can just as easily be a test for precognition. As the website explains, "The game offers multi-sensory feedback, reinforcement, and an opportunity to pass, meeting all the requirements needed for learning this skill. The purpose of the trainer is to allow you to become aware of what it feels like when you psychically choose the correct square."

The site notes that in a year-long NASA program with 145 subjects, many were able to significantly improve their scores. Four of the subjects improved their scores at the 100-to-1 level or better. We found that with practice, our scores certainly improved.

The website also suggests precognitive skills achieved through the app can be profitable: "This approach has been used with surprising success on Wall Street." However, no details were provided, and the website includes the somewhat humorous disclaimer, "*Your* results might be different from the stock market winners."

We use the app as a tool for finding out whether we're in the flow at the beginning of the day. It's a simple but effective way for priming yourself for experiencing precognition. And if you frequently score 12 or higher, then developer Russell Targ would like to hear from you!

Keeping Track of Your Hits

Once you become aware of how precognition works in your life, it's a good idea to keep track of your hits in a journal, computer file or even on your phone. A record helps to bolster self-confidence and provides a handy reference to events, people and situations that may be emerging in your life.

In the coming chapters, you'll find activities you can try that will help you cultivate an inner climate in which precognitions can occur. Think of yourself as a shaman who is summoning the future, inviting it to appear to you before it arrives so that you are better prepared for what's around the bend.

Hooking Up with the Future

Precognition is accurate anticipation of future events without any objective clues.

—Stanislav Grof

In 1909, Carl Jung and Sigmund Freud got together in Vienna. The two men had met before and exchanged numerous letters about their respective views on psychology, the mind and the unconscious. Even though they were friends at the time, an undercurrent of tension existed between them that Jung later attributed to the differences in their views about the human psyche. Freud saw Jung as his protégé, the one who would continue to explore his theories about sexuality, the id and the ego. But Jung's research had begun to diverge from Freud's and was leading him deeper into the world of parapsychology, myth, religion and symbolism.

At this particular meeting, Jung asked Freud about his views on precognition and parapsychology in general. Freud dismissed it all as nonsense. As Jung, stung by his reaction, held back a sharp retort, he suddenly experienced a curious sensation, as if his diaphragm was made of iron and was turning scorching hot. Then there was a loud cracking sound in a nearby bookcase and both men bolted to their feet, alarmed that the bookcase was about to topple over on them. Jung exclaimed, "There, that is an example of a so-called catalytic exteriorization phenomenon."

"This is sheer bosh," Freud retorted.

Jung insisted it wasn't and predicted that in a moment it would happen again: "Sure enough, no sooner had I said the words than the same detonation went off in the bookcase. To this day, I do not know what gave me this certainty. But I knew beyond all doubt that the report would come again."

Freud just stared at him and Jung didn't have any idea what the look meant: "In any case, this incident aroused his mistrust of me."

Jung first wrote about this episode in his autobiography, *Memories, Dreams, Reflections*, and since then it has been retold in any number of books. It has been cited as the point where the friendship between the two men started to unravel, and as an instance of synchronicity, of psychokinesis—mind over matter—and of precognition.

But if one of us experienced something like this and wrote about it, it wouldn't make the impact that it did when Jung related it. What makes it notable is that Freud is considered to be the father of modern psychology and that Jung, whose name is often preceded by *the great Swiss psychologist*, devoted his career and, ultimately, his entire adult life, to "what Heraclitus called the 'boundaries of the soul,'" writes Robert Hopcke in *There Are No Accidents*. "He consistently applied scientific methods to examine so-called 'irrational' phenomena and to elucidate the psychological meaning and function of such experiences in human life—paranormal experiences, extrasensory perception, UFOs, psychokinesis and the like."

Jung's labyrinthine path reads like the *Star Trek* motto—daring to go where no one has gone before. He explored areas considered to be taboo by psychologists like Freud, whose mechanistic approach to psychology left Jung with too many unanswered questions. His exploration became intensely personal and much of his struggle was recorded in *The Red Book*.

When *The Red Book* was published in 2009, Stephen A. Diamond reviewed it in *Psychology Today* as a personal record of Jung's tortuous quest to "salvage his soul." Diamond, like other psychologists, notes that *The Red Book* is the personal story of Jung's "insidious descent into what many believe to have been madness, and his eventual return to the world a transformed man. This alchemical process took almost 20 years, starting shortly after the acrimonious split from Sigmund Freud and the Freudians when Jung was in his late 30s. This loss catalyzed what Jung would come to call a massive 'mid-life crisis' in which much of his libidinal energies were withdrawn from the outer world and redirected inwardly to his inner life."

In Jungian terms, then, that cracking sound in the bookcase could have been symbolic of the *breaking apart* of the friendship between Jung and Freud. There was no apparent cause and effect between Jung's holding back his sharp retort to Freud's dismissal of the paranormal and the explosive sound in the bookcase. And, since the event was meaningful to Jung, it qualifies as a synchronicity. It's also an example of psychokinesis—matter manipulated by the mind—or, in this case, by a powerful emotional response that couldn't be verbalized and found another means of self-expression. Then there's the precognitive element to the experience. Just moments after Jung told Freud the sound would happen again, it did.

This experience encompassed the very areas that eventually consumed Jung's research and his life. It undoubtedly proved to him that when deep unconscious forces are activated, when we experience a major transition in life, synchronicities peak.

But we don't have to wait until our life is locked in some sort of crisis before we hook into the future. In our daily life, we're surrounded by signs, symbols and patterns that carry hints about it. Sometimes the message is obvious; other times, it requires interpretation. The journey can be bewildering and frustrating, but we don't have to experience that "insidious descent into . . . madness" to be transformed. We just have to pay attention.

The Broken Plate

During a family trip to Asheville, North Carolina, in October 2015, we went into a shop where our daughter, Megan, decorated a ceramic plate that was a gift for her roommate, Erin. A year earlier, Erin's parents had bought a house for her and she had asked Megan to move in with her. They had agreed to a year's lease, which was coming up for renewal on December 2, and had talked about living together in the house for several years. The place sat on an acre of land that backed up to a lake, so Megan's dog had plenty of space to run, and there was enough room for Megan to convert one of the bedrooms into her art studio. She has known Erin for a decade, since they both interned at a dolphin facility in the Florida keys. It was an ideal setup and Megan had been happy in this place.

The message Megan inscribed on the plate was a tribute to their long friendship: *Megan & Erin, Friends Forever.* The plate was to be mailed to Megan once it had been fired.

A few weeks later, when we were visiting Megan in Orlando, we noticed the ceramic plate from Asheville on the counter. It was broken and chipped. A tube of superglue sat beside it. "What happened?" Rob asked.

"Oh, Erin put it in the dishwasher and it broke when we took it out," Megan replied. "I'm going to fix it with superglue."

Later that evening, Rob remarked that he didn't think the broken plate was a good sign about the continuation of the living arrangement. I felt it was just a fluke. My argument was, *C'mon, sometimes events are just stuff that happens, right?* But Rob kept referring back to the broken plate, how it was like a symbol from a dream that you're supposed to pay attention to.

Shortly before Thanksgiving, Megan and I returned from a road trip. As soon as we walked into Megan's place in Orlando, I spotted that chipped and broken plate on the counter, still not repaired. In fact, when Megan attempted to glue it back together, it had slipped from her hands and more pieces had broken off. That night when Erin got home from work, she seemed strangely preoccupied, uneasy. She said she was just stressed from work. I, obsessing about the broken plate, felt otherwise.

Fast-forward to November 30. Megan had arrived back in Orlando after the Thanksgiving holidays and had gone out and bought a Christmas tree for her and Erin to enjoy. But when she walked in the house that evening, Erin informed Megan that her brother had gotten a job in Orlando, a surprise to everyone, and wanted to live in the house. Megan would have to move out by the end of January. She had two months to find other living arrangements and was devastated.

Rob had recognized the sign and Megan and I refused to acknowledge it.

In retrospect, it's similar to the cracking sound in the bookcase that signaled the end of Jung's friendship with Freud. It wasn't as immediately dramatic and didn't spell the end of the friendship between Megan and Erin, but it was an exclamation point at the end of their living arrangement.

If all of us had heeded the precognitive warning message of the broken ceramic plate, would we have encouraged Megan to start looking around for other living arrangements? Probably not. The broken plate provided only the larger picture, that their living arrangement wouldn't continue, and it didn't offer any details about how or why this might transpire. Also, Megan would have felt that by preparing herself for a move she was bringing that particular future path more fully into physical reality. Yet, the path unfolded anyway, a shock but perhaps also an opportunity.

We don't live in a random universe, as Robert Hopcke said in his book *There Are No Accidents: Synchronicity and the Story of Our Lives.* But even when we're paying attention and sense the future through a sign or symbol, are we ready to act on that information?

Robert Moss's Wallet

In *The Three "Only" Things: Tapping the Power of Dreams, Coincidence & Imagination*, author and dream researcher Robert Moss recounts an incident that happened to him shortly before the stock market crash in 1987. He was in an airplane restroom when he accidentally dropped a wallet with his credit cards and checks from a brokerage account into the toilet. He barely managed to snatch it out before it was flushed away.

"Had this been a dream, I might have written a one-liner like: 'If you're not very careful, your stock market investments will go down the toilet.' Unfortunately, in 1987, I was not yet fully aware that incidents in waking life speak to us exactly like dream symbols. I failed to harvest the message, neglected to take the appropriate action to limit the risk to my brokerage account—and saw a large percentage of my net worth go down the toilet."

The incident was clearly a hint about the future, a warning specifically about his assets. But the message eluded Moss just as the message of the broken ceramic plate eluded Megan and Trish.

The Wedding Ring

When Trish's sister was married to her first husband, she called Trish in a panic one day. Her wedding ring had disappeared. Mary had searched all over the house but couldn't find it. She thought she had taken it off when she had washed her hands earlier at the kitchen sink and wondered whether it had slipped off the edge and gone down the drain. She took apart the pipe, hoping to find the ring, but it never showed up.

Trish felt it was a bad portent for the marriage, which had its share of problems, but she didn't voice this to her sister. Not too long afterward, Mary and her husband got divorced.

Suppose Mary had understood the event as symbolic of the state of the marriage? Could she have taken steps to rectify the relationship? Could the marriage have been saved? Perhaps. But it's also possible that the marriage, like Megan's living arrangement, had run its course and it was time for a change. Sometimes, signs and symbols like these are simply hints or warnings about what's approaching and our best course of action is to prepare ourselves internally for the seemingly inevitable change.

Getting Stung

Some years ago, Trish and her coauthor Phyllis Vega had gone to a writers' conference on Amelia Island off the Georgia coast to promote their book, *Power Tarot: More than 100 Spreads That Give Specific Answers to Your Most Important Questions*. They checked into their hotel room and as Phyllis was washing her hands, she suddenly squealed, "I just got stung by a bee!"

"A bee?" Trish hurried over to the sink, and sure enough, the dead bee lay in the basin and Phyllis's hand was starting to swell. "How'd it get in here? The balcony door isn't even open."

"Who cares how it got in," Phyllis said. "What's it mean?"

In this incident, the meaning was painfully obvious. "That we're going to get stung in some way at this conference," Trish replied.

Downstairs, Phyllis bought Benadryl for the swelling in her hand and they went on to the exhibit room. Authors were opening boxes of their books and setting up their tables. The conference organizer came over to them: "Ladies, so wonderful you could make it. Your shipment of books was delayed and will be here first thing tomorrow morning, just in time for the opening of the conference. Not to worry."

Phyllis and Trish exchanged a glance. They resigned themselves to the reality that the bee knew better. Their books never arrived.

Becoming Aware of Signs and Symbols

Once we become aware that signs and symbols in our waking life can be interpreted like their counterparts in dreams, we have a distinct advantage in sensing the future. You might ask yourself a question about a future matter, and watch for the first thing to appear that's somewhat unusual. Can you interpret it as a symbol or sign? If the meaning isn't immediately obvious, then poke around on one of the numerous websites about dream interpretation until you find an answer that resonates with you. Or look for a book like Denise Linn's *The Secret Language of Signs* or any of Moss's books, which are excellent resources. If the sign involves an animal, consult any book by Ted Andrews, the master of animal oracles.

In a journal or computer file, jot down the date, the issue you asked about and the particulars for the sign or symbol. Where were you when it happened? Was the weather a factor? What time of the day or night was it? What were you thinking and feeling right before it happened? The more details you provide, the likelier it is that you will recognize the event or situation when it occurs.

Types of Precognition

Just as scientists, researchers and writers have categorized extrasensory perception into various types—clairvoyance, telepathy, clairaudience, precognition and so on—they often break down each category into a specific type. Remote viewing, for example, is actually clairvoyance—viewing an event as it's happening elsewhere. Clairaudience—hearing sounds or voices not within the range of human hearing—is also a form of mediumship, communication with the dead.

This same kind of categorization has also happened with synchronicity, the granddaddy of the paranormal. In the last fifteen years or so, as interest in synchronicity has exploded, academics, scientists and psychiatrists have begun to explore and write about it. One of these individuals is Bernard Beitman, MD, a visiting professor of psychiatry at the University of Virginia and author of *Connecting with Coincidence: The New Science for Using Synchronicity and Serendipity in Your Life.*

He's the first psychiatrist since Jung who has proposed a serious study of synchronicity—Coincidence Studies—and hopes that he can help people find useful coincidences in their life with greater frequency. Beitman breaks down synchronicity into five categories:

- *Synchronicity—when a thought is mirrored by a meaningful exterior event*
- *Serendipity coincidences—finding what you need right when you need it*
- *Seriality—a string of similar events that are noted*
- *Simulpathity—feeling another's distress at a distance*
- *Instrument—synchronicities or serendipities that motivate you to make a change or changes that work out to your benefit*

In an e-mail, Dr. Beitman wrote, "Synchronicity and serendipity are old names for broad categories, with synchronicity sometimes including serendipity. If you just use synchronicity and serendipity, then synchronicity to me is more psychological and serendipity is more about getting something you need."

Coincidences, Beitman says, can be categorized along several lines, like a cube with several faces: Process, Forms, Use and Explanation. *Process* is the occurrence that triggers the coincidence. *Forms* include pairs and series of coincidences, the mind-environment of the individual and the actual environment. *Use* pertains to what we do with it, how it's used—in decision-making or by providing something that's needed. *Explanation* is just what it sounds like. Is the coincidence due to probability, something personal or a mystery? *Personal* would include psi, so precognition would fall here. *Mystery* can include quantum physics and God.

We did something similar in our book *The 7 Secrets of Synchronicity: Your Guide to Finding Meaning in Signs Big and Small*, where our categories for the phenomenon are called secrets:

- *The knowing—coincidence is recognized as meaningful*
- *The heart—synchronicities are deeply intertwined with our emotions*

- *The theory—synchronicity is the granddaddy of all paranormal phenomenon, including precognition*
- *The creative—creativity lies at the heart of synchronicity*
- *The clusters—synchronicity manifests itself in clusters of numbers, names, objects, words, symbols. This is similar to Beitman's seriality category*
- *The trickster—synchronicity can reveal itself with a twist of humor or wry irony so startling it stops us in our tracks*
- *The global—when synchronicities manifest themselves through global events, and the universe seems to be addressing us as a collective*

In retrospect, we would add several other categories to these secrets: any form of divination as our most personal engagement with synchronicity, travel synchronicities, animals as oracles and messengers, and synchronicity as an opportunity to engage the transcendent, the divine.

Robert Moss, in *The Three "Only" Things: Tapping the Power of Dreams, Coincidence, & Imagination*, has nine categories for coincidence:

- *There are things that like to happen together (clusters, seriality).*
- *Thoughts are actions and produce effects.*
- *Coincidence multiplies when we are in motion (physical or metaphorical travel).*
- *Life rhymes (like clusters that involve similar words or names).*
- *The world is a forest of symbols.*
- *Every setback offers an opportunity.*
- *To find our way we may need to get lost.*
- *Look for the hidden hand.*
- *The passions of the soul work magic (similar to engaging the divine).*

One of these categories needs a bit of explanation—*look for the hidden hand.* Here, Moss is referring to the nature of coincidences, how they seem to be orchestrated by a hidden order: "Events that manifest at discrete points in space and time . . . are the result of a single movement on another plane. Coincidences are homing beacons. They are secret handshakes from the universe."

Just as coincidences and synchronicities have been categorized and labeled, so has precognition. One of the clearest and simplest categorizations of precognition was spelled out in Arthur W. Osborn's 1961 book, *The Future Is Now: The Significance of Precognition.* He groups precognitions into five broad categories:

- *Precognitive warnings*
- *Precognition of death*
- *Precognitive knowledge of trivial events*
- *Precognition of significant events in a person's life*
- *Longer-range precognitions*

To Osborn's broad categories, we would add precognition of mass events—natural or man-made disasters—which we cover extensively in the next chapter on planetary empaths.

Impulses

An example of the first type of precognition, from Osborn's files, happened to his wife when she followed an *impulse*. She was invited by a friend to go for a drive and usually would be delighted to do so. But without thinking, she replied that she couldn't go that day. It wasn't true and she was astonished that she had lied. In other words, she'd followed an impulse that bewildered her. Later that day, Osborn's wife learned that her friend had gone for a drive with her daughter and young grandchild and had stopped for afternoon tea: "While they were returning to the car, another car struck the child and killed her."

Precognition often speaks to us through impulses. We feel the urge to do or say something that seems to defy logic. All too often, we ignore the impulse because it might embarrass us or others or because we can't immediately explain why we feel the way we do. But the next time you feel such an impulse, don't dismiss it as a personality aberration.

When Megan was in college, January was the month when students were involved in independent study projects—ISPs—that take many students off campus for the entire month. Two of Megan's roommates were doing their ISPs elsewhere, so it was just Megan and a young man who had moved into her campus apartment about two months earlier.

There had been some issues with this guy—namely that he often talked to himself in his room, shouting and ranting about how awful he was, what a terrible person he was and no wonder he wasn't liked. Megan and her roommates had overheard these rants and discussed asking the guy to move out. They thought he needed professional help.

Late one night, Megan was in her room, alone in the apartment except for the young man, and she heard him yelling out in the kitchen, talking to himself again. "I had this impulse to record what he was saying, so I turned on the recorder on my phone," and she recorded him shouting about how much he hated this group or that group, conservatives, liberals, hippies, everything and everyone and how he was going to BLOW THEM ALL UP. She was totally freaked out and locked herself in her room.

The next morning, Megan went to the resident director with the recording and said she wanted the guy out of her apartment. Her impulse to record the conversation caused the resident director to take the situation seriously—otherwise it might have been her word against his. So, Megan's precognitive impulse, like that of Osborn's wife, perhaps prevented some terrible scenario.

When we feel an impulse—as opposed to experiencing a sign or symbol—we don't have time to think about it. It's like instinct—we either act on it or we don't. And when we don't, we often regret it.

Years ago, when we lived in a townhouse in Fort Lauderdale, our cat disappeared. When Fox didn't return after two days, I knew that something was wrong. I sensed the cat was trapped somewhere. Rob, meanwhile, had a strong impulse that the cat would return by midnight on Saturday. He felt confident about it.

Just before midnight that Saturday, six days after disappearing, we heard a knock at the door. It was our next-door neighbor, holding Fox in her arms. She'd found her outside our door. The cat's front paws were badly scraped and she smelled like perfume. We figured someone had found Fox and had been keeping her inside. But Fox had tried to get out and finally made a break for it and returned home, right at Rob's deadline.

Rob had a similar impulse a couple of years later when he lost his wallet. He was confident that the wallet somehow would return to him. He'd lost the wallet while windsurfing on a lake near the house and hoped it had fallen out before he had gone into the water. However, he couldn't find it on the shore where he'd rigged his sail. He knew that if he'd accidentally taken it with him and lost it in the lake, chances of recovering it were probably nil. Yet he remained confident he would get it back, even though he had no logical reason to support that belief.

He didn't do any of the things people normally do when they lose wallets—no calls to credit card companies, no request for a duplicate driver's license, no contact with his auto insurance company. For three or four days, he visualized the wallet returning to him, visualized it so intensely that he could feel its weight in his hand, in his back pocket. He believed the wallet had been found already.

That same week, a lawn man had stopped by our house, soliciting business. We already had someone doing the lawn, but Rob and the man chatted, then the guy left. A few days later, this same man was fishing with a net in the lake where Rob had been windsurfing and dredged up Rob's wallet. He returned it, complete with all the cards and water-soaked cash, and said he was relieved that Rob was alive and not on the bottom of that lake. Not only did the wallet return, as Rob had foreseen, but he'd met the man who found it a few days before it was discovered.

Out of the blue on September 28, 2009, I thought of my former fiction editor, Kate Duffy, and had an impulse to e-mail her to find out how she was doing.

Kate had been my fiction editor from 1997 to 2008. We had worked on twelve books together and during that time, I came to appreciate how rare she was as a fiction editor. She understood that novelists do their best work when they write about what they love and always gave me complete creative freedom.

But more than this, Kate understood the terrain of the human heart. When my mother was diagnosed with Alzheimer's and we had to put her in an Alzheimer's unit, my dad moved in with us, and Kate called frequently to find out how we all were doing. In May 2000, Kate happened to call when I was sitting at my desk, sobbing, and I told her I would have to call her back.

Kate wouldn't let me off the phone until I told her what had happened—that I'd just been told by a doctor that my mother wasn't a candidate for hip replacement surgery because of the Alzheimer's and that she was now doomed to live out the remainder of her life on morphine. Kate talked me through it. When my mother died and my dad passed on several years later, she was there to talk.

A few months later, I felt something had happened to Kate and called her cell phone, which I'd never done before. Kate was on a train, headed home. Her father had just died.

When I was nominated for an Edgar Allan Poe Award for a novel Kate had bought, Kate sent roses. When I won the award, I sent roses to Kate.

At a romance writers' conference in Orlando in 2005, the last time I saw Kate, we stole away at 9 p.m. one night to watch *Lost*, a show we both loved, drank wine and laughed and talked politics and life. On my way home the next day, a sensation swept over me that I would never see Kate again. A few minutes later, one of my car's tires went flat. At the time, I didn't associate the thought with the flat tire.

The relationship between novelists and their editors is often complex, particularly when the relationship spans more than a decade. You may be friends, but you're always aware the editor has the final say on what you write. So, in April 2008, when I learned from my agent that my publisher wouldn't be renewing my contract, I was devastated. Kate called me later that afternoon—something she certainly didn't have to do—and told me how much she had enjoyed working with me. I understood it was business, so it didn't feel like a dismissal. It felt like what it was—Kate reaching out one last time to offer encouragement, options and reassurance.

Since we were both big Obama supporters, it seemed fitting that the last email we exchanged was right after Obama had won the election.

Trish: We're watching the birth of a whole new paradigm! Yahoo!!!

Kate: Went to bed in tears.

And that was it until September 28, 2009, when I felt an impulse to e-mail Kate. Even though the impulse had been strong, I didn't act on it. The next morning, a mutual friend told me Kate had died the previous day.

This type of precognition straddles categories. In 2005, when I had felt I wouldn't see Kate again, there was a finality about the feeling, just as there is in the first two examples you'll read in the next category, precognitions of death. But the urge to e-mail Kate four years later was a definite warning conveyed through an *impulse*. I didn't act on it because we hadn't been in touch for more than a year and I thought I would look foolish or that Kate might misconstrue the contact. By not acting on the impulse, I missed a chance to say good-bye and to thank Kate for everything she'd done.

Interestingly, in 2015, I wrote a short story that I submitted to *Ellery Queen Magazine.* Nothing paranormal in it, straight mystery/suspense. While Megan and I were driving back from the conference we'd attended in Asheville, I started thinking about how the short story could be expanded into a novel about reincarnation. By the end of the long drive, I had figured out the structure, characters and most of the plot. And immediately began to doubt it.

That night I dreamed that Kate and I were hanging out, talking about writing and books. Kate apologized for not renewing my contract back in 2008 and advised me to write the novel. I felt the dream was putting me on notice that the short story would sell and that I should write a novel based on it. Less than two weeks later, I heard that *Ellery Queen* had bought the short story, and shortly after I began writing a novel based on it.

Precognition of Death

This section in Osborn's book includes precognitive dreams and visions about death as well as well-documented predictions made by psychics. The most common type of future sensing is about death, and studies indicate that the bulk of them occur during dreams. The simplest and most direct type of precognitive death dream is like the one we wrote about in the introduction, where someone handed Trish a note that read, "Your mother has just died." It came true three weeks later.

One of the most intriguing cases in this section of Osborn's book concerned a female artist and her precognition about her brother's death. In June 1955, the artist, whom Osborn identifies as "Miss D.P.," walked into a bank in New South Wales, where she lived. In the glass doors, she saw her brother coming toward her. Whenever they met unexpectedly in town, he would tip his hat at her and, with an exaggerated courtesy, would say, "How do you do?" It was a joke between them.

They spoke briefly that day outside the bank, then went their separate ways. As he stood at the door, he glanced back at her and she was overwhelmed with the certainty that even though he was in perfect health, she would never see him again. Six months later, he and his family went on vacation. While they were in Portland, he was hospitalized, underwent surgery and died unexpectedly of a postoperative thrombosis. On the morning of his death, D.P. received a call from her sister-in-law, telling her that her brother had died.

Several hours later, she received a letter from her brother, written just before his operation, that he was fit and healthy and there was nothing to worry about. But she had somehow known six months earlier that his life was drawing to a close.

This particular story resonated for Trish. In the late 1970s, she became involved with a pilot, who was recently divorced with two small children. The source of his income was somewhat mysterious, but appeared to be inherited from his wealthy New England family. At one point, they flew to Panama so he could retrieve his Cessna, which had been impounded by the Panamanian government because he lacked the proper papers. During that trip, she discovered that his plane had been impounded because he was a suspected drug smuggler.

They eventually returned to the United States without his plane. The last time she saw him was outside her home in South Florida, when he was leaving for another trip to Panama to try to reclaim his plane. She had the overwhelming sensation that she would never see him again and said as much. He just laughed. "I'll be back," he said.

He did return to the United States some months later, but moved to Martha's Vineyard with a woman he'd recently met. A short time later, he hanged himself from the living room rafters.

This kind of precognition has no basis in reason. It's a fire that burns in the pit of your gut, races across the surface of your brain, drives nails into your heart. It's when your body screams, *Pay attention.* You may not have any inkling about the particulars, about all the interconnecting details. But you've been warned about the big picture, just like Moss's wallet, like the broken ceramic plate, and you can try to prepare yourself for it.

Precognitive Knowledge of Trivial Events

This category is fascinating because it's so mundane. These types of precognitions are important to the people who experience them, but they aren't earth-shattering. They aren't about mass events that involve great numbers of people and don't revolve around pivotal life transitions. They're personal and concern the minutia of our daily life.

This type of precognition may be more common than we realize, and may sneak into our awareness while we're driving, daydreaming, falling asleep, dreaming or engaged in something enjoyable. One of the most comical examples in Osborn's book about this type of precognition concerns a pig! And keep in mind that the incident occurred in the mid-1900s, when life was much different.

A bishop's wife in Hereford, England, dreamed that her husband was away and that she was reading prayers in his absence. After she finished her prayers, she walked out into the dining room and saw an enormous pig standing between the dining room table and a storage cabinet. In real life, after prayers had been said, a pig escaped from its sty and was discovered standing in the exact spot where the bishop's wife had seen it in her dream.

Does it get any more trivial or absurd than that? Yet, for the bishop's wife, this precognitive experience may have blown open her awareness that what she perceived in her normal life wasn't all that existed. Maybe the experience *awakened* her.

These trivial events can involve virtually anything, even an astrology book. Some years ago, Trish dreamed that her book *Your Intuitive Moon: Using Lunar Signs and Cycles to Enhance Your Intuition* sold to Russia. She could even "see" the pages written in Russian, the strange symbols and scribblings of that alphabet. The next morning, she received an e-mail from the woman in charge of subsidiary rights at her literary agent's company informing her that the book had sold to Russia. This experience was personally important to her; it proved she could sense her future. But it certainly didn't impact anyone else.

Writer Terry Crowley was standing in her living room in South Florida one day in 1981 and a sense of peace washed through her that was almost like a meditative state. "Natalie Wood was on TV, doing a White Rain Shampoo commercial, and a voice in my head said, *She's going to die soon*. It shocked me because she was still relatively young and seemed healthy. I wondered why in the world I would even think that."

Several months later, on November 29, 1981, forty-three-year-old Natalie Wood drowned off the island of Catalina. Terry believes that the only reason she experienced this precognition was because Wood was her favorite actress and perhaps she was being prepared for her death. While the event was significant to Wood's husband and loved ones, it was trivial in the overall scheme of Terry's life. But perhaps it was her emotional connection to the actress that drew the experience.

Our neighbor, Annette, often experiences synchronicity and as Trish was working on this particular section, she dropped by to tell us about something she'd experienced a few hours earlier. "*A synchronicity!*" she announced. But it turned out to be the kind of precognition that fit well into this section about trivial events.

Annette was at our local grocery store and had a sudden impulse to buy a couple of cans of Arizona Iced Tea, a product she hasn't bought for more than a year. She thought it would make a special treat for her son or daughter. After she left the grocery store, she swung by the house to pick up her son so they could run some errands and figured she would unload the groceries later.

As Dawson got in the car, he saw the bags of groceries in the backseat, with the cans of Arizona Iced Tea poking up from the bag. "Mom, you're freaking me out. As I was riding my bike home from school, I was dying for a can of cold Arizona Iced Tea!"

Sensing a future that involves Arizona Iced Tea is hardly the kind of precognition that changes or saves lives. But a big chunk of our life consist of trivialities and when we recognize what looks like a hidden order in the scheme of things, we're uplifted, buoyed; we feel like we're in the *flow.* The incident surprised Annette enough for her to tell us about it. Dawson, who is only fourteen, already grasps the concept of synchronicity; now he also understands the idea of precognition.

Sensing the future about trivial events sometimes involves clusters—names, songs, objects and numbers—just as it does for major events. In late 1982, Rob was driving a couple of friends, Hanna and George, to the Miami airport. George was a minister in a free-wheeling New Age church in Negril, Jamaica, and Hanna, his Norwegian girlfriend, had known Rob before she'd become involved in George's church. Rob had recently separated from his first wife and filed for divorce, a major life transition that contributed to the intensity of the conversation. They were discussing deep stuff, spiritual belief systems and cosmic questions. Zen stuff. Zen, as in the Zen of the moment, of peace, of meditation, of breathing and happiness.

Suddenly, Rob noticed the license plate of a passing car that read "ZEN 665." George blurted, "It would be really remarkable if we saw ZEN 666."

A few minutes later, a yellow sports car passed them with that very license plate: ZEN 666. The precognition was trivial in that it affected only the three of them. They'd asked, then it had appeared like something out of the biblical book of Revelation. But Rob understood what it meant for him, that he had to adapt a Zen-like attitude during his divorce, go with the flow and not offer any resistance.

For months afterward, Rob talked about the Zen story to anyone who would listen. The odds of that event happening were probably astronomical but the personal message for him couldn't have been clearer. More than a year later, he spotted a red sedan with the same license ZEN 666. This sighting served as a confirmation for him that he had emerged on the other side of his divorce with greater wisdom.

Precognition of Significant Events in a Person's Life

As we said earlier, significant events in life usually involve major turning points—birth and death, marriage and divorce, a move, a professional or financial change, a graduation or illness. Not surprisingly, precognitions often swirl around during these transitions to alert and prepare us for what's coming.

Writer Sharlie West lost her husband in 1989. A year later, her mother had a stroke and Sharlie had to put her in a nursing home because she couldn't care for her. But the facility was close to her house and she was able to visit her mother frequently. During one visit, she and her mom were talking and, out of the blue, Sharlie blurted, "I should have married Jimmy B. He always cared for me."

Her mother was puzzled by the remark; Sharlie hadn't mentioned the man in 40 years. "He was head over heels for you," her mom said.

They had a good laugh about it, then Sharlie forgot about the conversation. Three weeks later, her mother passed away. Not long afterward, Sharlie and a friend were sitting in her living room when she suddenly felt that someone was thinking about her: "It was so intense I could feel the person in my mind and even see his image—middle-aged, salt-and-pepper hair, glasses. No one I knew. I mentioned it to my friend, who shrugged and said it was my imagination."

Shortly afterward, Sharlie received a letter of condolence from Jimmy B and recalled her conversation with her mother. She thought the timing was interesting. But the stunner happened when Jimmy stopped by her house and Sharlie realized he was the same man she'd seen in her vision. Yet, the Jimmy she remembered had dark hair, no glasses and was thinner than the man who stood at her door. It would have been impossible for her to imagine him in the present, as he looked now. Three weeks later they moved in together and more than 20 years later, they're still together.

Sharlie's precognition involved three major life transitions over a period of about a year—the death of her husband and of her mother and an encounter with the man she would marry. Despite the tragedies that precipitated Sharlie's precognition, her story ended happily. Many of Osborn's cases in this category don't have happy endings, but underscore the point that some precognitions can be quite literal.

Longer-Range Precognitions

On a Facebook group on synchronicity, one of the participants, a psychiatrist, asked: Why do some people have precognitions and others don't? Or is it that most of us have precognitions and we just don't pay attention to them?

The correct answer is probably the last part of his question. *Paying attention* is another term for *mindfulness.* When we are mindful about how we live, we are engaged not only with our external daily life, but with our internal life as well—dreams and emotions, flashes of intuition, impulses, and the needs, desires and passions that fuel us. It means we are connected to the larger picture of who we are and may become, and that we are somehow connected to every other person on the planet. For the planetary empaths you'll read about in the next chapter, that connection extends to the planet, to the earth as a living entity. They feel what the planet feels.

How far out in the future can a precognition go? Several days? Weeks? Years? Decades? A century? Nostradamus lived in the 16th century and made predictions that extended to the late 3700s. Edgar Cayce's predictions, many of them made in the 1930s and 1940s, stretch into the 22nd century. But most of us don't strive to see the future of humanity in short or broad strokes. We're interested in our personal future, what tomorrow, next month, or next year might hold in store for us and how or if we can improve what we see.

We may experience something that unfolds over years. Or we may experience a precognition that happens within minutes, days, hours, weeks or months.

Wolfgang Pauli, a theoretical physicist who won the Nobel Prize in physics in 1945—and an early supporter of Jung's theory on synchronicity—was perplexed by one of the unsolved mysteries of modern physics: the value of the fine structure constant, which involves the number 137.

A prime number is a positive integer that can't equal the product of two smaller integers. It can only be divided by one and by itself. That makes 137 a particularly baffling number. In *Deciphering the Cosmic Number: The Strange friendship of Wolfgang Pauli and Carl Jung*, Arthur I. Millet has an eloquent name for 137—*the DNA of light.*

The significance of the number was discovered in 1915 by Arnold Sommerfield, Pauli's mentor. "From the moment 137 first popped up in his equations," writes Miller, "he and other physicists . . . quickly realized that this unique 'fingertip' was the sum of certain fundamental constants of nature, specific quantities believed to be invariable throughout the universe, quantities central to relativity and quantum theory."

The number perplexed so many physicists that Richard Feynman, winner of the Nobel Prize in 1965 for his contributions to the development of quantum electrodynamics, said that physicists should put a sign in their offices to remind themselves of how much they didn't know. The sign would read: 137.

Pauli wrestled with the implications of this number for most of his life. At the age of 58, he was admitted to a hospital in Zurich for a routine procedure. When he learned he would be in room 137, he supposedly said, "I will never get out of here." And he didn't. He died not long afterward, in the hospital.

In essence, the number 137 was a precognition that shadowed Pauli for his entire adult life.

During WWII, Carl Jung was on a train returning home from Bollingen, Switzerland. He couldn't read the book he had with him because from the moment the train started to move, he was overwhelmed by the image of someone drowning. As he wrote in *Memories, Dreams, Reflections*, "It struck me as uncanny, and I thought 'What has happened? Can there have been an accident?'"

At Erlenbach, he got off the train and walked home, still disturbed by the image. His second daughter's family was living with the Jungs then and as he walked into the garden, her children were there, and were visibly upset. It turned out the youngest boy had fallen into the water at the boathouse; he couldn't swim and had nearly drowned. This had taken place, Jung writes, at exactly the time he had seen the image when he was on the train.

But had the time been exact? Who glances at a clock when a kid who can't swim falls into a lake? The unconscious informs us "of things which by all logic we could not possibly know," Jung writes in his autobiography. "Consider synchronistic phenomena, premonitions, and dreams that come true. The unconscious had given me a hint."

On August 19, 2009, we had a precognitive experience that came to pass eleven days later. At the time it happened, we were clueless about its meaning and significance. When we have talked about this experience with Megan, she thinks we're making too big a deal out of it. *Mom, shit happens.* We think it's more than that.

We had moved Megan back to college on Florida's west coast and were on our way home on its east coast. There's a stretch of highway where mostly sugarcane fields cover land that was once part of the Everglades. Along this stretch, hundreds of swallows sweep across the terrain at dusk, nabbing insects on the fly, oblivious to cars.

Swallows are small birds and at dusk, they look like punctuation points against the waning light. They swooped and dived (literally "skydived"), often winging away from our car at the last second. Then two of them, one after another, hit our windshield. At some deep level, we sensed it might be a sign—a bad sign!

On August 30, *eleven* days after we moved Megan back to college, we met her midway across the state for her *second* skydive, for her *20th* birthday. Her appointment was for 12:30, but the group didn't get airborne until around *2 p.m.* She was jumping *tandem*, with an instructor.

The pattern was unfolding: *2nd dive, 20th birthday, two swallows, a tandem* (*two* people) jump at *2 p.m.* The tandem jumpers left the plane last. We were standing outside the terminal, watching the jumpers with four of Megan's friends. And suddenly, something happened to Megan's parachute. It seemed to just float away.

An instructor standing next to us exclaimed, "Wow, look at that."

"What just happened?" we asked anxiously.

"The first chute failed. Don't worry. They'll free fall for a few more seconds, then the *second* chute will open."

Those seconds were a nightmare.

The *second* chute opened and they landed safely. Afterward, Megan said she didn't even realize anything unusual had happened and wasn't a bit frightened by the experience. However, another experienced skydiver said it was an unusual occurrence. It didn't happen to him until his 1,200th skydive.

Meanwhile, we were stunned as we recognized the link between the failed chute with the dreadful implications and the swallows that had hit the windshield of our car eleven days earlier. We had sensed it was significant, precognitive, but simply didn't have the means to decode it until the day it happened.

But all of these types of precognitions pose the same fundamental question: can the future be changed? Can we, as individuals who have sensed the future, change what we've seen?

In Chapter 8, you'll read about the hypnosis of French actress Irene Muza and what she said about her own future—her death—while under hypnosis. Could she have changed the circumstances of her death? It seems doubtful. In the last chapter, we try to answer the question about how malleable the future might be.

At the time the two swallows hit our windshield, we knew about Megan's upcoming skydive because it was our gift to her for her 20th birthday. If we'd been paying closer attention to the birds—the sky acrobats—one of us might have made the connection to Megan's pending skydive long before the moment when we were standing on the ground, staring upward and watching her and her instructor fall out of that plane. In retrospect, it seems so *obvious*, especially since the swallows had struck our car just a few miles from where the skydiving school was located.

If we had been able to figure it out, we would have given Megan a different gift for her 20th birthday and avoided skydives completely. But she might have paid for it herself and the whole thing might still have happened. After all, in future events that *involve us but are not happening to us personally*, we are just witnesses, participants, secondary players in someone else's story.

One long-range precognition happened to a friend, Adele Aldridge, a writer, an artist and expert on the I Ching. She is now illustrating all 64 hexagrams of the Chinese oracle and every single changing line within these hexagrams. The total is staggering: 960 changing lines. You might say that this project is a huge part of her life's story. Another chapter in her life story involved a man on a billboard, the trigger for a precognition that didn't unfold until nine years later.

Adele's Billboard Man

The story began when Adele attended a two-week seminar on Hermann Hesse and Carl Jung in the Berkshires. During that time she became close friends with a Jungian therapist, Vivian, who was also a handwriting analyst and had a radio program in New York on the subject.

One day during the seminar, Adele received a postcard from Ted, the man she was in love with, who was spending those two weeks with his sons on Fire Island. She asked Vivian to read the postcard—not for content, but to analyze his handwriting. She took one look at it and told Adele to drop him immediately, that Ted wasn't good for her. Ted was the love of Adele's life and she didn't want to hear about it. So, she tucked the card away and that was the end of their conversation about Ted.

However, while Vivian was giving Adele this advice, Ted was with another woman on Fire Island. When Adele found out, she went ballistic. She'd had warning dreams that had predicted this, but had dismissed them as *just dreams*. Never again would she say that.

Adele ended the relationship with Ted immediately and went through such excruciating emotional and physical pain that she began therapy with Vivian: "I was desperate. So desperate that I learned to drive into Manhattan, which I had refused to do until that point."

During the nine months that she drove to Vivian's office near the Metropolitan Museum, she would pass a huge billboard on the West Side Highway with a picture of the Winston cigarette man. His eyes, she recalls, were a deep-set blue that gazed straight into the camera, so that on a billboard they appeared to follow you. They were slightly narrowed in thought and looked as if they were saying, *Keep out of my way*.

"He was striking. But, hell, he was a Winston cigarette ad. He's supposed to look like that. Yet, this picture was hauntingly riveting to me. He was very attractive and I *hated* him. Every time I saw that billboard, which was once a week for months, I got angry."

Sitting in bed one winter night, with the icy wind howling outside her window, Adele was reading a magazine and came across the same ad that was on the billboard. She stared and stared at the picture, trying to understand *why* she hated this man so much: "He was incredibly handsome with high cheekbones and piercing blue eyes, but he looked narcissistic and full of contempt for women. My soul was bleeding from my 'men wounds' and I couldn't stand to think of all the women this man had hurt. I saw contempt in his face. I spat full force at the picture."

Adele was so shocked by her reaction that she never told anyone about it, not even her therapist. At this point in her life, she was feeling deeply wounded by her relationships with men and his picture seemed to embody that wound.

That spring, she put her house on the market and several months afterward, moved to California. "All the nonsense about the man on the billboard was forgotten."

About six years later, Adele had a puzzling and disturbing dream that she was awakened by four figures who walked silently into her room, carrying a stretcher. Lying on the stretcher was a huge man, unconscious, with his head bandaged and his arm in a sling. The four figures dumped this man next to her and silently indicated that she was to take care of him. It was like a hospital stay for him. In the dream, she glanced up "at this huge creature lying next to me, looked at his profile and noted that in some way he reminded me of Christopher Reeves. I recorded in my journal that he looked like Superman."

Still in the dream, she became afraid of the man and jumped out of bed and ran down the hall to the bathroom. A voice told her that she *had* to get back to bed and deal with this man, that she didn't have a choice in the matter. Then she woke up, relieved that she'd been dreaming and perplexed that it had felt so real.

Nearly three years later, on a Sunday night in July, she and her friend Jill went to listen to music at the No Name Bar in Sausalito. Since 1959, it has been at the same location, 757 Bridgeway, and has been frequented by many of the great musicians and actors—Eartha Kitt, Jefferson Airplane, Bob Dylan, Alice Cooper, Woody Harrelson, Clint Eastwood. Adele and Jill sat down in the bar, music reverberating around them. One of the things they talked about was how all the men they'd met in California were always saying that Adele and Jill *had too many expectations.*

When the band stopped for a break, a tall good-looking dude from the band came over, plunked himself in front of them and said, "Do you come here often? Do you like jazz?" The tone in which he said it, Adele remembers, indicated he knew what he was saying was a cliché. He looked her in the eyes and said, "My guru told me the way to be happy is not to have any expectations."

Adele bolted to her feet and burst out, "That's it! I'm outta here!" She headed for the ladies room and left Jill sitting there with him.

She didn't realize that while she was in the restroom, Jill told him that having no expectations was a desecration of passion. "I'm sure he had no idea what he had walked into but I have to give him credit," Adele said. "As soon as I came back, Mr. No Expectations bowed his head humbly and said, 'Okay, I bombed. Can I begin again? Please?'"

His name was Jeremy and when the band called him back to the stand, he asked Adele and Jill to stay for another set. He returned to their table at the end of the next set, and he and Adele made a date for the following Tuesday. Even though Adele knew she'd never met Jeremy, he seemed familiar to her, "the kind of familiarity I might attribute to someone I'd known in another life."

On their second date, driving into San Francisco, Jeremy shoved a picture into Adele's hand. It was an old promo postcard of himself as a model for—yes, the Winston cigarette ad! The same ad she'd seen on the billboard nine years earlier. "I screamed. I'm glad I was sitting down because I got dizzy. Jeremy was very cool and asked me what was the matter. I told him I used to have a love/hate relationship with this picture years ago." He had put on a lot of weight since his modeling days and nine years had passed, which is why she hadn't recognized him initially.

Adele and Jeremy the Billboard Man lived together off and on for a year and a half. Her family and friends thought she was out of her mind when she let him move in with her.

> *"Living with Jeremy was like living with a beautiful wild animal. His beauty fascinated me. It was like observing with awe a beautiful painting or a tiger in the wild. I equated that wildness to something like an awesome part of nature—Victoria Falls or the Zambezi River. I think he was a wounded creature, but*

his physical strength and beauty enabled him to live without any self-observation, and so lots of his talents were not fully developed. One of his charms was his complete ability to live in the moment. Contemplation of the moment was out of the question. It was one hell of a lot of chaos and problems, but also a lot of fun experiences. My relationship with this man was the best and the worst. I loved him and I hated him. Both are equally true."

Shortly after they moved in together, they were lying in the semidarkness and she was trying to wrap her head around the realization that he was the guy whose picture she'd spat at nine years ago. She glanced over at him and gasped. The dream she'd had nearly three years earlier came flooding back and she exclaimed, *"It's you! I dreamed this!"*

When Adele told him the dream and the part about him looking like Superman, he replied, "I once understudied for Christopher Reeves."

Several weeks before that night in the No Name Bar, Adele had another powerful and mystifying dream that portended the future with Jeremy. She heard a knocking at the front door and when she opened it, a huge black bull was standing there, snorting. Terrified, she slammed the door shut and bolted it. Then she could see that the bull had kicked a hole in the door with its hooves and she woke up. "Jeremy was a Taurus (the bull). After we were living together for a while, he had a temper fit and bashed a door in. I had to call the police."

So, how is it that an image on a billboard and in a magazine elicited such strong emotional responses in Adele *nine years* before she met the Winston man and *3,000 miles* [over 4,800 km] *away* from where she'd first seen his picture?

"This wasn't something I was going to be logical about," she points out. "I had no choice."

Do the people who figure into our personal stories at any moment in our lives reach out to us across time and space? If we live within an interconnected universe where all time is simultaneous, then at some level we are all sensing our futures and our emotions, dreams; hunches and impulses may be the clearest indicators of that fact.

Your Story

In subsequent chapters in this book, you're going to encounter a lot of weird stuff. But just because it's weird doesn't discount its validity. Each of us has a story that is sculpted by the work we do, the people we love, our passions and issues, our personal and professional lives. And these things may not have anything to do with what we post on social media.

Take a few minutes to think about the people in your life and the various roles they play. What glimpses of the future have you experienced with, through or about any of these individuals? What were the circumstances, the details? What was the precognition? How quickly did it occur? Were the details exact? How was *your* story changed by your experiences?

Hooking Up

Among millennials, *hooking up* is a phrase that means you are intimate with someone. But when you sense the future in the way that Adele did with Billboard Man or as Pauli did with the number 137, it *is* a kind of intimacy. Your worldview shifts dramatically and when that happens, when your beliefs change at such a profound and fundamental level, everything you experience changes.

Belief, intentions, thoughts and emotions are powerful indicators that we may be sensing the future about an event, situation or relationship. Some visionary researchers and writers, such as Rupert Sheldrake, Dean Radin, Robert Moss and others, contend that our deepest beliefs actually create our reality, that our consciousness is an attractor. Even Jung stated that "like attracts like."

This idea is echoed in the voluminous material from Seth, "a personality essence no longer focused in physical reality" who was channeled by writer Jane Roberts.

Seth

These days, a lot of people claim to channel spirits who provide advice on life: Bashar, J. Z Knight and Ramtha, Esther Hicks/Abraham. But the most famous and credible in this group is Seth, channeled by Roberts from the late 1960s until her death in 1984.

Early on, Jane and her husband, Rob Butts, recognized the material as important and Butts took copious notes on each session. Until Roberts's death, Seth dictated more than 6,000 pages on the nature of reality and Roberts published more than 20 books "written" by Seth.

Psychologists who conversed with Seth were startled by the breadth of his knowledge. Eugene Barnard of North Carolina State University spent several hours talking with Seth and later wrote to Roberts's publisher about his impressions: "The best summary description I can give you of that evening is that it was for me a delightful conversation with a personality or intelligence or what have you, whose wit, intellect, and reservoir of knowledge far exceeded my own." Part of their conversation appears in *The Seth Material*, published by Prentice Hall in 1970.

There are numerous references to Seth and Jane in books by New Age writers and thinkers such as Louise Hay, Wayne Dyer, Esther and Jerry Hicks, Marianne Williamson, Michael Talbot and Fred Alan Wolf. Theoretical physicist Stanton Friedman wrote a book connecting the Seth material to quantum physics.

Bridging Science and Spirit: Common Elements in David Bohm's Physics, The Perennial Philosophy and Seth was published in 1990 and updated in 1994. Friedman takes complex quantum theories and illustrates how they coincide with Seth's statements about the nature of reality and David Bohm's theories on the holographic nature of reality, where "any event happening anywhere is immediately available everywhere as information." If this is true, then we have access to our future selves. It would explain why Adele felt such hatred and fear toward the image of a man she wouldn't meet for another nine years.

This holographic notion of reality coincides with Seth's view that consciousness is the basis of all reality, the creator of reality, and that the consciousness of each and every one of us is dependent upon every other. "The strength of one adds to the strength of all," Seth says in volume one of *The Unknown Reality.* "The weakness of one weakens the whole. The energy of one recreates the whole. The striving of one increases the potentiality of everything that is, and this places great responsibility upon every consciousness."

In other words, we're all in this together.

Five Easy Things

"Why would *anyone* want to see the future?"

We heard this at a party. The middle-aged man was saying it to his wife, who was about to have her cards read by another guest. The wife looked surprised by his reaction, and blurted, "Because if I don't like what's coming, I can change it."

There are five easy things you can do to not only glimpse your future, but to change it:

1. **Follow your impulses.** Think of them as flashing hazard lights. Do this. Turn here. Call him. Go home. You feel compelled to act uncharacteristically, to do or say something that strikes others as illogical, unreasonable or nuts.
2. **Keep a journal.** Record your dreams and the synchronicities and precognitions you experience. Decode them. Mull them over. Learn the language of your inner world.
3. **Set your intentions.** Do this whenever you need an answer to something. Do it as a daily practice. Write it down. Repeat it to yourself. Mean it.
4. **Pay attention to signs and symbols.** We live in an ocean of signs and symbols that chatter constantly, a white noise that we can tune in on. The hawk that flies overhead as you're struggling to connect details in a creative endeavor could be saying, *Look at the big picture. See what's coming up.* A friend or lover has criticized you or you're beating yourself up for something, and the first thing you hear on your car radio is Taylor Swift's "Shake It Off," and the line "It's gonna be all right."
5. **Believe and follow through.** You have to believe, of course, that what you're feeling or sensing about the future isn't just wishful thinking or triggered by paranoia or abject fear. With an impulse, you won't have time to ponder and debate with yourself. You either follow it or you don't. But interpreting signs and symbols can be tricky unless you set your intentions before you set out on that bike ride, hike, drive or flight to wherever. It can be tricky as soon as you open your eyes in the morning. But you'll learn to navigate your way through it all and to take appropriate action.

Planetary Empaths

"What you got, son, I call it shinin on, the Bible calls it having visions, and there's scientists that call it precognition. I've read up on it, son. I've studied on it. They all mean seeing the future."

—Stephen King, *The Shining*

On May 1, 2015, two days before the 7.8 magnitude quake in Nepal, Jane Clifford of Wales was in her garden when she experienced such violent shaking she had to stretch out against the ground to stabilize herself. The next day, she told a friend that a massive earthquake was coming and the loss of life would be huge. Her friend's response was that quakes were going on all the time, but Jane insisted that her premonitions concern the ones that hit the global news.

When she woke up on the day of the quake, she felt shock, grief, terror, loss, and knew the quake had happened. "For hours, I struggled to clear those emotions, then I heard on the radio about Nepal and I knew there was more to come."

What's Going On?

In 2010, there were 373 major disasters that killed 296,800 people, more than the number of deaths by terrorist attacks in the past 40 years. These catastrophes impacted the lives of another 208 million. In all, the UN News Centre placed the cost of these catastrophes at close to $110 billion.

That year began with the catastrophic quake in Haiti on January 12, followed by the 8.8 quake in Chile on February 27, and then the devastating quakes in China and the eruption of Iceland's volcano Eyjafjallajökull that disrupted international air travel for weeks. Between May and August of that year, floods, mudslides, landslides and rockslides killed thousands. In September, a 7.1 quake threw New Zealand into chaos and a tornado touched down in Brooklyn and Queens, New York, rare for that area. In late October, Indonesia's Mount Merapi started erupting, killed more than 350 people and left nearly 400,000 refugees. In early December, Colombia experienced the heaviest rain in 40 years, and it created massive flooding and landslides.

In spite of acute attention in the media to erratic weather patterns, municipal authorities were caught off guard when Hurricane Sandy slammed into the Eastern Seaboard of the United States in the fall of 2012 and impacted 24 states. A storm surge hit Manhattan on October 29, flooding streets, tunnels and subway lines, and cutting power in and around the city. New Jersey was hit especially hard, with economic losses that totaled $30 billion. More than two million households lost power, nearly 350,000 homes were damaged or destroyed and 37 people lost their lives.

On January 14, 2016, Berkeley Earth, an independent nonprofit focused on land temperature data analysis for climate science, released its report on 2015 ahead of official reports from NASA and the National Oceanic and Atmospheric Administration (NOAA). The report stated that 2015 was "unambiguously" the hottest year on record: "For the first time in recorded history, the Earth's temperature is clearly more than 1.0 ° C (1.8 ° F) above the 1850–1900 average. 2015 was approximately 0.1° C (about 0.2° F) hotter than 2014, which had tied with 2005 and 2010 as the previous hottest years. 2015 set the record with 99.996% confidence. The analysis covered the entire surface of the Earth, including temperatures from both land and oceans."

In a press release, the organization's executive director, Elizabeth Muller, stated, "A year ago, we announced that 2014 was not a clear record, but only in a statistical tie with 2005 and 2010. Now, however, it is clear that 2015 is the hottest year on record by a significant margin."

In May alone, there were three billion-dollar weather disasters—a calamitous heat wave in India, mass flooding in China and the ongoing drought in California and other western states. Even skeptics of climate change, who insist that human activity doesn't affect climate, now concede the planet is getting hotter.

The National Weather Service pegged 2015 as South Florida's hottest year on record. December temperatures soared up to 14°F (nearly 8°C) above normal. April 2015 was the hottest on record since 1907, when Teddy Roosevelt was president. On April 26, 100°F (38°C) temperatures were reported in South Florida, a first ever in April for the state. In November 2015, heat records were broken all over Florida. On Christmas Day, the temperature in Manhattan was 70°F (21°C) and people were out and about in shorts and T-shirts. In December 2015, a heat wave shattered more than a thousand high-temperature records in the central and eastern United States.

But not everyone has been surprised by these weather patterns and disasters. Some people literally felt them coming.

Who Are They?

Planetary empaths is a term for precogs who are particularly sensitive to major disasters that affect or attract the attention of large numbers of people. They experience physical, emotional and psychic symptoms hours and sometimes days before natural or man-made disasters. They come from different states and countries, from different cultural, ethnic and spiritual backgrounds, and most seem to be women. The intensity of their symptoms appears to be connected to the severity of the disasters and often subside once the catastrophe has occurred.

The symptoms aren't connected to any known physical conditions or ailments and include, but aren't restricted to:

- *Abdominal pain or discomfort*
- *Bleeding from the ears*
- *Clicking or ringing in the ears*
- *Extreme vertigo*
- *Heart palpitations*
- *Insomnia*
- *Migraines that last for days*
- *Nausea for no apparent reason*
- *Nosebleeds*
- *Poltergeist phenomena*
- *Profound sadness*
- *Strange, vivid and powerful dreams about disasters*
- *Tingling or vibrating that runs up and down the arms and legs*

Inside a Planetary Empath

On March 11, 2011, at 2:46 p.m. Tokyo time, a 9.0 magnitude earthquake shook northern Japan for six minutes, moved the main island of Honshu eastward by 8 feet (nearly 2.5 m), shifted the earth on its axis by almost 4 inches (10 cm) and shortened the length of a day by a microsecond. The quake unleashed a tsunami that raced across the Pacific, triggering tsunami warnings and alerts for 50 countries and territories. Waves over 100 feet (30 m) high slammed into Honshu's shoreline and swept 6 miles (nearly 10 km) inland, destroying everything in their path. Nearly 16,000 people died. The tsunami struck the Fukushima nuclear plant and created the largest nuclear disaster since Chernobyl in April 1986.

The triple disaster caught the Japanese government, the Tokyo Electric Power Company and other authorities by surprise. But none of it surprised Debra Page, a paranormal researcher in Southern California, who began experiencing debilitating physical symptoms up to a week before the quake. Debra's ears rang constantly; she suffered from extreme vertigo and excruciating migraines. She couldn't sleep, couldn't function; a sense of profound sadness left her paralyzed and she ended up in the emergency room several times.

"I had severe ringing in my left ear, always a precursor to a quake or volcanic eruption." Four days before the quake, other symptoms surfaced: severe vertigo, nausea, a crippling fatigue and inexplicable nosebleeds. Debra knew that the impending quake, wherever it would occur, would be bad.

"Even though I was born intuitive and empathic, nothing prepared me for how those qualities would progress through my life," Debra said. In the early 1990s, she began to notice that her intuitive flashes were expanding to include world events. The curious thing was how these flashes translated into physical symptoms. Days before a world event, she would feel a profound grief and heartache that nearly crippled her. "Then I started noticing a pattern. The grief episodes would precede an event—either a natural or man-made disaster—and disappear when the event happened: Princess Diana's death, the beginning of the Gulf War, the shootings at Columbine, at Virginia Tech, the 2008 financial debacle."

Before the quake and tsunami in Sumatra, Indonesia, in 2004, Debra and her husband were out running errands. Suddenly, her left ear had a long, sustained ringing and she experienced simultaneous visions of destruction and flooding: "I knew many would die. I was so disoriented my husband had to hold me up until it was over. I told him what I was witnessing. I was horrified. I knew it would happen in three days, but didn't know *where* it would happen."

One afternoon shortly before the Japanese earthquake of March 2011, Connie Cannon was in a grocery store in Saint Augustine, Florida. Suddenly, the ground shifted abruptly beneath her and she grabbed on to a shelf to keep her balance. Her head hammered, her vision blurred and nausea gripped her. She barely made it out of the store to her car. Her husband and the other people around her didn't experience anything at all.

"Prior to higher magnitude earthquakes, no matter where they are going to occur, I begin to experience a sense of impending doom," Connie says. "This is quickly followed by an *edginess*, then the physical symptoms kick in. My ears click and ring and sometimes thump. Walking becomes a real issue, as if I'm trying to walk on a rocking, undulating boat at sea and I must hold on to the walls to keep my balance. The nausea is like seasickness. Although I have Parkinson's, there's a distinct difference between those symptoms and the planetary event warnings."

Before the 6.3 quake in New Zealand on February 21, 2011, Natalie Thomas, an Australian medium and mother of five, began to experience a great sense of agitation that came out of nowhere and "dreadful sadness akin to grief or a broken heart." Most of the time when these feelings begin to surface, it's as if a switch has been flicked on that allows her to feel the energy of events. The only thing she can equate it to is a sense of "being broken open."

Backstory

We started gathering information about planetary empaths in early 2010, when we began receiving emails from visitors to our synchronicity blog who described a spectrum of physical symptoms that they believed portended an impending natural disaster. Some of these people said the symptoms were similar to what they had experienced before other disasters—9/11, the Indonesian quake and tsunami in 2004, Hurricane Katrina in 2005 and Hurricane Andrew in 1992. In other words, the symptoms had been consistent throughout their adult lives. They had a means of comparison.

We didn't have any idea what the nature of this disaster might be until January 12, when a 7.0 quake struck 15 miles (24 km) southwest of Port au Prince, Haiti, at a depth of just 8.1 miles (13 km). According to the Disasters Emergency Committee (DEC), an organization in the United Kingdom, 3.5 million people were impacted by the quake. The death toll was enormous—more than 220,000, with another 300,000 injured—and the destruction massive.

DEC estimated that the quake resulted in nearly 25 million cubic yards (19 million m^3) of rubble and debris in Port au Prince, "enough to fill a line of shopping containers stretching end to end from London to Beirut." At one point, 1.5 million people were living in camps. In October, there was an outbreak of cholera that killed nearly 6,000 and left more than 200,000 infected.

After the initial quake had occurred, the planetary empaths reported that although their symptoms had subsided, they were still experiencing severe discomfort, indicating that the event wasn't over yet. Sure enough, within the first nine hours after the quake, the United States Geological Survey recorded 32 aftershocks of 4.2 or greater, and on January 24—*twelve days* after the quake—there were 52 aftershocks measuring 4.5 or greater. Only then did the empaths report that they were free of their symptoms.

9/11

Those numbers are indelibly imprinted on human consciousness. It's the day the world changed. Not surprisingly, planetary empaths experienced a spectrum of symptoms hours and even days before the first World Trade Center tower was hit.

From Barbara Martin:

> *"About a week prior to 9/11 I felt a shift in the atmosphere around me, followed by several days of restlessness and a knowing that something important and horrible was about to happen. Slightly after 2:00 p.m. GMT (UK) on September 11, I thought I heard cries coming from a great distance. It wasn't until several hours later that I learned about the events at the World Trade Center. After correlating the time difference between London, England and New York, I realized that the time I heard the cries occurred when the first plane hit the tower. Now I really pay attention to anything I experience that seems out of the ordinary."*

Connie Cannon's symptoms began three days before the disaster, on September 8, while she was at a wedding. "Suddenly, I felt as if a blowtorch was aimed directly into my throat, and all the life-force energy flowed down and out of my body through the soles of my feet. I had to grab my friend to keep from falling."

Her throat was burning so horribly she could barely breathe or speak and could hardly keep from falling. Another friend went to get her husband. Even though she was supposed to drive the bride and groom to the reception, she wasn't able to do it. Her husband had to drive her home. She didn't have a fever or physical symptoms of any kind, just that blowtorch burning in her throat and absolutely no energy.

She crawled into bed and remained there until Tuesday morning. She had no idea what was wrong with her. She felt as if she were "dead but breathing." She couldn't get up or function. "On Tuesday morning, the TV was on, and as soon as the first plane hit the first tower, I was perfectly normal again . . . fully alert, fully restored, no blowtorch in my throat."

Beyond Anecdotes

Numerous studies have shown that people respond physically between one and ten seconds before a startling event. In most of these studies, frightening pictures, such as a slithering snake or a human-size insect, were randomly mixed with nonfrightening images, such as a tranquil beach scene or an awe-inspiring mountain landscape.

Julia Mossbridge, a Northwestern University neuroscientist, examined more than two dozen of these studies. She and her team eliminated studies where they found experimental flaws or bias. "The claim is that events can be predicted without any cues. This evidence suggests the effect is real, but small. So the question is: How does it work?"

Mossbridge coauthored research in a study that was published October 17, 2015, in the journal *Frontiers of Perception.* The authors believe that presentiment—an older name for precognition—is a real, physical effect that obeys natural laws—ones that we don't understand. The study, not surprisingly, has come under attack by mainstream scientists, who don't accept the validity of presentiment. "While the statistical methods used in the study are sound, that doesn't mean presentiment is real," said Rufin VanRullen, a cognitive scientist at the Center for Research on the Brain and Cognition, in an e-mail to Tia Ghose, staff writer for LiveScience.com.

While the study doesn't apply directly to planetary empaths, it may be the closest form of the ability that can be studied under laboratory conditions and replicated. Interestingly, some scientists have connected awareness of big events with a "global mind" phenomenon.

Global Consciousness Project

The Global Consciousness Project (GCP) monitors what researcher Dean Radin calls the "global mind." Based at Princeton University and cosponsored by the Institute of Noetic Sciences, the project was started by Princeton's Dr. Roger Nelson, who defines the *global mind* as the combined consciousness of everyone on the planet.

The project collects data from a network of random number generators located in up to 70 host sites around the world at any given time. According to its website, global-mind.org, "When human consciousness becomes coherent, the behavior of random systems may change. Random number generators (RNGs) based on quantum tunneling produce completely unpredictable sequences of zeroes and ones. But when a great event synchronizes the feelings of millions of people, our network of RNGs becomes subtly structured. We calculate one in a trillion odds that the effect is due to chance. The evidence suggests an emerging noosphere or the unifying field of consciousness described by sages in all cultures."

Data are transmitted to a central archive that now contains more than fifteen years of random data. Nelson explains that the project's purpose is to scrutinize "subtle correlations that may reflect the presence and activity of consciousness in the world. We hypothesize that there will be structure in what should be random data, associated with major global events that engage our minds and hearts."

If you repeatedly flip a coin, it should result in an equal number of heads and tails. But with events of extreme global interest, the concentrated and emotional outpouring results in a noticeable difference in the percent of heads versus tails. When 9/11 occurred, it became a collective story of humanity. The most powerful country in the world had been attacked in its financial heart by disaffected men from the richest oil producer on the planet, who had commandeered commercial jets with cardboard cutters.

Radin, chief scientist for the Institute of Noetic Sciences, noted that on 9/11, thirty-seven of the random number generators were active. The fluctuations in the bell curve analysis indicated that anomalies began *two hours* before the first plane hit the World Trade Center. "That means that on that fateful day, the GCP's 'bells' collectively rang out around the world with an unusually pure tone," Radin said.

It also means that the fluctuations were *precognitive*, that the global mind's awareness of an imminent mass disaster rippled throughout time, into the future.

New Paradigms

Are planetary empaths the human equivalents of random number generators? Are they the 21st century shamans who can tap into the flow of human experience in a way that eludes the rest of us, in a way none of us would consciously choose—but that might help save lives? Like most shamans in traditional cultures, the empaths are usually not happy campers. They are disturbed by the abilities that disrupt their life and make it difficult for them to live normally.

What can we learn from them? How can they hone their abilities so they can pinpoint longitude and latitude, the exact place and the nature of the disaster? Is such a thing even possible? Is a new paradigm under construction here or have planetary empaths been around in one form or another for millennia?

One of the earliest modern examples of planetary empaths that we found was in *Forbidden Universe: Mysteries of the Psychic World*, published in 1975. The author, Leo Talamonti, recounts how during WWII, Lucia Alberti, who lived in Vienna, used to experience violent headaches and panic on the days leading up to an air raid. This fact was apparently so well known that "her friends would ring her up to know whether a raid was to be expected or not."

From the oracle at Delphi to Nostradamus and Edgar Cayce, the world has always had prophets and seers. But planetary empaths may be the quintessential result of the 21st century and an increasingly chaotic and divided world. They are radically different from other prophets in that their physical bodies and emotions are the conduits of precognitive information.

They don't have the luxury that Nostradamus did, whose visions came to him while he stared into a brass bowl filled with water. They can't distance themselves from the information as Edgar Cayce did when he entered a self-induced trance. They must deal with *physical* symptoms that are often so debilitating it's difficult to function, to go about the business of their daily lives.

The challenge for these individuals lies in defining the symptoms. Some know that a clicking or ringing in one ear or the other indicates an earthquake is imminent, or that feeling hot and flushed indicates a volcanic eruption is about to occur. But location eludes them. Geographical coordinates don't accompany the symptoms. Most of the time they don't even know on which continent the catastrophe will take place.

On March 9, 2011, two days before the triple catastrophe in Japan, we received the following e-mails from some of the empaths.

"No sleep the night before last," wrote Debra Page. "Now I am having an epic migraine. One of the worst I have ever had. I can't function. I do feel something is going to happen. I have had two poltergeist phenomena today: loud stomping with sounds of a door slamming."

From Connie Cannon: "Just a heads up about the planetary symptoms . . . They were so bad beginning late yesterday afternoon that I had to go to bed early. My heart went into AFib at 10:40 p.m."

Sharlie West wrote: "I dreamed about 9/11 a month before it happened. Interestingly, it was in reverse, i.e., the people and buildings were upside down. Also, it was in black and white. Now I am feeling that something else equally big is about to happen. I don't know the kind of big I'm feeling. It's elusive."

From Jenean Gilstrap, a poet from Louisiana: "One of the physical symptoms I've had is an unsteady gait/walk. It was obvious enough so that my little grandson, when he saw me grabbing the walls as I walked down the hall, asked me what was wrong. I remember thinking that I felt as if I were on the big ferry going across the local bay."

From Nancy Atkinson, a counselor in Nevada: "I'm feeling ill at ease . . . a tingling in my heart area . . . more tingling that runs down my legs."

On March 12, the day after the catastrophic quake and tsunami in Japan, we received an e-mail from Dave, one of the few men who has commented about planetary empath symptoms:

"I've had some weird symptoms in the past few days. My ears have had a persistent 'airplane ears' and they feel constantly blocked in a weird sense. I also have ringing in my ears. Now, as I play drums, I pretty much signed up for tinnitus. But this ringing is . . . different. It's much higher frequency, and sometimes it feels like it isn't there, then other times it is. I've also felt quite on edge, and don't have the focus I did a few days ago. Even more, I've felt absolutely shattered. My average sleep pattern for the last three years was about 3 a.m. to 2 p.m. but over the past few days, I've been crashing at 9 p.m. It's 1:30 a.m. now and I'm struggling to keep my eyes open. Weird indeed. I have a feeling we are *not* out of the woods."

At about the same time that Dave was writing us, the emergency battery power for the high-pressure core-flooder system for reactor 3 at Fukushima ran out. Less than two hours later, the fuel rods in reactor 3 were exposed.

In early April 2013, we began receiving e-mails from several empaths about severe physical symptoms they were experiencing. We eventually realized these symptoms were connected to the bombing at the Boston Marathon on April 15, 2013:

- *I feel as if I have a high fever and my eyes are burning like crazy, the way eyes burn from being exposed to a lot of fire and smoke. I just feel completely BAD, full-body BAD. This involves severe heat, probably fire, lots of death and/or injuries.*
- *I have severe bone aches, specifically in my legs and arms.*
- *Dizziness, vertigo, crippling pain in lower spine, deep bone marrow aches.*

On April 14, the day before the bombings, Jenean Gilstrap reported that she'd been having left ear vibrations, palpitations and dizziness. She was sitting outside on her daughter's deck, moved her chair slightly and suddenly "felt the earth tremble" and jerked her chair back.

Her daughter noticed and asked her what was wrong. Jenean replied, "Didn't you feel that? The earth just trembled and I thought I was going to fall off the edge."

Her daughter laughed and said it was all in her head.

The next day, of course, Jenean realized she'd been experiencing symptoms related to the bombings.

Ridicule is one reason these empaths are often reluctant to talk about their experiences. It's easy for other people to write off ringing in the ears or vertigo or a sense that the earth is rocking and rolling as being "in your head," that is, *you're imagining it.* In Western society, we're taught to distrust and dismiss our intuition and the validity of our own experiences. We're taught that skepticism is the only course that is *reasonable and logical* even when our own experiences tell us otherwise.

"Most biologists, agriculturists, and doctors have been brought up to believe that the mechanistic theory represents the triumph of reason over superstition, from which true science must be defended at all costs," writes British biologist Rupert Sheldrake in *Seven Experiments That Could Change the World.*

We've found that planetary empaths consistently report symptoms *prior* to major disasters. Rather than dismissing these folks as hypochondriacs or overly imaginative, we should recognize the possibility that they represent an emergence of something new in human consciousness. When that recognition reaches a tipping point, then perhaps the abilities of planetary empaths will expand or they will be able to train themselves to pinpoint the nature of the catastrophe, the time and the place where it will occur.

If these empaths were at that point now, perhaps the attacks in Paris on November 13, 2015, might have been mitigated, if not prevented.

Attacks in Paris

On the afternoon of November 11, 2015, we were in Orlando, visiting our daughter, when we received an e-mail from one of the empaths we've written about. She asked whether any of the other planetary empaths had reported symptoms.

"About 40 minutes ago, I began to feel very 'sick' (stomach), feel as if I have a fever . . . I don't. Temp is actually low: 97.2 degrees [36.2°C]. Also, am crying for no reason . . . feel an intense, overwhelming sense of great sadness enveloping me that has no basis in my life. I can't be still. Am walking, pacing the floor, and feel extreme nervous energy."

Connie Cannon said she had checked the usual worldwide geographical sites for any kind of earth events and decided that whatever she was feeling hadn't happened yet. Based on the strength of her symptoms, she felt that whatever was imminent was huge and would be accompanied by "untenable grief and/or loss." She felt it might not be a planetary event, but some type of human action: "A massive school shooting or something on that order. I do sense many people involved. I hate this. Absolutely hate it. When it [the event] manifests, the symptoms will dissipate."

We started checking the various earthquake sites. There had been a 6.9 quake off the coast of Chile that afternoon, followed by powerful aftershocks. No tsunami warning was issued and no damage or injuries were reported. This quake didn't appear to be what the empath was feeling. We checked for other planetary events—volcanic eruptions, tornadoes, flooding—but couldn't find anything, so we agreed with her that event hadn't occurred yet.

In a subsequent e-mail, Connie wrote that while reading a book, an attempt to escape her physical symptoms, the number 242 flashed into her mind. She felt it was relative to whatever pending event she sensed.

We Googled the number, checked latitudes and longitudes, turned the number inside out, but couldn't find anything connected to an event that had occurred that day.

We returned home on November 13, and that evening turned on the news and heard about the terrorist attacks in Paris. The attacks, at several different locations around the city, appeared to have been well coordinated. At the Bataclan theater, where hundreds of young people had gone to see a US rock group ironically named Eagles of Metal Death, the assailants took hostages and threw explosives at the people trapped in the theater. The scene there was described as carnage, with blood and bodies everywhere.

Another attack happened at a restaurant and bar in Paris's tenth arrondissement, where two unmarked men got out of a car armed with AK-47s and shot and killed eleven people. Two explosions went off outside a Parisian stadium where a soccer match between France and Germany was under way. The French president was attending the match and was evacuated to safety. He promptly placed the city of Paris under mandatory curfew, the first time since 1944, and closed the country's border. Later in the evening, he clarified that by saying that border patrols and inspections had intensified.

Less than a week after the attacks, the Belgian jihadist suspected of being the ring leader in the Paris attacks was subsequently killed. The final death toll was 129, with 368 injured. Neither figure was the one the empath had foreseen. We still don't know how or whether the number 242 is connected to the tragedy in Paris.

Possible Scenario

Is there a way these empaths could be trained—or could train themselves—to bring forth more specific information so that the event could be prevented or mitigated? Well, maybe.

Perhaps planetary empaths could attempt to answer the five interrogatives that are at the heart of journalism: *Who? What? When? Where? Why?* With practice, their answers might provide enough information to save lives.

Who? Is there a person or persons behind this upcoming catastrophe? Can you describe them? Their appearance, their nationality?

What? Is the event natural or man-made? If natural, what type of event is it? Volcanic? An earthquake? Tsunami? Tornado? Something else? If the event is man-made, what is its nature? Is it hot or cold? Explosive? Gunfire? Does it involve water or fire?

Where? Location. What direction is it from the empath's location? Can you pick up any names of an actual city or country?

When? How far into the future does this event take place? Minutes, hours, days, weeks, months? This specificity would be important in determining whether the effects of the event could be mitigated or prevented.

Why? What motivates the people involved in any kind of man-made disaster? Is it religion, a particular set of beliefs, madness, something else?

Although we're all precogs to some degree, most of us would definitely not seek to become planetary empaths. At the extreme, their physical symptoms are so crippling that they fall into bed with ice packs on their heads and the world fades to black around them.

People in this state might not want to answer questions from others, and may be incapable of doing so themselves. That's the first big wall. But if they could get around it, if these empaths could learn to ignore their symptoms or disassociate from the pain and discomfort, we might be able to answer a sixth interrogative: *What if?*

What if the date and location of the Paris attacks had been provided by an empath?

What if the name of the stadium or the theater or even the restaurant could be pinpointed?

What if an empath could see the time of day?

Are planetary empaths the emerging shamans of what eventually becomes the vastly changed planet that our children and grandchildren will inherit? We need to pay attention to them and, somehow, decipher what they are experiencing.

A History of the Future

People like us, who believe in physics, know that the distinction between past, present and future is only a stubbornly persistent illusion.

—Albert Einstein

Whether it's called precognition, presentiment, augury, premonition, divination or prophecy, sensing the future has been a part of life for millennia. Those with the ability were known as shamans, seers, diviners, augurs, prophets and oracles, and they were typically well respected in their community. They counseled powerful leaders in times of war and peace, and they guided common people on their paths.

Some made significant marks, and a few are remembered to this day for their remarkable talents. Still others, self-appointed prophets among them, are best remembered for being wrong.

It's Armageddon, Baby!

One particular prophecy that stands out in the category of "That was really wrong" are the notorious predictions of specific dates for the end of the world, variously known as Armageddon, the Apocalypse and the Second Coming. A related term is the Great Tribulation, which refers to a period of hardship, disaster, famine, war and despair following Armageddon. These prophecies are invariably embarrassing for the prognosticators the day after the predicted apocalyptic event when the sun rises and life continues on.

To name a few:

- *The oldest known prediction of the end of the world, according to an article on Smithsonian.com, is recorded on Assyrian tablets from the 28th century BC. "Our Earth is degenerate in these later days; there are signs that the world is speedily coming to an end; bribery and corruption are common; children no longer obey their parents; every man wants to write a book and the end of the world is evidently approaching." We're not too sure about the accuracy of the translation about books, since the prophecy itself was written on a clay tablet! But even Isaac Asimov used this quote in* The Book of Facts, *which he edited.*
- *Italian painter Sandro Botticelli believed he was living during the end times in 1504, according to an inscription on his painting* The Mystical Nativity.
- *Jacob Bernoulli, a prominent mathematician in his day, predicted that a comet seen in 1680 would return and collide with Earth in 1719. The comet has yet to make a reappearance.*
- *William Miller, a Baptist preacher, predicted the end of the world would come in 1843, then 1844. Apparently, some of his followers weren't deterred by the no-show for the end times, and went on to become founding members of the Seventh Day Adventists . . . who are still waiting for the end.*
- *The Jehovah's Witnesses probably have the worst record on predictions for Armageddon. Generically, Armageddon is synonymous with end times. For the Jehovah's Witnesses, it means the armies of heaven will eradicate all who oppose the kingdom of God, wiping out false religions and wicked humans on Earth, leaving only righteous humans. All governments will be banished and Jesus and 140,000 humans will rule for 1,000 years. Predicted years for this big event include 1914, 1915, 1918, 1920, 1925, 1941, 1975 and 1997. Apparently, they didn't bite at the millennium, but you've got to give them credit for trying repeatedly.*
- *The end times were abundantly predicted in the 1980s. Pat Robertson predicted mass destruction on Earth in 1980, 1982 and 1985.*
- *Hal Lindsey, who wrote* The Late Great Planet Earth, *predicted a pretribulation rapture in 1981. Nice that some good folks go directly to heaven in their current body and escape what's left behind. When no rapture or tribulation occurred, he explained the postponement a few years later in* There's a New World Coming: An In-Depth Analysis of the Book of Revelation.

- *Edgar Whisenant, a former NASA rocket engineer and Bible student, and Colin Deal, an author of prophecy books, both predicted the Second Coming for 1988. The following year, Whisenant did it again. Unless it's a secret, we're still waiting.*

- *In the 1990s, as we pushed toward the millennium, more prophecies of doom and the Second Coming were predicted. Louis Farrakhan said the looming Gulf War would be the "War of Armageddon," the final war. He was clearly premature, as worse wars followed.*

- *Rollen Stewart predicted the Second Coming in 1992, as did the Mission for the Coming Days. Two years later, Harold Camping predicted the Second Coming, and that same year some Jehovah's Witnesses said it was finally time for Armageddon.*

- *If it seems we're picking on the faithful believers in the old-time religion, here's the New Age version. Elizabeth Claire Prophet predicted the end times for March 15, 1990, by way of thermonuclear war. This end-times believer even endorsed herself by putting prophecy in her last name. She followed a New Age belief system influenced by theosophy and Alice Bailey. She said her prophecies came from ascended masters during the 1960s and 1970s. Possibly, they were ascended tricksters. Not the most humble of prophets, she donned the title vicar of Christ, wrote several books and advocated survivalism.*

- *In 1997, a cult called Heaven's Gate predicted Earth changes and a major UFO abduction scenario that would coincide with Comet Hale-Bopp's appearance. A mass suicide followed as believers expected to catch a ride on the UFOs.*

- *Just after the Islamic State, or ISIS, was established in 2006, its founder, Abu Ayyad al-Masri, ordered his lieutenants to prepare to conquer Iraq within weeks. He said that the Mahdi was going to come and they would surely have amazing victories. The Mahdi is the prophesized redeemer of Islam who will rule for seven, nine or nineteen years—depending on the interpretation—before the Day of Judgment when the world will be rid of evil. At the time, ISIS was viewed in the West as a "junior varsity" terrorist organization. They were pummeled and no Mahdi appeared. But the failed prophecy didn't deter ISIS, which is known for using end-time prophecies to recruit followers as it rampages across the Middle East.*

- *In spite of previous failures during the last century, some prophets-in-training returned with prophecies for the new century. In 2007, Pat Robertson predicted a Great Tribulation. That same year, Hal Lindsey revived his prophetic nature and predicted the Second Coming.*

- *Harold Camping returned with a prediction for the Second Coming and rapture for May 21, 2011. He even put up billboards, but later postponed the Second Coming until October 21. Since money would be useless after the rapture, Camping encouraged followers to send him their savings so he could promote the upcoming event. No doubt some were poor and disappointed when they woke up on October 22 and found they remained earth-bound.*

- *The 5,126-year Mayan calendar ended on December 21, 2012, and in the weeks and months before, there was a lot of talk about end times. But anyone who took a closer look at the subject realized that a new calendar began the next day as the Fourth World moved into the Fifth World. Welcome to the Fifth World.*
- *More recently, megachurch pastor John Hagee predicted that the tetrad of lunar eclipses and blood moons between April 2014 and October 2015 would signal the start of end times. Meanwhile, Hal Lindsey pushed back the Second Coming to 2018.*

While these enthusiastic believers in Biblical prophecy have been eager to bring end-time revelations to the masses, they're batting zero in accuracy and give precognition a bad name. Yet, if we move beyond rigid religious interpretations of earlier prophecies, it's not difficult to imagine that the world is moving toward some sort of apocalyptic event, possibly a combination that involves war, pestilence and environmental disaster that would drastically reduce the world's population. Rather than taking place on one particular date, the events—if action isn't taken to prevent them from occurring—could unfold over a generation or longer.

When it comes to making prophecies, it seems that the pagans had a much better track record than the end-time forecasters. At least that's true for the famed Oracle of Delphi. Historians, in fact, have found that more than half of the known prophecies by the oracle—and hundreds have survived—were historically correct.

The Delphi Oracle

For hundreds of years, the famed Delphic Oracle advised kings and commoners about future events. The Oracle was a succession of prescient women who were known as Pythia. They performed their sacred duties under the guidance of priests at the Temple of Apollo, located on the slopes of Mount Parnassus.

Built around a sacred spring, Delphi was considered to be the omphalos—the navel of the world. The virgin priestess of Apollo sat on a tripod over a fissure and breathed vapors rising from the abyss. The fumes induced a trance, and Pythia muttered or shouted messages that were interpreted by attendant priests, who conveyed their translations to the supplicants.

"Such prophecy," wrote Socrates, "is akin to madness, but it is a madness which is the special gift of heaven, and the source of the chiefest blessings among men. For prophecy is a madness, and the prophetess at Delphi and the priestesses of Dodona, when out of their senses, have conferred great benefits to Hellas, both in public and private life, but when their senses were few or none."

If longevity is a key factor in judging the success of an enterprise, then the Oracle of Delphi was an astonishingly successful mystical endeavor. It dates back to 1400 BC, and survived until the fourth century AD. While Pythia was appointed for life, the temple priests were the power behind the mystical throne. They monitored and interpreted Pythia's mumblings, but sometimes the priestess needed no such intermediary.

That was the case in AD 67 when the Roman emperor Nero vacationed in Greece. Eight years earlier, the brutal ruler had killed his mother, and that event would come into play when he visited the Oracle at Delphi. As

Nero approached the adyton, a sunken chamber below the floor of the temple that measured just 9 by 12 feet (2.75 by 3.66 m), Pythia was perched on her seat and inhaled the sweet fumes rising from the fissure. Several priests were stationed nearby and anxiously awaited to hear what Pythia would tell the unstable young emperor.

Pythia's long hair cascaded over her shoulders and partially covered her face as she raised her gaze. Her wide-eyed, crazed demeanor shifted to anger at the sight of Nero, and she shouted: "Your presence here outrages the god you seek. Go back, matricide! The number 73 marks the hour of your downfall!"

That was the last declaration that Pythia would ever make. Nero was infuriated and had Pythia buried alive in the sacred chamber, along with the bodies of the temple priests, whose hands and feet were chopped off by the emperor's henchmen.

Nero thought the number 73 would be his age at death. He was only 30 years old, so he didn't worry about it. The number actually related to Galba, who was 73 when, in AD 68, he succeeded Nero after the emperor, fearing that he would be overthrown, committed suicide.

Alexander the Great, like Nero, had little respect for Pythia. He visited the Delphic Oracle hoping to hear a prophecy that he would soon conquer the entire ancient world. To his surprise, the oracle refused to reply and told him to come back later. Enraged, Alexander dragged Pythia by the hair out of her chamber until she screamed, "Let go of me; you're unbeatable." The moment he heard those words, he let her go and said, "Now I have my answer."

About 500 predictions made by the Oracle of Delphi have survived, including one from 550 BC that was initiated by Croesus, king of Lydia, who set out to unite all Greek cities in Asia under his rule. He conquered several cities, but became concerned about the growing threat of the Persians. He decided to test several famous oracles before he would ask about his chances against the Persians. He asked the oracles to tell him what he was doing on a particular day.

He sent messengers to Greece and Libya, where the oracles were located. He instructed the messengers to wait until the 100th day after their departure before making their inquiries to the oracles.

On that day, the king chopped up a lamb and a tortoise and placed the pieces in a brass cauldron, covered it with a lid and boiled the contents. The answer from the Oracle of Delphi was the one that impressed the king the most: "I count the grains of sand on the beach and measure the sea; I understand the speech of the dumb and hear the voiceless. The smell has come to my sense of a hard shelled tortoise boiling and bubbling with a lamb's flesh in a bronze pot: the cauldron underneath it is of bronze, and bronze is the lid."

Confident of the oracle's abilities, Croesus decided to seek counseling from Pythia regarding a question about war with the Persians. He sent substantial treasures of gold and silver to the oracle and his messenger posed the question. The oracle responded, "If Croesus goes to war, he will destroy a great empire."

Croesus was pleased with the answer and made preparations to confront the Persian army. The ensuing battle was indecisive, with both sides suffering substantial losses. Croesus withdrew for the winter, releasing his army and planned for a new attack in the spring. However, the Persians pursued him and massacred his cavalry, and Croesus was dragged away in chains.

The oracle's prediction had come true. Croesus had destroyed a great empire—his own. Such ambiguous answers from the oracle were commonplace over the centuries. It was as if the gods were covering their bases by offering such trickster responses to the inquiries from the rich and mighty.

In 480 BC, the Greeks were again faced with a battle against the Persians when King Xerxes and his army were plotting against Greece. Before the Battle of Salamis, the Athenians sought counsel with the oracle. In this case, Pythia's prophecy was unambiguous. Pythia told the Athenians they were doomed. "Now your statues are standing and pouring sweat. They shiver with dread. The black blood drips from the highest rooftops. They have seen the necessity of evil. Get out, get out of my sanctum and drown your spirits in woe."

However, the Athenians didn't believe they would be defeated, so they returned to the oracle a second time. Again, Pythia told them to leave.

"Await not in quiet the coming of the horses, the marching feet, the armed host upon the land. Slip away. Turn your back. You will meet in battle anyway. O holy Salamis, you will be the death of many a woman's son between the seed time and the harvest of the grain." The Persians soundly defeated the Athenians, destroying the Spartan army and proving the oracle correct.

If the oracle was only occasionally accurate, it wouldn't have survived for centuries. Historians have studied the massive collection of readings that survived and found that more than half of them pointed to historically correct events that followed the prophecies.

However, in some instances, Pythia simply offered savvy advice, telling questioners to figure it out for themselves. That was the case in 83 BC, when the great Roman orator Cicero consulted the oracle and asked how he should find greatest fame. He was told: "Make your own nature, not the advice of others, your guide in life."

Cicero was subsequently defeated by Julius Caesar, but he went on to cultivate his oratory skills in the courts and preserved Rome from the Catilinarian conspiracy, which earned him great fame. He'd followed the lead provided by Pythia and achieved his goal.

By the fourth century AD, Rome was becoming Christian and its pagan past was waning. That spelled the end for the Oracle of Delphi. However, a Roman leader visited the oracle and said he wanted to revive classic Greek culture. The response, which has survived, might be the final prophecy from Pythia: "Tell to the king that the cavern wall is fallen in decay; Apollo has no chapel left, no prophesying bay, no talking stream. The stream is dry that had so much to say."

Apollo was no more and the time for reviving Greek culture was over. The Christian era had begun.

Over the next thousand years, prophecy—like art—in Western civilization would be heavily influenced by biblical themes. However, at the beginning of the 16th century, a new prophet would be born, one whose prophetic writings seemingly peered well into modern times. Interestingly, he secretly followed a path of prophecy that flashed back to ancient Greece, and in particular to Branchus, the son of Apollo.

Nostradamus

One of the world's most famous seers, Nostradamus, was born Michel de Nostredame on December 14, 1503. His life story, as well as his prophecies, have been passed down over the centuries, and numerous books have been written about him. He was born into a prosperous family in Saint-Rémy, Provence, in southern France, where his father was a notary. The family was originally Jewish, but converted to Catholicism to avoid persecution that was rampant in Europe in the 15th and 16th centuries. The French king Louis XII had ordered all Jews to be baptized or face dreadful consequences.

Michel's ancestors were merchants and doctors, and a similar future awaited him. He excelled in his studies and after he received his doctorate at the Montpellier University, he changed his name to the Latin version, Nostradamus. However, an incident from his youth foretold of the real direction his life would take.

While attending a Catholic school in Avignon, he made his first prediction. Having seen two young pigs at the barnyard, a black one and a white one, he said the white pig would be killed by a wolf and the black one served for dinner. After the rector found out about the prediction, he ordered to have the black pig slaughtered and buried, and to serve the white pig for dinner immediately. The cook rushed to fulfill the order, but was told at the barnyard that the white pig had been snatched by a wolf that had entered the barn through the roof, and only the black pig was left. Unsure of what to do, the cook served the black pig for dinner.

Nostradamus's love of astrology and his talent for prophecy were encouraged by both of his grandfathers, who were physicians to the king and his son, and part of the king's touring group of scholars and artists. King René had been extremely tolerant of Jews, unlike his successor, Louis XII. Nostradamus spent much of his youth living with his grandfather, Jean de Saint-Rémy, and excelled at mathematics and astrology, while learning Latin, Greek and Hebrew.

He studied liberal arts at Avignon University and wanted to become an astrologer, but conceded that it would be wiser to study medicine. In 1522, he began at the University of Montpellier. Three years later, he passed his exams and received his medical license. He headed off to the countryside with his medical and astrology books to practice medicine just as the plague was sweeping through Europe.

He spent the next ten years battling the plague, saving hundreds of lives from the deadly disease as he traveled from town to town on his mule. His formula was simple: fresh air, clean water and lemon juice mixed with water, which contains vitamin C. But it defied the medical practices of the time that actually discouraged cleanliness and advocated bleeding patients. However, his results were recognized and the Provence Parliament granted Nostradamus a lifetime pension in 1546. As a result, he remained financially independent until the end of his life.

While pursuing a busy life as a physician, Nostradamus studied occult sciences, including alchemy, with doctors and pharmacists on numerous evenings. By 1529, the plague had subsided and he returned to his studies. He successfully defended his approach to medicine against arguments by doubters and received his doctorate of medicine at Montpellier. He was already famous and a large crowd showed up for his oral exam that was held before the entire faculty. He taught for three years at Montpellier, but left when he faced restrictions on what texts he could use.

Nostradamus moved to Agen, where he practiced medicine, was happily married and had two children. But the plague swept through the town in 1537, taking the lives of his wife and children. The loss of the doctor's family was considered scandalous and most of his wealthy patients deserted him.

He took to the road again, roaming the countryside, seeking a new life and avoiding Church Inquisitors who were investigating him. Nostradamus redeemed himself after he arrived in Aix in 1544 in the midst of the plague to find that all the doctors had fled or died. He went to work tirelessly for 270 days, administering his cure and saving people and the city.

Afterward, he received his pension for life, but didn't retire. He moved on to Salon to fight the plague, then to Lyon. He went back to Salon-de-Provence, where he spent the rest of his life. He married a rich widow and lived a comfortable life. He also found time to pursue his interest in astrology and other occult practices. He was a devout Catholic by day, but at night he followed the way of Branchus, the son of Apollo, who had received prophetic abilities from his father.

When the time was right, he would sit on a brass tripod in front of a brass bowl filled with water, divinatory tools designed after the ones used by Branchus in his mystical explorations. Nostradamus would move into a meditative state by staring at the flame of a candle. As he sank deeper into trance, he heard voices and glimpsed visions in the brass bowl. When he foresaw a religious war approaching that would result in the downfall of the French king, he wanted to warn his fellow citizens. Yet he was wary of persecution and waited until 1550 to publish his prophecies in an almanac.

His first book in the almanac included a section containing twelve four-line poems called quatrains, which provided a general prophecy for each month of the coming year. The success of the book augured well for future editions and he began writing one for each coming year. Meanwhile, he worked on a more ambitious project, his ultimate book of prophecy that would describe the future of mankind for centuries. In fact, that's what he called it. He planned ten volumes of the *Centuries*, each featuring 100 quatrains, many set hundreds of years in the future.

Seven of the *Centuries* books were published in 1555. Thanks to the success of his almanacs, he became the darling of the nobility and was called to the Paris court at the behest of Catherine de Médici, the French queen who was particularly impressed with the seer's abilities.

Nostradamus had predicted that French king Henry II would either unite the French Empire that was divided between Catholics and Huguenots, or he would die from a jousting accident. The king's own astrologer had earlier warned Henry II not to participate in any tournaments during his 41st year. The astrologer, Luc Gauric, said that if he did so, he would die of a head wound. Nostradamus's 35th quatrain predicted the accidental death:

The young Lion will overcome the old one
On the field of combat in single battle
He will pierce his eyes through a golden cage
Two wounds made one, then he dies a cruel death.

It was fulfilled on July 9, 1559, during a tournament celebrating the wedding of the king of Spain to Henry II's daughter and Henry's sister to the Duke of Savoy. Henry II and his opponent, Gabriel Montgomery, were garbed in full armor, both with shields bearing images of lions.

When Montgomery's lance shattered, a splinter pierced Henry's gold-plated visor and penetrated his head behind his eyes. He was blinded and died ten days later. Ironically, the match had ended as a draw, but the king tested fate by insisting on a second match, even though Montgomery had tried to withdraw.

The news of the cruel death resounded throughout France. The queen was furious and a mob burned Nostradamus in effigy and called on the Inquisition to send the prophet to a fiery death. Nostradamus prepared for the worst, but Catharine de Médici overcame her anger and placed Nostradamus in charge of her children's education.

Nostradamus's precognitive abilities sometimes turned to mundane events. During his first visit to the court, he became ill with gout and remained for days in his room. One day, a page for a noble rushed to Nostradamus's door and, without identifying himself, called out for help. He had lost his lord's prize hunting dog.

Nostradamus responded: "What troubles you, king's page! You are making a lot of noise over a lost dog. Go along the road of Orleans. There you will find the dog led on a leash." The boy hurried away, following the suggested road, and found the dog being led back to Paris by a servant. The page was baffled by how Nostradamus knew he was a king's page and on which road he would find the dog. The story spread in the court and Nostradamus's fame expanded.

While his prophecies extended to events thousands of years in the future, his final forecast was his own death. According to Jacques Chauvigny, his aide and biographer, one evening he wished Nostradamus good night and the seer replied, "You will not find me alive at sunrise." He had also written about his death in his last almanac. The final prophecy read:

On his return from the Embassy,
the King's gift put in place.
He will do nothing more.
He will be gone to God.
Close relatives, friends,
brothers by blood
(Will find him) completely
dead near the bed and the bench.

And that was just what happened. On the morning of July 1, 1566, Nostradamus lay breathless on the floor in his study. He had collapsed between his bed and bench. He was 63 . . . and a prophet to the end.

But Nostradamus wasn't quite done with his amazing predictions. His body was placed upright in a coffin behind a wall of Salon's Church of the Cordeliers. There it would remain until 1700. In that year, the city fathers decided to move his coffin to a more prominent wall of the church. A rumor had spread since his death that a secret document would be found in the coffin that would help decode his prophecies. When the coffin was moved, it was briefly opened. No such document was found. Instead, the skeleton supposedly wore a medallion inscribed with the year 1700.

Many of his prophecies were related to the histories of France and England, the rise and fall of empires, including the French Revolution. He cited 1792 as a key year in the revolution. That turned out to be the year the revolutionaries discarded the old calendar for a new one to mark 1792 as the year they thought a new age would begin.

Although Nostradamus's prophecies are often puzzlingly obscure to present-day readers, they've been of particular interest over recent decades because many were linked to the 20th century and major world events. Among them are prophecies related to the Bolshevik revolution, the murder of the Russian royal family, the rise of Hitler, Mussolini and Stalin, the Holocaust and the defeat of Nazi Germany in World War II.

Here's an excerpt about the collapse of the Soviet Union: "The new Babylon, augmented by the abomination of the first Holocaust, will last no less than seventy-three years and seven months."

If the Soviet era started at the dissolution of the Russian Constituent Assembly by the Bolsheviks on January 19, 1918, and ends at the 1991 coup, that's exactly 73 years and seven months.

Of course, Nostradamus was not always correct on dates. For example, he predicted a serious attack on New York City in 1999, when he wrote:

The year 1999 seven months
From the sky will come the great King of Terror.
To bring back to life the great King of the Mongols,
Before and after Mars to reign by good luck.

—Centuries X, quatrain 72

That quatrain today reads like a precursor to 9/11, but two years and two months ahead of time. The following quatrain is also suggestive of the attack on the World Trade Center. The mention of 45 degrees could refer to the angle of viewers from several blocks away who watched the burning buildings. After all, those who were closer, instead of looking up at the higher angle, would no doubt be fleeing the scene.

The sky will burn at 45 degrees.
Fire approaches the New City.
In an instant a huge scattered flame
Leaps up.

—Centuries VI, quatrain 97

Other famous prophecies from Nostradamus, and their common interpretations include:

The Great Fire of London, 1666:

The blood of the just will be demanded of London,
Burnt by the fire in the year 66.

The Rise of Napoleon, which included an anagram of his name:

PAU, NAY, LORON will be more of fire than of the blood,
To swim in praise, the great one to flee to the confluence.

Louis Pasteur, the French chemist:

Lost, found, hidden for so long a time,
the pastor will be honored as a demigod.

Adolf Hitler:

From the depths of the West of Europe,
A young child will be born of poor people,
He who by his tongue will seduce a great troop;
His fame will increase towards the realm of the East.

Beasts ferocious from hunger will swim across rivers:
The greater one will cause it to be dragged in an iron cage
When the Germany child will observe nothing.

Second World War:

The two greatest ones of Asia and of Africa,
From the Rhine and Lower Danube they will be said to have come,
Cries, tears at Malta and the Ligurian side.

Atomic bombs:

Near the gates and within the cities
there will be two scourges the like of which was never seen,
famine within plague, people put out by steel,
crying to the great immortal God for relief.

Death of the Kennedy brothers:

The great man will be struck down in the day by a thunderbolt,
An evil deed foretold by the bearer of a petition.
Another falls at night time.
Conflict at Reins, London and a pestilence in Tuscany.

Death of Princess Diana:

The penultimate of the surname of Prophet
Will take Diana [Thursday] for his day and rest:
He will wander because of a frantic head,
And delivering a great people from subjection.

Skeptics say Nostradamus's prophecies are ambiguous, that meaning can be attributed to them after dramatic events, such as 9/11 or the death of Princess Diana, and that the connections cited are mere mind games played by believers. In fact, the prophet is a favorite target of skeptics on the Internet, where numerous websites and blog posts dissemble the quatrains and scorn those who find meaning in the prophecies.

If there were only a handful of puzzling quatrains that seem to identify events, then the criticism would ring true. But when we examine Nostradamus's entire collection of prophecies, as well as the recorded precognitive events that took place in his life that weren't set in quatrains, then the mystery of the man and his prophetic words can't be dismissed so easily. In a sense, Nostradamus's volumes of quatrains are like astrology. You can find meaning in the movement of the cosmos, as he did, or you can see nothing but empty space and shiny objects in the night sky.

While Nostradamus is probably the best-known prophet, because so much is known about his life and his volumes of prophecies, Harriet Tubman is much better known for her efforts to free slaves than for her precognitive abilities. But without them, it's doubtful she would've accomplished as much as she did.

The Conductor of Premonitions

Harriet Tubman was born a slave in Maryland in the early 1820s and was nearly killed at age twelve when she refused to help an overseer hold a boy who was attempting to escape slavery. The overseer hurled a 2-pound (1-kg) piece of lead that struck her in the forehead. After that, Tubman was never the same. She received no medical attention for the wound, and a hole remained in her forehead, which she covered with masculine hats. In addition to the horrible headaches and blurred vision, she began glimpsing future events. She was able to escape from slavery in 1849 and became a leading abolitionist before the American Civil War.

She returned to the South numerous times to rescue both family members and nonrelatives from the plantation system. She helped 300 slaves escape and was never caught, a fact that she attributed to her precognitive abilities. She said she was able to see into the future to where the slave hunters would be searching for her. She took frequent short naps and supposedly was able to travel out of her body and foresee which houses were safe havens for runaway slaves, where they would be fed and given a place to sleep for the night.

She became known as the Moses of her people and the most famous "conductor" on the Underground Railroad, an elaborate secret network of safe houses organized for that purpose. Although her visionary abilities developed after her head injury, she often said she inherited her talents from her father, who could see the future.

In early 1858, Tubman had a vision that she would meet abolitionist John Brown, who advocated the use of violence to disrupt and destroy the institution of slavery. In April of that year, she was introduced to him. Tubman shared his goals and tolerated his methods. When Brown began recruiting supporters for an attack on slaveholders at Harpers Ferry, he called on "General Tubman" for help. After Brown was executed, Tubman praised him as a martyr.

When the Civil War broke out, Tubman worked for the Union Army as a cook and nurse. But because of her background and unique abilities, she quickly became an armed scout and spy. In fact, Harriet Tubman was probably America's first psychic spy when she guided the Combahee River Raid, which liberated more than 700 slaves in South Carolina.

Biographies of Tubman's life written in recent decades tend to skirt her precognitive abilities and make reference to her being deeply religious. Possibly researchers have hesitated exploring that aspect of Tubman's life because they thought it might denigrate her legacy, exploit her life's work or even bring into question the integrity of the researcher.

In spite of her difficult life and the many dangers she faced, Tubman lived until the age of 92 and died in 1913.

The Nazi's Astrologer

Karl Ernst Krafft was a Swiss-German astrologer, statistician and researcher. After he graduated from university, he spent nearly a decade writing *Traits of Astro-Biology*. This ambitious tome focused on Krafft's theory of "typocosmy," a method of forecasting the future based on the study of an individual's personality.

Krafft was sympathetic to the Nazis and followed the rise of the Nazi party with great interest. He wrote to a member of the secret intelligence service about the possibility of an assassination attempt on Hitler that would occur between November 7 and 9, 1939. But his message was disregarded. On November 8, 1939, a bomb exploded in Munich's Bürgerbräukeller, a beer hall, only minutes after Hitler had left. Krafft then sent Rudolph Hess a telegram reminding him of his earlier prediction and was promptly arrested by the Gestapo.

When Krafft proved that he could accurately predict events with astrology, the Gestapo released him and in 1940 the Nazi party requested that Krafft apply his knowledge to their cause. Joseph Goebbels hired him to translate the prophecies of Nostradamus believed to be related to the Nazis. Krafft was the right guy for the job. He believed that Nostradamus had predicted the supreme reign of the Third Reich and in January 1940, Krafft went to work for Goebbels. At the time, the Gestapo was arresting and eliminating astrologers and occultists.

Many of the Nazi attacks were believed to be based on the astrological calculations made by Krafft, who said that if the Nazis were to be victorious, the war needed to end by 1943. Krafft eventually fell out of favor with the Nazis, was imprisoned and died en route to the Buchenwald concentration camp in 1945.

The Sleeping Prophet

Writer Jess Stearn named his book about Edgar Cayce *The Sleeping Prophet* and the name stuck. But Cayce, known for his uncanny prophecies, didn't sleep through his precognitive utterings. He knew how to relax and enter a deep meditative state where he connected with an underlying reality outside of the everyday world and glimpsed visions of the future. In retrospect, many were startlingly accurate, others not so much.

If we are to accept the work of his biographers, Edgar Cayce's childhood was as astonishing and unusual as his accomplishments as an adult. Born in a small town in Kentucky on March 18, 1877, Cayce played with imaginary friends he called the "little folk" and talked with his dead grandfather. He also saw a woman with wings who guided him. At age ten, he was taken to a church service and given a Bible. He supposedly read it a dozen times by the time he was twelve. Even though his later psychic readings often contradicted dogmatic religious beliefs, he became a lifelong Christian, Sunday school teacher and missionary.

As a youngster, he didn't apply himself to his schoolwork and when his father punished him for his inability to pass a spelling test, Edgar heard the voice of the woman with wings, who had first appeared to him the day before. She told him to lay his head on his spelling book and rest, and "they" would help. His father agreed to give him a break and when he returned to drill him again, Edgar knew all the spelling words. He later applied the same technique with other books and became the top student in his class. When his teacher asked how he knew all the answers, Edgar said he could see pictures of the pages.

Shortly after the turn of the century, a severe bout of laryngitis left Cayce unable to speak. His recovery was aided by hypnosis and, eventually, by self-hypnosis. While in a trance state, Cayce said his inability to speak was related to a psychological paralysis. Possibly, it related to his subconscious hesitation to pursue the controversial career that he was about to embark upon—the readings for which he became famous.

For more than 40 years, Cayce answered questions from a meditative state that he easily entered. He would stretch out on a couch, close his eyes and fold his hands over his stomach. While he gave readings on health, dreams, meditation, religion, reincarnation and other topics, he is best known for his prophecies.

Like many others before and after him, Cayce predicted apocalyptic events related to Earth changes, possibly from a pole shift, which would take place either in the 1930s, 1960s or 1990s. He predicted that 1998 would see either the rising of Atlantis, the sinking of California or the Second Coming of Christ. He also predicted that the "greater portion of Japan must go into the sea," that northern Europe would be changed as in the twinkling of an eye. These Earth changes would occur as a result of a tilting of the Earth's rotational axis.

Fortunately, Cayce was wrong on the timing of Earth changes, but in the second decade of the 21st century—100 years after he made such predictions—it's now widely accepted by scientists that the Earth is changing as a result of climate change.

Stock Market Crash—1929

During a reading in 1925 for a 26-year-old physician, Cayce said that the young doctor would come into a great deal of money. However, he was advised to be cautious with investing his wealth because of "adverse forces that will come then in 1929."

In March 1929, just six months before the stock market crashed, Cayce severely warned a New York stockbroker about what was to come: "We may expect a considerable break and bear market, see? This issue being between those of the reserves of nations and of individuals, and will cause—unless another of the more stable banking conditions come to the relief—a great disturbance in financial circles. This warning has been given, see?"

World War II

In 1935, in response to a question about global affairs, Cayce warned of catastrophic international events on the horizon that sounded remarkably like a world at war:

> *"As to the affairs of an international nature, these we find are in a condition of great anxiety on the part of many; not only as individuals but as to nations. And the activities that have already begun have assumed such proportions that there is to be the attempt upon the part of groups to penalize, or to make for the associations of groups to carry on same.*
>
> *This will make for the taking of sides, as it were, by various groups or countries or governments. This will be indicated by the Austrians, Germans, and later the Japanese joining in their influence; unseen, and gradually growing to those affairs where there must become, as it were, almost a direct opposition to that which has been the theme of the Nazis (the Aryan). For these will gradually make for a growing of animosities.*
>
> *And unless there is interference from what may be called by many the supernatural forces and influences, that are active in the affairs of nations and peoples, the whole world—as it were—will be set on fire by the militaristic groups and those that are for power and expansion in such associations . . ."*

The Essenes

Years before the discovery of the Dead Sea Scrolls—texts attributed to a then little-known sect called the Essenes—Cayce described the mystical-oriented community in 171 readings:

> *"Before this we find the entity was during those periods when there was much turmoil in the land of Judea, when there was the announcing of the prophet, of the new teacher, and all Judea had gone out to John. The entity then was among those that had been of the students of the Essenes. There was a direct connection with many that had been prophesying, had been searching the records of or for the coming of the new light, to those that had been hemmed in by tradition and by the acts of peoples in a political and religious purpose in the land."*

The language Cayce used was sometimes awkward, as in this reading: "This was a part of that group of Essenes who, headed by Judy, made those interpretations of those activities from the Egyptian experience—as the Temple Beautiful, and the service in the Temple of Sacrifice. Hence it was in this consecrated place where this selection took place."

Death of President Kennedy

In 1939, Cayce predicted the death of a president during a time of civil unrest: "You are to have turmoil—you are to have strife between capital and labor. You are to have a division in your own land, before you have the second of the presidents that next will not live through his office . . . a mob rule!"

Cayce referred to two presidents who would die in office. The first was Franklin D. Roosevelt, who died in April 1945 during his fourth term. John F. Kennedy died in office in November 1963 at a time when racial tensions and societal change were building.

Blood as a Diagnostic Tool

In 1927, Cayce foresaw a medical advancement that at the time sounded like science fiction: "There is ever seen in the blood stream the reflections or evidences of that condition being carried on in the physical body. The day may yet arrive when one may take a drop of blood and diagnose the condition of any physical body . . ."

La Niña and El Niño

In a reading in 1926 about the future of wheat crops and weather patterns, Cayce described a connection between temperature changes in deep ocean currents and weather changes: "As the heat or cold in the various parts of the Earth is radiated off, and correlated with reflection in the Earth's atmosphere, this in its action changes the currents or streams in the ocean."

Today, we know that temperature changes in the currents of oceans have dramatic effects on our weather. They are known as La Niña and El Niño.

By the time of his death in 1945, Cayce had achieved widespread fame, but it would be decades before some of the terms he used would become commonplace. He frequently talked of spiritual growth, meditation, the Akashic record, holistic health, auras and soul mates. Such terms are now so familiar that Cayce could be called the godfather of the New Age.

Tools for Tuning Into the Future

Divination is turning out to be much more trouble than I could have foreseen, never having studied the subject myself.

—J. K. Rowling, *Harry Potter and the Half-Blood Prince*

With practice, anyone can ask a question and glimpse the future as it is most likely to unfold from that moment in time. This may come as a surprise to those who feel they have no such abilities. Yet, by taking advantage of certain readily available tools, you can hurl open the window to events before they unfold. When you do so, you're stepping into the world of divination.

Throughout time and across cultures people have peered into the future with divination tools—the I Ching, tarot cards, astrology charts, patterns made by tea leaves or the toss of bones, numerology and scrying. The principle of synchronicity lies at the heart of every divination system. When you toss coins or lay out cards, they form a pattern intrinsic to that moment. The pattern, Carl Jung pointed out, is meaningful only if you're able to verify the interpretations through your knowledge of the subjective and objective situations, as well as the unfolding of subsequent events.

The term *divination* comes from the Latin *divinare,* meaning "to foresee," and it probably was practiced even before humans learned to control fire. Diviners among the ancient Babylonians read patterns in animal entrails, in smoke, oil on the surface of water and through the behavior of animals. The Druids favored crystal balls and read patterns in knotted tree roots, the calls and movements of birds and the patterns of clouds and stars. The ancient Greeks had their Oracle at Delphi, of course, but also divined patterns in dreams, in the murmuring of springs and by tossing small stones or pieces of wood, knucklebones or dice.

In Mesoamerican religious life and in every civilization from the Olmec to the Maya and Aztecs, divination was a part of daily life and scrying was commonly practiced. This system involved looking at any smooth or translucent surface—water, stones, crystals, mirrors—with the belief that images about the future would appear. "The history of divination has no starting point and no destination. It is woven so tightly into the spiritual life of humankind that we cannot imagine a time when some form of divining was not used," wrote Dianne Skafte in *Listening to the Oracle.*

Eventually, divinatory tools were created. Around 1,200 BC, the Chinese used a divination system called *fuji*, similar to a Ouija board, which was followed a millennium later by the I Ching. Tarot cards arrived in Europe from Turkey near the end of the Middle Ages, where related card games had existed for centuries.

Divination remains the most immediate and tangible way to sense the future. By making use of these tools, we tune into a deeper order of reality and enhance our intuition, and that allows us to see future events more clearly. Charlene Berlitz and Meg Lundstrom, writing in *The Power of Flow: Practical Ways to Transform Your Life with Meaningful Coincidence*, agree: "If we are facing a major decision, divination can show us the ramifications of our choices from a wider perspective and loosen our attachment to things turning out a certain way."

Any question you ask a divinatory tool is personal, a one-time experience that can't be replicated. So, like art, it falls outside the scientific process. It exists as a subjective reality, one where you can confirm your own anecdotal encounters and explorations with any of the following methods.

I Ching

I Ching, which means "moving" or "changing," is a divination system that originated thousands of years ago, probably as part of shamanic practices in China. What's known for certain is that the first text describing the system was written at least 3,000 years ago. The method was introduced to the Western world in 1950 by Richard Wilhelm, a European who spent most of his life translating ancient Chinese texts. The divination system is based on 64 hexagrams derived by tossing three coins six times. Originally, bones were used and later stalks of yarrow.

An I Ching hexagram consists of six horizontal lines, either broken or unbroken. Using the coins, heads (yang) equals three points, tails (yin) equals two points. So, two heads and a tail would equal eight, whereas two tails and one head would equal seven. Eight is a broken line; seven, an unbroken line. Totals that are entirely yang (nine—three heads) or yin (six—three tails) are considered to be changing lines, with extra significance. That means six changes to a broken line, and nine changes to an unbroken line, hence creating a second hexagram.

Confused yet? It's simpler than it appears. Read on.

Any time you obtain a hexagram with changing lines, it means the situation you asked about is evolving and the second hexagram describes the final outcome. But let's stick to basics for right now. Here's an example of a hexagram without changing lines:

This is hexagram #48, The Well, and the Richard Wilhelm/William Baynes translation describes it this way:

"The well remains in its place; it has a firm, never-failing foundation. Similarly, character must have a deep foundation and a lasting connection with the springs of life. The well itself does not change, yet through the water that is drawn from it, it exerts a far-reaching influence. The well is the image of a tranquil dispensing of bounty to all who approach it. Character also must be tranquil and clear, so that ideas of what is right can become clear."

Other authors have attempted to clarify and simplify Wilhelm's somewhat obscure translations. Here's a description of hexagram #48 from *I Ching Prescriptions: Choosing Change*, by Adele Aldridge, PhD: "It is time to go to the well of the foundation of life, and draw on the inexhaustible spring of the divine in your own nature. Penetrate the deepest part of yourself that gives you life. All humans contain within them the same basic characteristics. Respect others as yourself. You can change where you live but you can't change your real nature that springs from deep within you."

The 64 hexagrams are created from eight possible trigrams, which are associated with eight images of nature: Heaven, Thunder, Water, Mountain, Earth, Wind/Wood, Fire and Lake. The hexagram illustrated here is formed from Wind/Wood and Water.

No doubt the ancient Chinese were in close touch with their physical environment, which provided clues to the meaning of life. That's why the trigrams are associated with elements of the physical environment. Most of us now live in cities, have running water, air-conditioning and heat, access to the Internet and the digital world, and all the other accoutrements of civilization. Yet, the physical environment remains keenly important for our future. The more time we spend in nature, the more balanced we become.

As Jung wrote in the introduction to the Wilhelm edition, whoever invented the I Ching believed that the hexagram "was the exponent of the moment in which it was cast."

In other words, when you toss the coins, the hexagram you receive is like a snapshot in time, making manifest the internal. In *The Invisible Landscape: Mind, Hallucinogens, and the I Ching*, authors and visionary scholars Terence and Dennis McKenna wrote that they believed the hexagrams of the I Ching were archetypes "that could shed light on one's fate if one properly consulted the oracle."

We asked the I Ching about the importance of precognition and tossed three pennies six times. The first five throws were all sevens (two tails and one head) and the last line—the one at the top—was a nine (three heads). So, that resulted in six unbroken lines, hexagram #1, Creativity, with nine as the changing line at the top. About hexagram #1, Wilhelm says, "These unbroken lines stand for the primal power, which is light-giving, active, strong, and of the spirit . . . Its essence is power or energy. Its image is heaven . . . The movement of heaven is full of power." Wilhelm notes that "the hexagram includes also the power of time and the power of persisting in time, that is, duration."

Aldridge, writing about hexagram #1, says: "Creativity is a force that comes from beyond yourself, through yourself. Imagine that you are a pinpoint of light, a focal point of energy that originated in a galaxy beyond."

Sounds like the power of precognition!

Due to the changing line at the top of hexagram #1, it changes to #43, Break-Through. Wilhelm says this hexagram signifies on the one hand "a break-through after a long accumulation of tensions, as a swollen river breaks through its dikes, or in the manner of a cloudburst." When applied to human conditions, he continues, it refers to a time when "inferior people" gradually begin to disappear.

Aldridge points out that the changing line is a warning about becoming arrogant with success; "After achieving fulfillment, if you are not careful, like Icarus, you may fly too high and fall." That would suggest that precognition can be misused, that seeing the future shouldn't be used for manipulative purposes or personal gain at the expense of others. She suggests: "Respond quickly to what's calling you now. Declare your decision. Let go of the past. Focus. Direct your plan into action. Trust your instincts. Be clear about where you are going."

In other words, these hexagrams seem to be saying that precognition is enlightening—"light-giving" power and energy, an ability that comes from outside of you. It's about breakthroughs, and a means of alerting you to what's ahead.

While the Wilhelm book is considered the bible of English-language I Ching interpretations, the author was a scholar and attempted to remain as true to the original interpretations as possible. As a result, some of the hexagrams that address the roles of women in ancient Chinese society are blatantly sexist by today's standards. But if you set aside your Western bias and distill the essence of the hexagrams, you can glean a lot of wisdom from this divination system.

I Ching Online

If you're not familiar with the I Ching and aren't ready to buy one of the I Ching books, you can go online for sample readings. Just Google "free I Ching readings." We did so and found a site called I Ching by Clarity, where we asked, "What's the message of our book?"

The answer was hexagram #30, no changing lines. Traditionally, this hexagram is called The Clinging Fire, but Clarity has renamed it . . . Clarity. Here was the reading:

"The ancient Chinese character for Clarity shows a flying bird, and a net to capture it. Birds are messengers; this one represents flashes of insight, the way things can light up and shine out clearly. We weave a net of concepts to grasp the message and hold its meaning in awareness. This is not passive seeing, but a meeting of outer and inner light."

The reading seems to suggest that the message of the book is about bringing clarity to the topic of precognition. For another interpretation, we went to a site, www.jamesdekorne.com, recommended by author Nancy Pickard, who has been using the I Ching for decades. Its interpretations are comprehensive and easy to grasp. About hexagram #30, DeKorne notes:

> **"Judgment:** Willed persistence gets results. Be receptive to your inner light, and reflect it in your life.
> **The Superior Man** cultivates his capacity to manifest his comprehension of the Work in his everyday choices."

This interpretation indicates the importance of showing how precognition can be used in daily life and how important it is to follow its guidance.

There are numerous I Ching apps for both Android and iOS operating systems. One of the best we found is I Ching Pocket App for Wisdom. It costs 99 cents, the interpretations are easy to understand and it has a section where you can make notes about the results. It's a great way to keep track of your readings—and how they eventually turn out.

On November 18, 2015, at noon, Trish asked the I Ching app whether *Ellery Queen Magazine* would buy the short story she had submitted a week earlier. The answer was interesting: hexagram #22, changing to hexagram #35. The app calls the first hexagram Radiant Beauty; Wilhelm calls it Grace. By either name, it's fantastic.

"Elegance and quiet beauty," says the app.

"Grace brings success," says Wilhelm.

Three changing lines brought a second hexagram: #35. The app calls it Advancement, Wilhelm calls it Progress. Either way, the end result is good. The app says: "Moving out of darkness, this is a time of brightness when clarity is rising and far-reaching. Things come easy . . ."

Wilhelm's take: "The symbol of rapid, easy progress . . ."

The I Ching's prediction proved to be correct. The short story sold less than a month later, on December 9.

Sometimes you ask the I Ching a question and instead of answering it, the oracle seems to address an underlying internal issue or challenge that needs to be resolved first. Your reaction? *That's not what I asked.* You feel like hurling the book or your iPad across the room. *You don't have any positive news for me? What good are you?*

The I Ching is making you aware of impediments that must be addressed first and that probably originate in your beliefs about that topic. Finances, relationships, career, kids, creative endeavors . . . those are usually the biggies.

Our advice? Be patient. Research the various meanings for the particular hexagrams you've gotten. Ask yourself the necessary questions about what the hexagrams are saying. Meditate on it. Ask for dream guidance.

Be alert for synchronicities. Better yet, set up the conditions for the synchronicity. The next time you get into your car, give yourself the suggestion that the first thing you hear on the radio will illuminate the situation.

Astrology

Like the I Ching, astrology is an ancient practice that's rich and complex in meaning. Even though it predates the scientific revolution, astrology remains a vibrant means of analyzing personalities and relationships—and predicting the future. It survives and even thrives as an alternative to the materialistic view, which doesn't recognize our spiritual nature. Like the I Ching, astrology works on the principle of synchronicity. In the case of astrology, particular patterns in the cosmos reflect aspects of one's life.

A natal chart or horoscope is a geometrical diagram of the heavens as seen from your birthplace at the moment you were born. The chart is determined by the date, time and place of your birth and looks like a circle with twelve unequal sections. These sections are known as houses and depict different areas of your life: self, finances, siblings and neighbors, family, partners, career and so on. Just as the I Ching coin toss is a snapshot in time, the moment you drew your first breath froze an instant in time. A birth chart, like a hexagram, forms a meaningful pattern, a blueprint of archetypal *potential.*

Many types of astrology can be used to assess patterns operating in your life in the coming days, weeks or months, or even years from now, as well as what's going on right now. Transits, the daily motions of the planets, have the most immediate and obvious effect, particularly when the slower-moving planets—Pluto, Neptune and Uranus—are involved. The longer a planet remains in a particular sign, the greater its impact on us as individuals, a society, a country, a world.

The zodiac consists of twelve signs, and each sign contains 30 degrees. The degree the sun occupied when you were born probably corresponds to a year in your life when some sort of transformative experience occurred—the birth of a sibling, a move, a parental divorce or remarriage, an accident, illness or some other defining event. The timing isn't always exact—give it leeway of about six months on either side.

Trish, whose sun is at 16 degrees 12 minutes of Gemini, experienced a defining event five months after her 16th birthday. Her parents moved from Venezuela, where she had been born and raised, to the United States. That year she also discovered astrology, which helped illuminate the ramifications of the move. For anyone over 30 years of age, this particular type of predictive astrology is a retro reading, since we've already experienced the significant event in question.

For our daughter, whose Virgo sun is at 8 degrees, the event was entering the gifted program in third grade, which made all the difference in her education.

If you don't know the degree of your natal sun, go to www.astro.com and put "free natal chart" in the site's search window for a free copy of your natal chart. Locate the sun—its symbol looks like a circle with a dot in the center. Next to it you will find numbers that indicate the degree of the sign in which your natal sun is placed. If you were born on October 14, 1950, for example, your sun would be in 20 degrees of Libra. This means there may have been a defining moment in your life when you were around 20 years old. If you're not yet at the age that corresponds with the degree of your natal sun, keep in mind that some pivotal event may happen when you reach that age.

Astrology can be so ridiculously complicated in terms of the future that you may feel as though you're ready for the loony bin before you even gain any insight. Keep in mind that there are several ways to glimpse the future: through transits as well as progressions (where your natal chart is progressed through time) and returns (where transiting planets return to where they were at your birth). There are also new and full moons each month, eclipses several times a year and a host of other influences. If you're new to astrology, the best policy is to keep things simple. Start with your natal chart and once you understand it, play around with transits so you can see how the daily motion of the planets may impact you.

A friend was concerned about her college-age son and asked Trish to take a look at his chart. He has Pisces on his ascendant considered the doorway to a chart, and Uranus was coming up to conjunct it. Uranus is all about freedom, rebellion, individuality, and it meant this kid was probably rebelling against authority, rules and regulations. Its function is to shake up the status quo, to "awaken" you to some facet of your life that needs attention, to shake out the stuff in your life that no longer works, so the new can rush in to fill the void. As it approaches and then conjuncts your ascendant, jarring events often occur.

Trish explained all this to her friend, gave her the time frame when Uranus would be conjuncting her son's ascendant and advised her to tell him to be cautious during that period. "No car races, skydives, climbing Mount Kilimanjaro or other risky behavior."

Several months later, the friend called. During the time frame Trish had provided, the son had two beers in his dorm one Friday night, then headed out to meet friends at a local restaurant. He drove right into a speed trap, was arrested for a DUI and spent fourteen hours in jail before his parents bailed him out. They'd hired an attorney, who reported that a dozen other college students had been arrested that same night, in that same speed trap, and there was a chance the charges could be dropped. Eventually, that's exactly what happened.

The son was deeply shaken by the time he'd spent in jail and has never again driven after drinking a drop of alcohol.

Scientists Who Were Astrologers

Everyone coming of age in the 20th or 21st century has been educated with an institutional bias against astrology. Science historians effectively have excised astrology from the biographies of the bright stars of the scientific revolution—Copernicus, Galileo, Tycho Brahe, Kepler and Newton. But modern science actually developed out of astrology. Three centuries ago, astronomers were knowledgeable about astrology. Four centuries ago, many astronomers practiced it. Five centuries ago, *every* astronomer was also an astrologer. We're not supposed to know that, though.

Google "Galileo," read a few of his bios and see whether you find any mention of astrology. You'll read that he was a mathematician, an astronomer, a physicist, an engineer and a philosopher. But not an astrologer. Meanwhile, an Italian astrologer and scholar, Grazia Mirti, has convincingly documented that Galileo created astrological charts his entire adult life. Galileo's fascination with the cosmos led to him being charged as a heretic by the Inquisition because he stated that Earth wasn't the center of the universe and that it actually revolved around the sun. He spent the final years of his life under house arrest.

Bruce Scofield, writing in *The Mountain Astrologer* (August/September, 1998) noted that Johannes Kepler "is a great embarrassment to the scientific community, though they cover this up with smoke and mirrors." Kepler practiced and enjoyed his pursuit of astrology. In fact, his motivations were so cosmologically astrological that historians paint him as having one foot in the Middle Ages and the other foot in the modern world. Science textbooks sanitize this image and focus almost entirely on his scientific achievements. There's a famous quote from Kepler that we've all heard in one form or another. In his 1610 publication *Third Party Intervening*, he discussed the conflicts between astrology and astronomy, and advised readers critical of astrology "not to throw the baby out with the bath water."

Astrological Predictions in the White House

Did you know that, from 1981 through 1988, the most powerful leader in the world followed guidance from the stars? President Ronald Reagan and First Lady Nancy Reagan received regular astrological readings from Joan Quigley. A top aide to Reagan once called Quigley the administration's "most closely guarded secret." She was kept on a $3,000 per month retainer and spoke to Mrs. Reagan two or three times a day.

Quigley, according to the former chief of staff, set the time for summit meetings, presidential debates, State of the Union addresses and Reagan's cancer surgery. Private phone lines were set up for her at the White House and Camp David.

Nancy Reagan called Quigley in 1981 after John Hinckley attempted to assassinate the president, and asked her whether she could have foreseen and prevented the attempt. After she answered yes, she became the White House astrologer until 1988, when her secret role was exposed by former chief of staff Donald Regan.

The former first lady later explained why she had turned to Quigley, who she had met in the 1970s on *The Merv Griffin Show*: "Very few people can understand what it's like to have your husband shot and almost die, and then have him exposed all the time to enormous crowds, tens of thousands of people, any one of whom might be a lunatic with a gun . . . I was doing everything I could think of to protect my husband and keep him alive."

In her book, *What Does Joan Say?: My Seven Years as a White House Astrologer to Nancy and Ronald Reagan*, Quigley didn't mince words when describing her role in the Reagan White House: "Not since the days of the Roman emperors—and never in the history of the United States presidency—has an astrologer played such a significant role in the nation's affairs of State."

The revelation of the existence of a White House astrologer caused a furor in the press. Hundreds of political cartoons were drawn mocking the Reagans. The vast majority were negative and sarcastic. The Reagan Library in Simi Valley, California, has 2,800 files documenting the media attention to the issue.

In spite of the attacks on the Reagans, there was never any evidence presented that the actions taken at Quigley's suggestions had any detrimental effects on the governance of the nation. Famed astrologer Sydney Omarr gave several interviews in which he defended the Reagans. He praised Nancy Reagan for consulting an astrologer before making major decisions, and said that "only the ignorant" would laugh at the First Lady's awareness of astrology. Omarr also said that the Reagans were not the only high-level politicians in Washington who paid attention to the cosmos. In an interview with the *Wall Street Journal*, he said that Richard Nixon and Henry Kissinger were also advised by astrologers.

Stars and Numbers

Sydney Omarr was only seventeen years old when he joined the US Army in the middle of World War II. He picked April 4, 1944, as the day to enlist because he liked all the fours, which in numerology (see next section) are about building foundations for an outlet for one's creativity. About a year after he enlisted, he was transferred to the US Air Force at a base located in Ontario, California, about 35 miles (56 km) from Los Angeles.

At "Camp Hollywood," as the base was often called, Omarr was assigned to Armed Forces Radio and began broadcasting "Sydney Omarr's Almanac," a weekly astrology report. His interest in astrology and numerology caught the attention of a reporter for *Wings*, the air force's newspaper, and Omarr was featured in a tongue-in-cheek article that would help establish his career. In the article, published in April 1945, he predicted that Japan would surrender in mid-August 1945. And in fact, Emperor Hirohito announced the unconditional surrender of Japan on August 15, 1945.

Sydney Omarr is best remembered as a longtime astrologer, based in Los Angeles, who wrote a newspaper column that appeared in 300 newspapers and authored annual sun sign books. But early in his career he favored numerology, which he eventually worked into his astrological predictions.

His birth name was Sidney Kimmelman, but he changed it when he was fifteen, after seeing a movie called *Shanghai Gesture*, in which Victor Mature portrayed a character named Omar. For numerological reasons, he added the extra *r* at the end of the name and changed his first name to Sydney with a *y* instead of an *i*. He was so fascinated with numerology that, at fifteen, he wrote a self-published booklet, *Sydney Omarr's Private Course on Numerology.* He sold mimeographed copies for two dollars.

We crossed paths with Omarr late in his career when Trish ghostwrote a book for him about the new millennium, and then they coauthored a book on spirit contact. After Omarr's death in 2003, we took over his sun sign series, *Sydney Omarr's Day-to-Day Astrological Guide*, which we wrote for a decade. In addition to the astrological elements, we included numerological readings on particular days as well.

Numerology

The Greek philosopher and mathematician Pythagoras, who lived 2,500 years ago, is called the father of numerology. He believed everything had numerical relationships, and that if these relationships were investigated, the secrets could be unveiled through divine grace. "The world is built upon the power of numbers," he wrote. Saint Augustine (AD 354–430) felt the same way: "Numbers are the universal language offered by the deity to humans as confirmation of the truth."

Modern numerology goes by the name Pythagorean numerology and is a multifaceted divination system that applies certain character tendencies to numbers and reflects a cosmic plan. In essence, it's a mystical relationship between numbers and coinciding events.

If you're familiar with numerology, you probably know your life path number, which is derived by adding together the numbers of the month, day and year of your birth until you reach either a single digit, or a master number, 11, 22 or 33. That number represents who you were at birth and the traits that you'll carry throughout your life. In other words, it's a general life reading.

We'll focus here on finding the numbers for your personal year and personal days as a means of glimpsing what's ahead for you. Let's start with the *personal year frequency*.

Add the numbers for your birth month and day to the number of the year in question. For example, Megan, born on August 31, would find her personal year number for 2017 by adding 8 + 31 + 2017 = 2056 = 13 = 4. If instead of 13, the two-digit number was 11, 22 or 33, she would stop there and use the master number. In this case, Megan's number for her personal year is 4, which suggests that 2017 will be a year in which she gets more organized, works harder and takes care of her obligations. She would be creating new foundations and paying attention to details.

To get the *personal day*, you add the number of the birth month and the birth day to the number of the day in question. So, if Megan wanted to know her personal number for May 11, 2017, she would add together 8 + 31 = 39 = 12 = 3 to 5 + 11 + 2017 = 2033 = 8; 3 + 8 = 11, a master number day. That means May 11, 2017, is a good day for Megan to work with others on a spiritual level. Higher awareness comes into play, whereas a two-day would focus on a more mundane level.

We asked Connie Cannon, a numerologist from Saint Augustine, Florida, for her take on personal day and year numbers: "I always look at my personal day frequency when I'm making appointments, signing papers or taking other actions. I sometimes will change plans if the frequency isn't compatible with whatever the appointment is about. I also look at the personal year when looking at my personal day. I always try to make doctor appointments on personal 11 days and sign contracts or make business decisions on a personal 8 day."

To get a second look and possibly a clearer picture on your personal day, add your personal day to your personal year. If Megan wanted more details about May 11, 2017, she would add 4 (the month and day of her birth, added to 2017) and 11, which would result in 6 for that day. That means she should remain diplomatic and tolerant, generous and sympathetic with those she's helping. Family and children play a role. She needs to remain balanced and concerned with what works best for her group or community.

What the Numbers Mean

Here are the keywords for the root numbers.

1—Taking the lead, getting a fresh start, a new beginning. Independent, inventiveness and pioneering, strong-willed and determined.

2—Cooperation, partnerships and sensitivity. A new relationship. Adaptable and considerate of others, diplomatic.

3—Creativity, self-expression and imagination. Harmony, beauty and the pleasures of life. Warm and receptive, communicative, optimistic and fun-loving.

4—Getting organized, hard work and methodical. Rebuilding, fulfilling your obligations. Establishing foundations, attention to details.

5—Freedom of thought and action, change and variety are key. Visionary ideas, quick thinking. Scattering of energy, but in a positive way.

6—Service to others, diplomatic, generous, tolerant and sympathetic. Family and children issues are highlighted. Balanced and community-oriented.

7—Mystery, secrets, investigations, research analyzing and detecting deception, exploration of the unknown, of the spiritual realms. Seeker of knowledge, a love of solitude.

8—Power and authority, decisive and commanding. Financial success, political skills, gaining recognition.

9—Completing a project and tying up loose ends. Looking beyond the immediate, setting goals, seeking a new approach. Reflection and expansion.

Master Numbers

The presence of master numbers indicates that the soul has had multiple life experiences in spiritual endeavors. These numbers don't mean that you're better than others, but reflect the possibility of working at a higher level of awareness. If you choose to do so, you face powerful challenges and take up responsibilities that can be overwhelming. It's virtually impossible for individuals to constantly remain in the master number vibration. So, those individuals at times resonate on the related root numbers 2, 4 or 6.

11—The higher vibration of 2 and implies working with others on a spiritual rather than mundane level.

22—The master builder, the higher level of energy directed to order, service and organization.

33—The master frequency of the teacher and counselor on the cosmic level as opposed to the mundane level.

Once you become accustomed to what the numbers mean for a particular day, you can prepare yourself and adjust your attitude, thoughts and actions accordingly. After all, how your day, week, month or year unfolds depends a great deal on your attitude toward yourself and your world.

The next divination system we'll look at delves into the tarot, a world of powerful and archetypal images.

Tarot

While astrology and numerology speak in symbols and the I Ching is chatty, the tarot is hauntingly visual. This system of divination dates back to 14th-century France and was probably imported from Turkey. It has links with the Kabbalah, the Jewish mystical practice, and ancient Egyptian symbols. The 78 cards of the tarot are divided into two sections known as the major arcana and the minor arcana. The major arcana's 22 cards represent an archetypal evolution in consciousness.

The Fool, the first card in the major arcana, symbolizes a peak moment, an intense euphoria that rises from the knowledge that we're all connected to something larger than we had imagined. The Fool is Pocahontas when she sings about the color of the wind, and represents the beginning of the magnificent journey ahead of us. Meditating on the Fool bolsters your courage, risk-taking and the creative expression needed to open up new areas in your life.

The last card, The World, ends the Fool's journey and suggests the goal has been reached. You're now the sage, the master.

The other 56 cards, the minor arcana, represent the synchronistic details of our lives and the steps along the path from The Fool to The World.

Robert Hopcke, a psychotherapist and author of *There Are No Accidents: Synchronicity and the Stories of Our Lives,* relates a humorous story about one of his clients who received a deck of tarot cards for her birthday. She initially used the deck with a "give-me-an-answer" attitude. One day she received an answer she disliked and drew the cards again, but all the cards were reversed, "that is, facing away from her, as if they didn't want to talk to her."

Shortly after 9/11, Trish's coauthor for *Power Tarot*, Phyllis Vega, remarked that nearly every client that she had recently read for seemed to be drawing The Tower. This card usually depicts a tower being struck by lightning. Flames shoot from the windows, people are falling or leaping to their death, everything is dark, ugly and terrifying. If there's any card that depicts the scenario of 9/11, this is it. In the months following the tragedy, the archetypes of destruction, chaos and death became embedded in our collective psyche as a nation. The Tower card reflected it.

Whenever The Tower appears in a personal reading, the archetype generally points to chaos—not destruction and death in the physical sense. Often the chaos catches you by surprise. Let's say you pull The Tower card several times in the days just before you're leaving for vacation—and it comes up when you ask questions that have nothing to do with your vacation. It may be indicating problems with your trip, so it would be wise to recheck your itinerary and ticket, leave for the airport earlier than usual and be sure you've packed everything you need. If you have a lengthy drive to the airport, be sure your car is in shape—gas tank full, tires in good condition, engine humming.

Getting to Know the Tarot

To familiarize yourself with the tarot, select a card each morning and use the meaning to get a sense of your day. If you practice waking up in a spirit of adventure and gratitude, then pretty soon it becomes second nature, and your life shifts accordingly. Sound like magical thinking? Indeed it is, and when you discover your innate power to change your life for the better, you recognize the world *is* a magical place, if we all would only recognize it as such.

Start by focusing on the major arcana cards. Allow the image to speak to the deeper part of you, then check your impressions with the meaning of the card. If you don't have a tarot book, you can refer to the abbreviated keywords for the following major arcana cards. As you learn the meanings of the cards, use the entire deck.

Let's say your card for the day is The Empress. That would suggest that you might spend some time in nature today, enjoying the beauty. It's also a good day for nurturing your creative side and creating balance in your life. The Empress often refers to your own mother, who may play a role in the day's events.

You might also draw a second card to glean more information. For example, if you drew The Hermit, you might be spending time alone today and doing some soul-searching as you seek inner guidance.

Be sure to have a tarot book that provides meanings that are easy to understand. One such book is *Power Tarot*, by Trish MacGregor and Phyllis Vega.

The Fool: A fresh start or a new beginning. Expect the unexpected. You're willing to take risks that shock other people around you. You believe that all things are possible. Trust your intuition.

The Magician: Seemingly magical influences come into your life and you sense solutions to your most pressing problems. You notice synchronicities that point to a deeper order of reality. You create what you need and want.

The High Priestess: Something is hidden in your life, a mystery or secret that eludes you. The answer may be found in your memories or dreams. Rely more on intuition than intellect. Remain open to information that flows from your unconscious. This card often depicts a period of time—two hours, days, weeks or months. It rarely points to an event two years out.

The Empress: Your life swells with abundance. You nurture and soothe the pains and anxieties of others. You're a good listener, an excellent counselor. Your home is your sanctuary, your sacred place. Pregnancy is a distinct possibility. If you're already pregnant, then you can expect an easy nine months.

The Emperor: Something you desire is starting to appear in your life, even if you can't see it yet. The more focused your intent, the faster the manifestation. Your greatest strength is the power of your will.

The Hierophant: You come up against the powers that be—corporate, religious or family. The clash of beliefs helps you clarify your own positions. Others offer advice, but you look within and make your own decisions.

The Lovers: A new relationship is right around the corner, or your current relationship is about to be transformed in some way. You feel divided about a major issue or relationship in your life. Your heart tells you one thing; your head tells you something else.

The Chariot: A journey is at hand. It can be a physical journey, usually by car, or a spiritual one, a journey of self-discovery. Either way, you're in the driver's seat and you create your destiny through your actions. It's also possible that a new car lies in your future.

Strength: You have the innate ability to deal with whatever life brings. You can overcome obstacles with ease. You seize control of your destiny and can attract the contacts and opportunities you need. If you're ill, this card signals that you'll soon be on the mend.

Hermit: You're ready to tie up loose ends, finish a project and move ahead. Your time of solitude or isolation is over. You reach out to others through a workshop, a course or a lecture as you move closer to your goals. Any travel is related to education or the higher mind.

The Wheel of Fortune: A turning point. You feel as if you're being nudged to move in a new direction and take a gamble. You could resist the urge, but you benefit by going with the flow.

Justice: Any legal issues wane. A judgment in your favor. Conflicts are resolved, harmony reigns. When you deal with others fairly, you get a fair deal in return.

The Hanged Man: Adjust your point of view. Reverse the established order of how you do things. Expect delays, but the standstill isn't permanent. If you're stuck in a rut, it could be that rigid ideas are blocking you. Let go of old ideas and associations.

Death: Do you fear the future? Are you clinging to the past? Expect a complete turnaround as old ways are turned inside out. Even though things might seem quite hopeless, your situation can suddenly make a dramatic improvement. Change is required.

Temperance: Tranquility comes your way by maintaining harmony and balancing opposites: success and failure, justice and compassion, joy and sorrow. Practice moderation in all things. Patience and perseverance pay off.

The Devil: This card represents your own fears and uncertainties. It alerts you that it's time to take charge of your life rather than allowing life's events to choose for you. The Devil can be exorcized by changing patterns of behavior and thinking that keep you feeling luckless and helpless. This card can also address that the "devil is in the details."

The Tower: A violent upheaval of some sort is in the offing. The card portends a shocking and surprising event, a wakeup call in which beliefs and structures break down. But it also implies that your slate is swept clean, enabling you to move forward.

The Star: One of the best cards in the tarot. Life works the way it should, doors open, new opportunities surface, your finances improve, your health improves, you meet your soul mate. Focus on your goals with confidence and belief that they will come true. Remain upbeat and positive. Your plans are about to bear fruit.

The Moon: You're haunted by anxiety and uncertainty. Your dreams and daydreams may hold clues about the source of what you're feeling. With work, relationships and finances, there are underlying mysteries and things seem to go through many phases. Your mother or another nurturing female may figure significantly in events. Intuition and emotions, your inner world, are highlighted. Know that whatever is bothering you will pass. This card can also be about timing—the next full moon.

The Sun: Empowerment. You're embracing opportunity and your life opens to new experiences. Your goals are much clearer now. You realize that you write the script of your life from the inside out, based on your deepest beliefs and your emotions. You're forgiving of others and you can afford to be generous.

Judgment: In all areas of your life, you're on the right track. You're promoted, your income increases, you and your partner commit to making things work—or you call it quits. You experience a spiritual awakening. If you're involved in legal proceedings, things shake out in your favor. Stick to the speed limit; otherwise, you may get ticketed and the fine will be hefty!

The World: Completion, success, fulfillment. You're ready to reap your rewards and move on to a new phase. You enjoy your triumphs now before you begin again as The Fool. The World is a reminder that the journey is the true goal.

The tarot, like astrology and the I Ching, probably isn't the simplest divination system. If you want to engage synchronicity quickly, try stichomancy.

Stichomancy

Stichomancy (from the Greek *stichos*, or "row") is quick and easy—and can be startlingly accurate. Think of a question or issue that concerns you. Hold it in your mind, randomly open a dictionary, Bible or book of your choice, and point to a place on the page. See whether the word or phrase your finger touches illuminates your question or concern.

Maybe you asked about the future of a new relationship, opened a dictionary and your finger pointed at the phrase *a lurking suspicion.* That confirms it. There's something not right about the relationship. You were hoping it would work out, but now you realize that you were just wasting your time with this person.

Or let's say you asked about your chances of getting a job that you've applied for and pointed randomly at this phrase *free of trouble or difficulty.* It seems to suggest that you have a good chance of getting hired. But it isn't specific enough because there are two job openings, an entry level and one with a higher salary that requires more experience. You're hoping for the latter. You then ask what your chances are for getting the better-paying job. You open the dictionary and your finger stabs down near the bottom the page. The word is *bud* and you are pointing at the phrase *begin to grow or develop.*

It looks as though you're more likely to get offered the entry-level job. You're disappointed, but then you notice that in parentheses next to the phrase is this: *a budding artist.* Now you remember that the lower-paying job actually sounded more interesting because there are creative possibilities. But you were focused on the more prestigious one. You realize that taking the entry-level job might be a better fit and you will have opportunities to work your way up in the company.

If you get an ambiguous answer, try again and rephrase your question. Or when you point at a word, read the entire sentence or paragraph. If you're using a dictionary, look at the nearby words above and below. Sometimes even a nonanswer can provide you with a bit of wisdom. For example, say you asked a question about a relationship and your finger landed on a blank space. What's it mean? Possibly that you have the free will to make choices or that the answer—for now—is unknown. However, if you already asked this question, your unconscious mind might be telling you that you already know the answer.

Sometimes an answer provides a hint or sets you on a trail of thoughts. For example, Rob posed the question, "What are the benefits of divination?" He opened the dictionary at random and dropped his finger onto the page. The words he pointed at were: *To wish longingly, or intently.* A reasonable response. When looking for a peek at the future, we're often wishing for a particular outcome. That response could even reveal a bit of humor and irony, as if the universe is saying that divination is wishful thinking. But then, where did that answer come from?

You might experiment with different books to see which one feels most appropriate for you for stichomancy. It could be a favorite novel or a book of fairy tales. The larger the book, the more possible answers you'll have. The symbolism of the source you use should also resonate for you. In other words, if you've read the Bible a dozen times or you've owned a well-paged copy of *Grimms' Fairy Tales* since you were a child, those would probably be good choices. You can also try this online, by navigating to one of the stichomancy sites. You type a question and a passage captured from a library of books appears on the screen. The response might seem irrelevant, but if you look closely you might find a phrase within the text that strikes you as a response.

The beauty of divination systems is that there are so many. They all work on similar principles and can bring you to the same place—that point of connection between the inner and external worlds, the space between. What these systems have in common is the creation of meaningful patterns intrinsic to the moment in which the question was asked. But you don't necessarily need cards or computer apps.

Divination also can be practiced in nature by becoming aware of signs, symbols and patterns that can be interpreted, especially when you go out into the world with a question in mind. The appearance of an animal or the shape of a cloud might provide an answer. You can easily look up the divinatory meaning of an animal online or through guidebooks.

Not only can nature and animals serve as divination tools, but animals themselves seem to have an instinctive means of foretelling dramatic changes in the world around us. We'll take a close look at that in the next chapter.

The Awesome Power of Nature

Animals have access to levels of reality that might remain hidden to us without their help.

—Mary Lou Randour

A 9.1 magnitude undersea earthquake erupted in the Indian Ocean on December 26, 2004, triggering a massive tsunami that slammed into the coastlines of eleven countries that surrounded the ocean. Nearly 250,000 people died. Yet, in Sri Lanka's Yala National Park, the largest wildlife reserve, there wasn't a single report about dead animals. According to the deputy director of the National Wildlife Department, elephants, wild boar, monkeys, jackals and deer had moved inland to avoid the killer waves.

Khao Lak, on Thailand's western coast, was hit particularly hard by the tsunami. But hours before it struck, elephants trumpeted and an hour before the tsunami crashed to shore with waves more than 30 feet (9 m) high, the elephants became agitated again and took off for higher ground.

Along India's Cuddalore coast, where thousands of people died, the Indo-Asian News service reported that buffaloes, goats and dogs were found unharmed.

The indigenous tribes of the Andaman and Nicobar Islands, which lie near the quake's epicenter, noticed the unusual behavior of dolphins, birds and lizards and retreated to higher ground. The tribes survived without a single fatality.

Even though premonitions in animals have been well documented over the years, mainstream science is slow to accept that it happens and typically offers alternate explanations. That was the case in 2004, when Florida was hit by four hurricanes in rapid succession—Frances, Charlie, Ivan and Jeanne.

Birds delayed their migration during these tumultuous weeks. When Hurricane Jeanne was still hours away from Gainesville, University of Florida biologist Thomas Emmel noticed that the butterflies in the university's enclosed rainforest took shelter among rocks and trees. When Hurricane Charlie was within twelve hours of southwest Florida, scientists at the Mote Marine Laboratory in Sarasota, Florida, noted the odd behavior among ten tiger sharks they had tagged. Eight of them fled the estuary for the safety of the open ocean.

In 1992, Hurricane Andrew slammed into Homestead, Florida, and nearly wiped it off the map. In its path was the habitat of crocodiles that live in the cooling canals of the Turkey Point nuclear power plant. Not a single dead crocodile was found in the aftermath of the storm. It's speculated that before the hurricane hit, they fled into open water or to the bottom of the 20-foot (6-m) canals.

"It doesn't make any difference if it's a hurricane, a fire or an earthquake," said Frank Mazzotti, a wildlife biologist at the University of Florida. "They start moving away from danger before humans pick it up. It's likely a combination of smell, vibrations and pressure."

But suppose it's something else? Suppose animals are natural precogs?

Animals Predicting Earthquakes

The first description of bizarre animal behavior before a quake came from a Greek historian, Diodorus Siculus. It concerned a cataclysmic earthquake that occurred in the winter of 373 BC and destroyed Helice, Greece, which was subsequently swallowed by a tsunami. Five days before, all sorts of animals—rats, snakes, weasels, centipedes, worms and beetles—fled the city. They supposedly "migrated in droves along the connecting road toward the city of Koria," writes Helmut Tributsch in *When the Snakes Awake: Animals and Earthquake Prediction.*

Pliny the Elder, an author and naturalist in ancient Rome, noted in his second volume of *Natural History* that there were four signs of a coming earthquake and one of those signs was excited animals: "Even the birds do not remain sitting fearlessly."

On July 26, 1805, a 7.3 magnitude quake struck the Molise region of Italy, killing more than 5,500 people. The worst damage was spread across more than 1,200 square miles (over 3,100 sq km). Minutes before the quake happened, oxen and cows started bellowing, dogs howled, rabbits and moles fled their holes, birds took flight. Horses became agitated and those in stalls leaped up, trying to break out of their halters. Hours before the quake struck, ants and reptiles left their underground nests. The night before the quake, swarms of locusts were seen headed toward the sea.

On April 18, 1906, a quake estimated to be close to 8.0 on the Richter scale devastated San Francisco. Hundreds of people were killed, several hundred thousand were left homeless and tens of thousands of buildings were destroyed. Fires broke out and burned for days. Prior to the quake, herds of horses stampeded, horses in harnesses ran off, while others stopped and screamed. Horses in several of the San Francisco fire departments became terrified and broke out of their stalls. But horses weren't the only animals that sensed the pending quake.

Cattle that had been in the upper hills retreated to lower levels, other herds stampeded, several cows were reported to have given birth prematurely to calves. Cats behaved strangely, rushing around wildly, terrified, hiding in corners; some mother cats carried their kittens to other locations. Dogs also sensed the pending quake, howling throughout the night before it struck.

Dr. George Pararas-Carayannis, who was director of the International Tsunami Information Center of UNESCO IOC from 1974 to 1992, has written extensively on unusual and erratic behavior in animals before quakes, tsunamis and other disasters. He notes that before an 8.5 quake on December 16, 1920, in the Haiyuan County, Ninghsia Province, in China, "wolves were seen running around in packs, dogs were barking unusually and sparrows were flying around wildly." Before the 7.4 quake on July 18, 1969, in the Pohai Sea on the coast of northern China, weird behavior was observed in "seagulls, sharks and five different species of fish." Based on observations of unusual behavior of giant pandas, deer, yaks, loaches, tigers and other animals, a warning was issued at the Tientsin People's Park zoo, two hours before the earthquake struck.

Pararas-Carayannis points out that surveys done in China illustrate that most incidents of unusual and abnormal animal behavior occur 24 hours before the quake hits; "In other parts of China where major earthquakes have been preceded by foreshocks, unusual behavior in rats, fish and snakes were observed as early as three days prior to the earthquake, but continuing to several hours, or even a few minutes before."

For hundreds of years, the Chinese and Japanese have used unusual animal behavior as part of their national earthquake warning system. It paid off big time in February 1975, when a 7.3 quake struck Haicheng, China, and destroyed most of the city's structures. A week before, residents had noticed abnormal behavior in animals—snakes came out of hibernation and into the snow, dogs acted restless and anxious and howled without apparent reason. Small animals deserted the city. In the first three days in February, the bizarre behavior intensified with cows, horses and pigs. Based on nothing more than the observations of the erratic behavior of animals, officials evacuated the city, and when the quake struck on February 4, more than 90,000 lives were saved.

But as British biologist Rupert Sheldrake points out in his book *Dogs That Know When Their Owners Are Coming Home*, the Chinese have also had "some spectacular failures," such as the 1976 Tanghan quake, in which 240,000 people died. Overall, though, Sheldrake believes the Chinese have been incredibly successful in predicting earthquakes "in contrast to their Western counterparts, who do not even try."

If you live in a Western country, can you imagine the officials in your area issuing an evacuation order based on nothing more than the erratic behaviors of animals? Can you even visualize CNN or NBC explaining why such an order was issued? Yeah, right.

Yet, if precognition exists in humans, writes Larry Dossey in *The Power of Premonitions*, then it probably exists in animals, too: "Animals might have an even greater precognitive sense than we do, just as their senses of hearing, smell and vision are often keener than ours."

The official stance of the US Geological Survey (USGS) is that there isn't any reliable technique for predicting quakes, not even strange animal behavior. In spite of thousands of anecdotes that span centuries, the USGS states on its website: "Because of their finely tuned senses, animals can often feel the earthquake at its earliest stages before the humans around it can. This feeds the myth that the animal knew the earthquake was coming. But animals also change their behavior for many reasons, and given that an earthquake can shake millions of people, it is likely that a few of their pets will, by chance, be acting strangely before an earthquake."

James Berkland, a retired USGS geologist in California, however, has a different opinion. According to his research, the number of missing dogs and cats increases significantly two weeks before a quake. The gravitational variations due to lunar cycles create "seismic windows" of greater quake probability. When the number of missing pets also rises, then a quake is likely. As a result, Berkland claims to be able to predict quakes with an accuracy greater than 75 percent just by counting the number of ads for lost pets in the daily newspaper, by the mass beachings of whales and dolphins and by correlating these events to lunar-tide cycles.

What about fish? Are they able to sense future quakes, too? In Japanese mythology and folklore, the oarfish is one predictor. This bizarre-looking creature, thought to be the world's longest bony fish, can measure from 20 to 50 feet (6 to 15 m) in length and lives at depths of several hundred feet. According to the *Japanese Times*, it's known in mythology as *ryugu no tsukai*, or messenger from the sea god's palace. When they come to the beach, it's an omen of an earthquake.

In March 2010, around the time of the 8.8 quake that struck Chile, Japanese fisherman discovered dozens of oarfish. Not long before the 2011 quake and tsunami in Japan, 20 oarfish stranded themselves on beaches in the area.

The Chinese also believe that fish can sense future quakes. In July 2015, *China Daily* reported that the seismological bureau in Nanjing has transformed seven animal farms into seismic stations, where the behavior of fish, chickens and black boars will be monitored for unusual behavior.

The inclusion of boars is interesting and was mentioned in *The Great Neapolitan Earthquake* by Robert Mallet, published in 1862. It concerned the quake in the Neapolitan territory in 1851, in which pigs exhibited depression and unease *ten days* before the quake. Three pigs in a pen outside a monastery kitchen were "furiously excited and biting each other like dogs." Tributsch notes this same phenomenon was observed two days before the quake in China on February 2, 1975, when a dozen young pigs were fighting and bit one another's tails off.

According to the keeper at the Hongshan Forest Zoo in Nanjing, these particular animals are sensitive to infrasound but not to other changes in environment or weather. Cameras will be set up across the park to monitor the animal behaviors. There are 200 black boars, 2,000 chickens and a 36-acre (146,000-sq m) fish pond. Zhou Hongbing, a breeder turned earthquake observer at one of the refurbished animal farms, said that breeders and observers have to brief the bureau in Nanjing twice a day about the animal behaviors. When they observe erratic behaviors, they notify the bureau immediately, through QQ, a Chinese instant messaging software.

"Seismological experts will analyze reported abnormalities to decide whether or not a possible earthquake is imminent," said Zhou in the *China Daily* article.

Special training at the bureau lists possible abnormal behaviors—chickens flying above trees instead of eating, a large number of fish jumping out of the water or toads moving en masse. Zhou Bing, division chief with Nanjing Seismological Bureau, says that potential animal farms must house more than three species and have a pond that covers dozens of acres, so that the experts have enough samples for cross-checks. Preferred locations should be in quiet neighborhoods away from factories or mines.

The article noted that since the 1970s, 58 kinds of animals have been found that exhibit abnormal behavior before earthquakes. These include wild and domesticated animals, such as boars, cats, dogs, pandas, fish, snakes, rats, skunks, ants and bees. Cave animals, such as rats and snakes, have been found to be more sensitive than those living above the ground, and smaller animals are more sensitive than their larger counterparts.

The Chinese will combine the observation of bizarre animal behaviors with more traditional means of predicting quakes. But they are clearly leagues ahead of the West in this area and seem to lack the skepticism about animal precognition that's so prevalent in our culture. It probably wasn't always this way.

When we lived in caves and tribes and foraged for food, our survival depended on signs in our environment. One type of sign involved wildlife. *Why are thousands of birds fleeing the forest? Why are elephants stampeding? Why are the wolves howling?* These days, we have our weather apps—radar that instantly shows where the storm cell is, where the front, tornado or hurricane is headed.

One afternoon at the dog park, we noticed that the sky was growing dark, the wind was picking up; we could smell rain in the air. We hadn't heard thunder or seen any lightning yet and figured there was a good chance the approaching front would simply circle our area and open up elsewhere. That happens frequently in South Florida. But when we saw a number of dogs cowering under benches—the dogs that usually hid at the first roll of thunder—we knew the storm would hit our area.

One woman was sitting at a picnic table, scrolling through her phone, and when Rob remarked that a storm was coming, she glanced up and shook her head. "Nope. The weather sites say the front will hit north of us." Her dog, though, was hunkered down under the table.

Five minutes later, the skies opened up and everyone and their dogs raced for their cars. Technology may be a marvel, but when we rely on it more than we do on our own feelings and observations of our environment, we rob ourselves of our ability to sense the future.

Animals Predicting Hurricanes

In 1992, category 5 Hurricane Andrew was predicted to slam into South Florida with such ferocity that on August 22, a watch went up along most of the state's east coast, from Titusville to the Florida Keys. A watch means that hurricane conditions, with sustained winds of at least 74 miles (119 km) an hour, are *possible* within a specified area. The next day, a hurricane warning was issued—hurricane conditions were now *expected*—and Andrew's track had been adjusted 83 miles (134 km) south, so that it extended from Vero Beach to the Florida Keys.

At the time, we were living about 100 miles (161 km) north of Miami, in Boynton Beach, with our daughter, who was three, and our two cats. Our area was included in the warning, so we made our preparations. This entailed dealing with everyone else in the warning area who was doing the same thing, rushing around for bottled water, food and supplies. It meant long lines at gas stations, grocery stores and Home Depot. Rob started putting up our hurricane shutters, a tedious, time-consuming job. We had aluminum panels for every window and sliding glass door in our house, and each panel had to be installed individually.

Our house backed up to a lake that was home to several types of ducks and an occasional alligator. A family of burrowing owls lived in our backyard and usually came out near dusk and hunted for food. We figured the birds would all be headed elsewhere and that our cats would be hunkered down somewhere in the house, as cats often do when a hurricane approaches.

But by midafternoon, with Andrew only several hours from landfall, it was business as usual in the animal kingdom. Even though the sky was overcast and the wind had picked up a little, a dozen ducks waddled along the edge of the lake, quacking noisily, our cats scampered out of the house to chase the ducks and Trish located the burrowing owls in their usual area in the yard. She went over to Rob, who was having trouble installing the panels on the sliding glass doors that overlooked the lake.

"The screws on these panels are stripped," he said. "I need to go to Home Depot."

"It'll be a madhouse. Besides, I think the National Hurricane Center is wrong about where Andrew is going to hit," she said, and told him why.

Rob thought about it, but not for long. "Let's just leave these panels off."

As it turned out, the animals were right. In spite of Andrew's category 5 status, with winds that peaked at nearly 180 miles (290 km) an hour, it was a tight, compact storm. Winds of 35 miles (56 km) an hour extended only 90 miles (145 km) from the storm. When Andrew made landfall in Homestead, we had no idea about the extent of the damage because for us, it didn't even amount to a summer thunderstorm.

On October 29, 2012, superstorm Sandy made landfall near Brigatine, New Jersey, as a category 1 hurricane. It's the second costliest hurricane in US history—Katrina still holds the number one spot—with $108 billion in damages and 1,833 deaths. Sandy is also the largest Atlantic hurricane on record, with winds that spanned more than 1,100 miles (1,770 km). The superstorm affected 24 states from Florida to Maine and west to Michigan and Wisconsin. The storm surge flooded the New York subway system, shut down the New York Stock Exchange for two days and left millions without electrical power.

Not surprisingly, stories emerged about the erratic behavior of animals before the storm. One of the most interesting stories came from Dr. Gary Langham, chief scientist of the National Audubon Society in Washington, DC. In the November 13, 2012, edition of the *New York Times*, Langham cited the behavior of the birds in his backyard during the days before Sandy struck.

"They were going crazy, eating food in a driving rain and wind when normally they would never have been out in that kind of weather," he said. "They knew a bigger storm was coming, and they were trying to get food while they could. We must remind ourselves that 40 to 50 percent of birds are migratory, often traveling thousands of miles a year between their summer and winter grounds. The only way they can accomplish that is to have amazing abilities that are far beyond anything we can do."

Steve Dale, one of the most widely syndicated pet columnists in the world and host of two nationally syndicated pet radio shows, posted a query on his website that came from a dog owner who was in the path of Hurricane Sandy. During the storm, the person's Labrador mix became badly agitated, crying at times, and the dog's behavior convinced him and his family to evacuate. It turned out to be a smart move. "Our street and a small part of our home flooded. What did our dog know? Was the dog warning us?"

Dale notes that some dogs are fearful and anxious during thunderstorms: "What you suggest, however, is that your dog actually went above and beyond, intentionally warning family members about the danger. Some animals do seem to have a beat on Mother Nature, sensing something about changes in the weather, for example, though we're not sure what that something might be. At some point, learning how animals are able to determine when super-storms are on the way could save many human lives. I'm glad you listened to your dog!"

In late October 2005, Hurricane Wilma was supposed to hit Palm Beach and Broward Counties in South Florida as a category 1 hurricane. But its prior history worried us. At the time, it was the most intense hurricane ever recorded in the Atlantic basin, with its lowest pressure at 882 millibars. At its peak when it was southeast of the Yucatán Peninsula, its winds were estimated to be 185 miles (298 km) an hour.

Twenty-four hours before landfall, on a morning that was warm, sunny and beautiful, we noticed squirrels frantically foraging for food in our backyard. Flocks of birds—black birds, wading birds, hawks—headed east toward the ocean rather than west toward the Everglades as they usually did in the evenings. They sensed that the storm was coming in from the Gulf of Mexico and would cross the state from west to east. Squadrons of frogs and toads hopped toward the nearest canal.

Our three cats hunkered down inside the house, in a back bedroom. Our dusky conure, Kali, usually spent her days perched on top of her cage, beneath a large tree in the backyard. But the day before the storm, she refused to leave the cage and huddled inside, agitated, squawking, gobbling at her seed and hiding slices of vegetable and fruits that we gave her. Our golden retriever was restless, uneasy and refused to go outside when we were stashing outdoor furniture in the garage.

We live adjacent to a sprawling equestrian community, and during a bike ride through Saddle Trails we noticed how unruly the horses were. Horses in open fields galloped wildly from one end to the other and refused to be led into trailers so they could be moved. In the canals around our neighborhood, where turtles usually basked on rocks in the sunlight and wading birds preened and spread their wings to dry in the heat, there wasn't a turtle or wading bird in sight. But huge schools of fish were visible in the canals. An exodus was underway.

By midafternoon, with Wilma less than 24 hours away, the weather was still beautiful, but we started closing the accordion shutters on our windows. On one that faced the lush backyard with its mango and palm trees and tropical plants, we found a swollen dark ball of several hundred fire ants huddled in a fold of the shutter.

These stinging ants are the bane of Florida homeowners. They build large nests in grass, foliage, around the bases of trees, all the places where your dogs run and your kids play. If you're unfortunate enough to step in a nest or drop an article of clothing on one—a cap, a shirt, a sock, a shoe—and then put that piece of clothing on, you could end up in the ER on the verge of anaphylactic shock.

When these suckers are threatened with lots of rain, they often form a ball so they can float if they have to. We hadn't had a drop of rain. We hosed them away, sprayed the periphery of the window with ant killer and sealed the inside edges of the window with duct tape so that if they squeezed through the bottom of the shutter, they wouldn't be able to get through the edges of the window and into the house.

That was really the point when we knew Wilma would be *bad*.

It struck the morning after we'd found the ball of fire ants. We didn't have any shutters for our heavy wooden front door or for the three skylights in the roof. But because our house had been built after Andrew, the skylights could supposedly withstand category 5 winds. So, we congregated in the kitchen with our daughter, dog, three cats and Kali. The wind caused the skylights in the living room and kitchen to vibrate violently, filling the rooms with a sound like a discordant orchestra. The front door shook so hard that we were terrified it would blow off its hinges and had some half-baked idea that if we took turns gripping the knob we would be able to prevent it from happening.

Our power went out—and didn't come back on until ten days later. Schools were closed for two weeks. Gas stations shut down. Sewage backed up. Canals overflowed throughout South Florida. For several days we had to boil our water. The aftermath was worse than the hurricane.

Wilma raged for about 30 minutes, then the wind suddenly stopped, the sun came out and we realized the eye of the storm had stalled over our area. We hurried outside to survey the damage—and our eyes were drawn upward to the hole in white fluffy clouds that revealed blue sky. In all of our years in Florida, this was the only time we had ever been outside in the *eye* of a hurricane, where it is dead calm.

There was no wildlife anywhere—no birds, crickets, squirrels, lizards, worms, butterflies, spiders, not even an ant. They knew the storm wasn't over. The backside of the storm was supposed to be less intense. But as the winds picked up and gathered ferocity, we quickly moved back inside the house. Wilma's backside, compounded with a spinoff of tornadoes, proved more powerful than the initial blast.

When it was over, we ventured outside in a kind of stupor. The trunk of Kali's favorite tree had been split down the middle. Our papaya trees had toppled, our mango trees looked as if they had been plowed under by tractors, our fence had collapsed, there were dead snakes and frogs and toads in our swimming pool. And when we opened the accordion shutters on those back windows, we found more dark balls of fire ants that had ridden out the storm and now scattered.

Stories like this are common among people who have lived in South Florida since 2000 or earlier. In the western part of communities in Miami-Dade, Broward and Palm Beach Counties, which were built where the Everglades used to be, wildlife is abundant. The creatures, both great and small, talk constantly. They are messengers who confirm, comfort and warn about what's ahead. But unless we're open and receptive to the chatter, we swat them, spray them, squash them, and the message never reaches us.

The Octopus That Picked Winners

In 2010, a strangely beautiful creature made a string of correct sports predictions that blew Las Vegas away.

In that year's World Cup competitions, Paul, a two-and-a-half-year-old octopus, correctly predicted the winning team seven times in a row, then went on to pick Spain as the World Cup finalist. At the time, Paul lived in an aquarium at the Sea Life Center in Oberhausen, Germany. He made these predictions when he was presented with two boxes containing food—mussels—that were marked with the flag of a national football team in an upcoming match.

Whenever he chose the box with a particular country's flag, that country's team invariably won. In four of Germany's six Euro 2008 matches and in all seven of their matches in the 2010 World Cup, Paul chose the winners. In the World Cup final on July 11, he correctly predicted a win for Spain against the Netherlands by eating the mussel in the box with the Spanish flag on it. His predictions were 100 percent correct for the 2010 World Cup and 86 percent correct overall.

So, how did Paul do this?

Science tries to explain it by noting that octopuses are the most intelligent invertebrates because they can be trained for learning and memory tasks. They apparently are also strongly attracted to horizontal patterns, says scienceforum.com, which notes that these patterns are found on the flags Paul favored—Germany, Spain, Serbia. Really? That's the best explanation?

On plusmaths.org, David Spiegelhalter attempted to answer the riddle about Paul in the article "Understanding Uncertainty: How Psychic Was Paul?" He notes that many animals around the world were also making predictions at the same time—porcupines, guinea pigs, even a parakeet named Mani in Singapore. But Mani was beaten by Paul when he mistakenly chose the Netherlands as the winner. Spiegelhalter does the complicated math on the odds that Paul is psychic and at the end of the article concludes, "If you believe that a hypothesis is impossible, then no amount of evidence will change your mind, and you have to put the events down to just chance. Call me biased if you want, but that's certainly how I felt."

Some scientists suggested that the sensitive chemoreceptors on Paul's tentacles are what enabled him to pick the winners. Since these chemoreceptors allows octopuses to taste food and smell water, it's possible that minor chemical differences on the surface of each box might account for Paul's decisions. Some people say that Paul could be trained to choose the right box by smell. The plastic containers reportedly have holes to help him choose.

But if someone training the octopus actually made the picks and *fed* Paul the answers, that, too, is pretty remarkable.

But why not give Paul the benefit of the doubt and attribute it to precognition, which Carl Jung considered to be an aspect of synchronicity—meaningful coincidence.

Whatever Paul's secret was, he's not telling. He died on October 26, 2010.

Animals Predicting Other Stuff

Cats and the Vet

As of 2015, there were 78 million dogs living in households in the United States. That's up 10 million from 2000. As of the same year, there were 85.8 million cat owners in the United States. What can these millions of pet owners tell us about their cats and dogs as natural precogs?

Most cat owners have stories about how their pets seem to *know* stuff before events occur, especially events that involve them, such as a pending vet visit. Rupert Sheldrake actually conducted a survey of veterinary clinics in the North London Yellow Pages and asked the vets, nurses or receptionists whether they found that some cat owners canceled appointments because the cat had disappeared: "Sixty-four out of sixty-five clinics had cancellations of this kind quite frequently." The single holdout had done away with appointments for cats and told owners to just come in with their pets when it was convenient.

Sometimes a cat will see the carrier in which it's going to be hauled to the vet and freaks out and hides or bolts from the house. But suppose there isn't any carrier in sight? Suppose the cat isn't even in the house when you call the vet to make an appointment for several days from now and yet the cat vanishes on the day of the appointment? Is that telepathy—mind-to-mind communication—or is it sensing the future?

We posted a question on Facebook about this: "Cat owners: Does your cat vanish on the day it is supposed to visit the vet, even if the carrier isn't anywhere in sight?" The responses were insightful and funny. Vicki DeLaurentis, one of the planetary empaths we wrote about, addresses the psychic/telepathic component between owners and their cats: "I had to put the carrier out days in advance so that I wasn't thinking about it. Otherwise, they would sense it!"

Adelita Chirino, who teaches dream workshops, had the most comical comment: "It's a veritable stealth operation at our house that involves at least two people. The carrier stays hidden until the last second; I deliberately keep my mind blank leading up to the corralling, because he knows, he always knows. Jim scoops up Sunny and I tilt the carrier up to enlist gravity. There are no guarantees!"

When our daughter was ten or eleven, a stray cat gave birth to five kittens on our back porch. We found homes for all of them except the runt, whom we adopted, a black and white male, Whiskers. By the time he was a year old, he invariably disappeared on the day he was supposed to go to the vet. We thought it was because he'd seen the carrier, so we started stashing the carrier in the garage several days before the vet appointment. It didn't matter. He still continued to vanish on the day of a vet appointment.

The next step we took was to make the vet's appointment when Whiskers was prowling around outside, so that he couldn't hear us or sense our intentions. It didn't make any difference. He always *knew*. In the end, the only way we could get him to the vet was to just scoop him up in the morning, get him into the carrier and show up unannounced at the vet's office. It meant a longer wait and a feistier Whiskers, but it was worth it.

The vet we use now for our cats and our dog welcomes walk-ins.

Oscar the Cat

In 2005, a kitten named Oscar was adopted from an animal shelter and became a permanent resident of the dementia unit at the Steere House Nursing & Rehabilitation Center in Providence, Rhode Island. The staff adopted him because they feel that animals make the facility a home. After all, Steere House is usually the final stop before death, where patients with dementia and Alzheimer's no longer recognize loved ones, can't talk and are lost in chopped-up memories of the past.

The staff in the facility noticed that Oscar had an unusual routine. Two to four hours before a patient died, the cat would walk into the room, jump onto the person's bed and curl up next to him or her, purring loudly. In the first two years after his arrival in 2005, there had been 25 deaths and he had been present for all of them. In only one instance was he *not* present and that was because the family asked that he be taken out of the room. Oscar wasn't at all happy about that situation. He made quite a fuss outside the patient's door and was removed from the floor.

One time, the nurses placed Oscar on the bed of a patient they thought would die shortly. But Oscar didn't stick around and the staff figured he'd gotten this one wrong. As it turned out, the patient survived for another two days. But in the final hours, Oscar was there, snuggled up next to the person, purring.

In 2007, Dr. David Dosa, a geriatrician and professor at Brown University who works with dementia patients, wrote about Oscar in the *New England Journal of Medicine*, and a furor erupted. The uproar worsened three years later when Dosa published a book, *Making the Rounds with Oscar: The Extraordinary Gift of An Ordinary Cat*. By then, Oscar had accurately predicted 50 deaths and the book catapulted him to fame.

It also triggered discussions about end-of-life issues. As Dosa writes in his book, "Cats may have nine lives, but we have only one and we're all terrified to talk about the ending of it."

When CBS News reported about this remarkable cat in 2010, it pointed out that Dosa can't explain scientifically how the cat makes his predictions, but he theorizes that Oscar "imitates the nurses who raised him or smells odors given off by dying cells, perhaps like some dogs who scientists say can detect cancer using their sense of scent."

After the televised story about Oscar on CBS, the theories ranged the spectrum of extremes. Glenn Beck's conclusion was fraud on the part of the staff. One person posted a comment on CBS's website, suggesting the cat was carrying a disease that caused the patients' deaths. The theories from experts were all over the map. They ranged from the cat's heightened sense of smell picking up on a pheromone given off by those who are close to death, to the motionless state of the patient. One science blog concluded that Oscar's ability was nothing more than "confirmation bias"—in other words, that a member of the staff probably noticed him curled up next to a patient who subsequently died.

As Larry Dossey writes in *The Power of Premonitions*, "Physicians of course are nervous about endorsing the existence of the afterlife or future knowing, thus the stampede to analyze Oscar in everyday terms."

But perhaps Oscar, like Paul the octopus, is a precog with a specific focus. Whereas Paul could predict World Cup winners, Oscar can predict within two to four hours when a person will die. Yet, skeptics go to great lengths to find alternate explanations.

After Dosa's book was published, the *Skeptical Inquirer* reviewed it, but the review was little more than a scathing attempt to debunk precognition in animals or humans. Joe Nickell, the author of the review, implied—as Glenn Beck did—that fraud was involved: "One wonders, was Oscar placed or coaxed into rooms of other dying patients?" This kind of innuendo was also leveled against Daryl Bern, the professor at Cornell who conducted the precognition experiments mentioned in the first chapter.

Nickell calls himself a prominent skeptic and investigator of the paranormal, but it's unclear in his "review" whether he actually *investigated* anything. Did he go to the dementia unit and observe Oscar? Did he speak to the staff? Did he attempt to understand how Oscar's ability works? He came at the material with the certainty that it couldn't be true and after dropping his innuendos about possible fraud, ended the review with a line that so many skeptics use when debunking the paranormal: "My guess is that Oscar is a magnet for fuzzy thinking."

That phrase *fuzzy thinking* implies that if you believe in anything paranormal, if you believe Oscar can actually predict these deaths, then you are cognitively impaired.

As for Dosa and his staff, they know that when Oscar curls up next to a patient, the family should be notified. "People actually were taking great comfort in this idea, that this animal was there and might be there when their loved ones eventually pass," Dosa said. "He was there when they couldn't be."

We were curious about what has happened with Oscar since the publication of Dosa's book in 2010 and Googled him. In 2013, Oscar had a severe allergic reaction and died for several seconds. He was revived and after being a patient for a few months at Steere House, returned to his normal duties. What an ironic synchronicity that a cat who does what Oscar does had a near-death experience. To date, he has accurately predicted more than 100 deaths.

No doubt anyone who has had firsthand experience with Oscar's uncanny talent to foresee death would consider it a meaningful coincidence. "At times," writes Robert Hopcke in *There Are No Accidents: Synchronicity and the Story of Our Lives*, "the synchronistic meaning of a coincidence seems almost capable of repairing and making whole what death has torn asunder."

The Precognitive Owl

Owls have been tagged as harbingers of death and of healing, of unspeakable evil and great wisdom. Across time, borders and cultures, the mythology and folklore about these birds involves extremes.

In Peru, owls are considered to be strong shamanic medicine. In Celtic traditions, owls symbolize the underworld. In ancient Greece, the owl was a symbol of wisdom, knowledge and philosophy. Zulus believe the owl is the sorcerer's bird. In Japanese culture, owls are thought to confer luck and protection from suffering. The Australian Aborigines believe owls to be the spirits of women.

Remember the opening scenes in the first Harry Potter book and movie? Owls sweep into the main hall and deliver mail to the students, a rainfall of envelopes and packages. This scene perfectly captures the long tradition of owls as messengers, but in the story they are literally mail carriers who travel freely across the boundary between the mundane world and the magical world of Hogwarts. In many shamanic traditions, owls are believed to move between the worlds of the living and the dead with equal ease, at home in both realms. Sometimes, owls are viewed as harbingers of death.

One Saturday morning in May 2000, our daughter came racing into the kitchen, where Trish was fixing lunch. "You have to see this, Mom," she said excitedly. "There's a burrowing owl on the fence outside Buddy's room."

Buddy was her name for Trish's dad, who was living with us at the time. He was in his late 80s then, struggling with the fact that his wife of nearly 50 years was in an Alzheimer's unit and that he had Parkinson's. Megan was excited because she'd never seen one of these owls close up before and was surprised it was just sitting on the atrium fence. These owls tend to emerge from their ground burrows at dusk and are rarely seen in the daylight.

Trish and Megan crept up to the sliding glass door that opened to the atrium outside her dad's room. Sure enough, the owl was just perched there, peering at them. It appeared to be standing on one leg. Trish and Megan went outside for a closer look. It didn't fly away as they approached and they could see that the owl wasn't just standing on one leg; part of its *left* leg was missing. By now, Trish felt alarmed. Her dad had both his legs and used a cane to get around. Yet, the owl was outside *his* room. If it was a harbinger of his imminent death, what was the missing leg about?

She thought she might be reading too much into it and after the owl flew off, they went back inside the house.

Early the next morning, Trish received a call from the Alzheimer's facility where her mother was confined and was told Rose Marie had broken her hip and was en route to the emergency room. Trish met her mother at the hospital and after X-rays and tests, was told that her mother's *left* hip wasn't broken—it had disintegrated. Due to her Alzheimer's, Rose Marie wasn't eligible for hip replacement surgery. The alternative was morphine and a nursing home. She died three weeks later.

Part of the owl's *left* leg was missing, Rose Marie's *left* hip bone was gone and her death ensued several weeks after.

It's unlikely that a skeptic would regard a one-legged owl as anything more than a curiosity. But when something like this happens to you, even when it involves the death of a loved one, you're filled with what Jung called a numinous quality, a sense of wonder and awe at the seamless quality of life. You feel as if the hand of the cosmos has swept into your life, magically shaken things up, and you no longer view yourself or the world in the same way. To Jung, synchronicity was evidence of an integrated reality he called *unus mundus*, an alchemical term that means *one world.*

In this view of reality, where everyone is connected—as opposed to the mechanistic view, where the universe operates like a giant machine—the owl's appearance was precognitive, a sign of what was coming less than twelve hours later.

Seizure-Alert Dogs

Roger Reep, a neuroscientist at the College of Veterinary Medicine at the University of Florida, is one of the few people in the United States to study seizure-alert dogs. In 1998, he and a colleague, Deborah Dalziel, surveyed 77 people between the ages of 30 and 60 who had epilepsy. The survey asked about quality of life, medical status, attitudes toward pets, ownership of dogs and their pets' behavior before and during a seizure.

Most of the respondents said they had the dogs for companionship, but in interviews with 31 people after the surveys, about ten percent said they felt that their dogs seemed to know when they were about to have a seizure. Even though the study was too small to be conclusive, it indicated that a dog's behavior isn't confined to any particular breed, age or gender and that a close emotional bond between owner and dog is important. Reep doesn't know why some dogs are able to predict seizures, but theorizes that it may be due to a smell triggered by nervous system activity.

The Epilepsy Foundation cautions consumers to be "very wary of any claims or programs that offer to train or provide 'seizure predicting' service animals." Jennifer Arnold, director of Canine Assistants in Alpharetta, Georgia, says, "There is no way at this point for us to know to what stimuli the dogs are responding." And that makes it impossible for trainers to train dogs how to be alert for the onset of a seizure.

PAWS with a Cause is a national, nonprofit organization that provides dogs as companions to assist people with epilepsy or other seizure disorders. On its website, it specifically states that its dogs "are NOT trained to protect or predict seizure activity." However, it also says that after several years with a client, "some may develop the ability to alert their owner of an oncoming seizure. This behavior is not guaranteed to develop, nor to be consistent if it does develop."

In the United Kingdom, however, it's a different story. Support Dogs, an organization run by a charity, guarantees on its website that its seizure-alert dogs are trained to provide "a 100% reliable warning up to 50 minutes prior to an oncoming seizure." This enables the owner to find a safe place to have the seizure.

The website has an information packet that spells out guidelines for applicants that include: a confirmed diagnosis of epilepsy, at least ten seizures a month, no pet dog already in the house, daily support so the dog's needs can be met. According to Rupert Sheldrake, this organization is pioneering the training of seizure alert dogs in the United Kingdom. The training manager, Val Strong, doesn't think dogs can be trained to recognize the signs of a seizure, but that they seem to do this naturally when an owner and dog have a strong emotional bond.

So, how do the dogs predict epileptic fits? Recent research suggests it may be due to smell, subtle changes in the owner's behavior or a detection of electrical disturbances in the owner's nervous system. Sheldrake notes that any of these possibilities would require the dog to be close to the owner. As he had seen in his research, though, and as dog owners attest time and again, some dogs react to their owners' thoughts and intentions at a distance, and some also seem to know when their owners have had an accident or are dying, even when they are hundreds of miles away; "It may therefore be worth considering the additional possibility that the dogs are not simply reacting to subtle sensory cues, but may be picking up signals of a nature as yet unknown to science."

This explanation might well be true for other facets of the paranormal, too. Since the 1930s when J. B. Rhine at the Duke Parapsychology Lab started researching ESP with Zener cards, scientists and researchers have tried, with varying results, to replicate psi under controlled conditions. These trailblazers have studied it all, from telepathy and clairvoyance, clairaudience and psychokinesis, remote viewing and precognition. And they have usually found that psi is a slippery trickster with its own inner order and refuses to behave according to rules imposed by researchers.

Yet ordinary people continue to experience psi in all its forms and add to the growing body of evidence that it not only exists, but it is accessible to everyone . . . including dogs.

When Nature Is Precognitive

The Cactus

Nature can be a powerful teacher and her lessons don't have to occur through natural or manmade disasters. To understand how nature often provides precognitive clues, it's vital that we pay attention and don't dismiss these experiences as meaningless. Yet, when it comes to communication with living things that are not human, many of us tend to be skeptical. Do animal communicators really hold conversations with dogs, cats and even wild creatures? Or are they saying how animals might respond . . . if they could think like a human? How about communication with plants? Is that possible?

In 1982, author Michael Crichton attended a conference held by Dr. Brugh Joy, a renowned healer and author of *Joy's Way: A Map for the Transformational Journey*. The conference was held at a facility in the desert and early on, Joy told the attendees to walk in the desert until they found a rock, tree or plant with whom they felt a particular kinship. Then they were supposed "to spend time with this teacher, and talk with the teacher and learn what the teacher had to teach us," Crichton wrote in his terrific nonfiction book *Travels*. So, he set out to find his teacher.

As other attendees excitedly reported finding a teacher, Crichton got annoyed because he hadn't. He finally found a cactus in an artificial rock garden in a meditation room. "I didn't like the cactus," he wrote. "It was common, a sort of phallic cactus shape with lots of thorns. It was rather battered, with scars on one side. It was not in any way an attractive cactus."

Days passed. Crichton kept talking to the cactus, visiting it, but the cactus refused to speak to him. Then finally one day on his way to the meditation room, he thought that if the cactus really was his teacher, it would speak to him: "And the cactus said, 'When are you going to stop running around and talk?' Irritably. Like a grouchy old man."

After this, Crichton kept firing questions at the cactus. It refused to speak to him. Every day, the same thing happened: no response. The conference continued and Crichton was exposed to new ideas—healing techniques, chakras, perceptual changes, the tarot and the I Ching. "On the final day of the conference, I visited the cactus to say good-bye. The cactus was just sitting there. It wouldn't speak to me."

Crichton told the cactus that he appreciated what it had shown him and said he'd enjoyed spending time with it. "Which wasn't exactly true because I felt frustrated a lot of the time, but I thought it was more or less true." Still no response. "Then I realized that from its position in the garden, the cactus could never see the sun set. The cactus had been years in that position and been deprived of seeing sunsets. I burst into tears. And then the cactus said, 'It's been good having you here with me.' Then I *really* cried."

Eight months after that conference, Crichton's life had completely turned around. He had changed his relationships, residence, work, diet, habits, interests, exercise, goals—in fact, anything in his life that could be changed, was changed: "These changes were so sweeping that I couldn't see what was happening while I was in the midst of them. And there was another change, too. I've become very fond of cacti, and I always have some around, wherever I live."

In a sense, his experience with the cactus was a precognitive trigger for Crichton, even though he didn't know it at the time. It was the synchronicity that blew his life wide open, shook out everything that no longer worked and made space for the new to rush in to fill the void. From this point forward, Crichton wrote some of his most entertaining and popular books. Among them were *Travels, Disclosure, Timeline, Sphere, The Lost World, Airframe* and, of course, *Jurassic Park.*

Okay, a skeptic could argue that Crichton imagined the whole conversation with the cactus. He was, after all, a Harvard-trained medical doctor who had never practiced medicine and had chosen to make his living through his imagination. Even before 1982, he had written a number of novels that included *The Andromeda Strain, Terminal Man* and *The Great Train Robbery*, all of which had been made into movies. And yes, his interaction with the cactus was subjective, lacked witnesses and replicable lab data.

But the fact that it caused such a powerful internal tectonic shift in Crichton, the kind of shift that pivots your life in a new direction, is the best testament to the *reality of this experience for him.* And that's the thing with precognition and its bewildering siblings. It's often so personal, so unique to you and your interpretation, that even if you explained it to someone else, the person wouldn't really *get it* because he or she isn't inside your skin.

Michael Crichton died in 2006. Toward the end of his life it seemed that he had taken on the curmudgeon personality of that cactus. He was an adamant climate-change denier and in his last novel, *State of Fear*, the bad guys were environmentalists. He went to great lengths in the novel to explain his prickly point of view via his main characters repeatedly lecturing readers.

The Precognitive Tree

One moonless October night, author Catriona MacGregor arrived home late from work. She had a bag of groceries over one shoulder and a briefcase over the other. It had been a long day and she was tired.

As she turned the corner to walk through the dark, empty lot next to her house, a soft, glowing light caught her attention. "A golden white light illuminated the lot warmly, like the delicate rays of the first morning sun," she writes in *Partnering with Nature: the Wild Path to Reconnecting with the Earth.* She glanced around, seeking the source of the light, and noticed a large tree in the center of the lot. She realized the bright light seemed to emanate from the tree. She kept looking around for another source of the light, didn't see anything and hurried on to her house, kind of freaked out.

Shaken, she set her groceries on the counter and opened the door for another look; "I looked toward the vacant lot hoping to see only darkness. Instead, the tree illuminated the lot and surrounding buildings as brightly as if the moon had come to rest gently on the soft grass."

Catriona ventured out onto the porch and stood facing the tree. Against the evening chill, its light felt warm. A sense of peace enveloped her. She experienced the sublime. "I knew that the light was the fire of the tree's divine spirit—the tree's very soul. There are no words to describe that which is known as intimately as a lover and yet remains unfathomable."

She finally went back inside the house, fell into bed next to her husband and dropped off to sleep. The next day her life unfolded as usual—she got her son off to school, then made her commute to work. She arrived home earlier than she had the day before and when the empty lot next to her house came into view, she was floored. "What I saw was not the beautiful tree that I had communed with less than a day before. Instead, I saw a ghastly two-foot [61-cm] stump surrounded by tiny clumps of wood arbitrarily spewed around the lot." Mulch. That was all that remained of the tree.

Catriona recognized what had occurred. "The tree, knowing of its impending demise, shone forth its inner light, sharing its everlasting soul with the rest of the world."

The tree had sensed its future and broadcasted it and she just happened to be the person who had tuned into it. No witnesses, no lab, no data other than subjective experience. Yet her experience, like Crichton's with the cactus, altered her path in life.

We experienced something similar in the aftermath of Hurricane Wilma. At the time, we tucked it away under the broad umbrella of synchronicity. But when we read Catriona's story about this tree, we realized our experience was precognitive.

Earlier in the chapter, we talked about how after Wilma had passed through, we walked out into our backyard. The top of the tree where our dusky-headed conure spent most of her days had been lopped off and the trunk had been split down the middle, as if a giant hacksaw had been taken to it. That tree had come from Trish's parents' backyard and we had carted it to our new home when we had moved in 2000. Every morning, we carried Kali's cage out to a spot under that tree, opened the door and she eagerly hopped out and climbed into the branches and spent the entire day there, living like a bird in the wild.

We both noted the symbolism of the tree's damage and thought it was connected to the death of Trish's father less than a month earlier.

Before we started cleaning up the damage in the backyard and removing the dead creatures from the pool, our daughter brought Kali's cage outside, opened the door and she eagerly climbed into her traumatized tree. We worked for hours as our dog and cats prowled the yard. At some point, Kali got spooked by the chatter of a neighbor's generator and suddenly flew away.

At one time, we had her wings clipped regularly, but stopped doing it when we realized she liked where she lived, that even when she flew off, she stayed close to home. Big mistake. In the aftermath of a hurricane, none of the usual rules apply.

We searched the neighborhood, called and whistled for her, left her cage in the backyard with the door open, her feeder filled with the treats she loved. As dusk collapsed into darkness and the season's first cold front moved in, we despaired.

Rob found her the next morning beneath a nest of fallen leaves across the street and brought her home. It was obvious that the cold front had been too much for her. She was sick but not a single vet was open in our county. The entire area had shut down in the aftermath of the hurricane. We cut up her favorite veggies and fruit, but she didn't eat or drink or chatter. The next night, as Trish held Kali against her chest, the conure died. Her ruined tree, split down the middle, had been the warning, the precognition.

"We have forgotten how to watch these signs, how to listen to the messages in the wind, and how to gain wisdom from trees," write Denise and Meadow Linn in *Quest: A Guide for Creating Your Own Vision quest.* "Very few people truly understand what forces have motivated their life or shaped their destiny."

We buried Kali under her favorite tree and today, a decade later, it still stands, bright and beautiful, strong and vibrant, the split mended.

Just as this last sentence was written, the bulb in the lamp in Trish's office—the main source of light—blinked out, like a punctuation mark at the end of the story.

Research Ideas

There are numerous books on the esoteric meanings of animals that can be helpful in understanding what your encounter with wildlife might mean in the larger scheme of things. *Animal Speak: The Spiritual & Magical Powers of Creatures Great & Small* by Ted Andrews is one of the best. The Internet also provides some terrific sites. Just Google "esoteric meaning of" and the name of the animal, then poke around on different sites until you find a meaning that resonates and feels right to you. Keep notes.

By researching the animal's behavior and life cycle, the number of young it typically has, the gestation period and its life span, you can glean a rough time frame for the event the animal represents. Let's say that mice have made themselves at home in your attic. What's the message? Mouse, according to Ted Andrews, represents details: "When mouse shows up as a totem, it is either time to pay attention to details or an indication that you cannot see the forest for the trees. You may be getting so locked into detail that you forget the bigger picture."

Presumably you'll know whether the mice represent something current. If you can't think of anything the mice might pertain to, then their presence might be addressing something headed your way. Since mice care for their young for about five weeks, Andrews pegs their power cycle as five to six weeks. But because the gestation period for a mouse is 19 to 21 days, the situation or event may arrive within a matter of weeks.

The next time you have an encounter with an animal, try the above suggestions, mark the date of the encounter on a calendar, jot down some of the details, then see what happens.

Renee and the Dolphin

Impulse. Need. Desire. Hunch. Any of these emotions can draw us to a particular time and place, where we become the vessel for the fulfillment of a precognition. In this story, a woman who spent years working with dolphins became that vessel for a dying dolphin.

Renee Prince earned a master's degree in experimental psychology so that she could work on interspecies communication with cetaceans. She spent years working with dolphins and orcas, always with the hope that it would lead to building some sort of mutual communication system between their species and ours.

> *"Unfortunately, after working with dolphins in captivity I came to realize that life in the tanks is ultimately an early death sentence for dolphins, and the brief life they do have is impoverished and intolerable. After two of my dolphins died, I left dolphin research, in part because I couldn't face another death of another one of my friends, and I had no power to change their situation. Captive dolphins and whales are, to the rest of the world, simply property to be sold, used and disposed of quickly when they no longer can serve human purposes. Since then I've lived with the guilt and pain of having left the dolphins behind."*

But even after Renee changed careers to work in the film business, she never forgot dolphins or her love for them. She lived near the beach in order to be near them and often jogged along the beach, always looking past the waves for the telltale arcs of fins or noisy exhalations of breath that meant dolphins were once again visiting her section of the beach. She would see them once in a while and would rush out to meet them, hoping they could stay and play.

One afternoon, she went jogging on the beach and was surprised that she was the only person on the beach, a strange event since she lived on a popular beach in the L.A. area. It wasn't long before she noticed a dolphin in the waves and could tell immediately that something was terribly wrong; "The surf was washing over him, tumbling him over and over. He was trying to get to shore. I knew immediately what was happening. The dolphin was in serious trouble and had to reach land because he was too weak to keep himself afloat. He was in imminent danger of drowning."

Renee ran out into the water and pushed out toward him. When the dolphin saw her, his eyes widened in fear just for a moment, then he headed directly toward her. "At that second, I had the odd, yet utterly certain feeling that this dolphin had been waiting for me. When we reached each other and I put my arms around him, just as I had always done with my own dolphin friends so many years ago, he relaxed against me and looked up at me with complete trust. I held him upright, keeping his blowhole above water, and he helped us head toward shore, moving his pectoral fins to steer us and slowly pumping his flukes."

Renee and the dolphin kept in constant eye contact and she talked to him, promising that she wouldn't leave his side. She told him she could call the marine mammal rescue center—a number she knew by heart—and that she would ride with him to wherever they could keep him, even if it had to be Sea World, the place she had fled long ago; "And I told him this time I wouldn't let Sea World keep him captive—I would make sure he was released back into the sea when he was well."

But as they reached shore, in water only a few inches deep, the dolphin wanted to turn around, to face back out to sea. Renee helped him turn and he came to a stop. "He lay back in my arms, looked deeply and calmly into my eyes, and died. I saw the light go out of him."

Somehow this dolphin, a deepwater species—*Delphinus delphi*—that never would have been near shore, had traveled untold miles away from his world. He had entered an utterly alien world where he somehow had known he would find the only human on the beach who could have seen him, known what he wanted, and helped him get to shore. "He died in the arms of someone who, he must have known, loved him instantly and without conditions; someone who knew dolphins and for years had longed with all her heart for another chance at contact with his kind."

It took Renee a long time to process this event. She had thought she was there to save him. She made promises to him, made plans to give him back his life, to help him heal. "When that didn't happen, I was horrified, angry at God, fate, the Tao—whatever. I was angry at myself. What if I had seen my dolphin earlier, before he was too weak to make it? Was there something I could have done differently or better so that he could have been saved? But I was left with no explanation, only the power and soul-wrenching synchronicity of our encounter. I've come to believe that my dolphin wanted to die in the embrace of love. I had given him that, I was sure."

The telepathic connection between Renee and the dolphin in the moments before it died—*in the embrace of love*—is also about a much larger picture, that of the earth as a living, organic being that speaks to us constantly. Gaia. Among its messengers are the creatures of the planet—with dolphins and whales as the ones with the greatest level of intelligence and understanding.

Dreaming the Future

I know some Tibetans who lived in Tibet prior to the 1959 uprising. Before their escape from Tibet, they did not know about the natural trails and passes by which to get over the Himalayas into India. Some of these people I met had very clear dreams of these tracks and, years later, when they actually had to follow the actual trails, they found that they were already familiar with them because of the very clear dreams they had had previously.

—Dalai Lama, from *Consciousness at the Crossroads: Conversations with the Dalai Lama on Brain Science and Buddhism*

On January 7, 2016, Trish and her psychic friend Millie Gemondo traded readings, as they frequently do. During the exchange, Millie told Trish to warn Rob to be careful when he went biking. She saw him falling off the bike and said it could be serious. Interestingly, six years earlier in late December, Rob had had a vivid dream that on January 7 he would fall from his mountain bike and die. A few days later, he related the dream to a friend with intuitive abilities, who told him he wouldn't die. "But you'll be paralyzed, and for you it will be like death."

Needless to say, on the day in question—prime riding time in South Florida—Rob avoided the challenging off-road trail where he often rides. He has continued that tradition every year. Several times, he remembered his dream date with death at the last hour. His regular riding partner, worried that the dream might have been about him, now also avoids riding January 7. That story might sound silly to a nonbeliever, but why challenge such a dream? Instead, Rob acted on it. He honors that day for life, rather than death.

Dreams, those mysterious and often baffling movies that play in our sleep, have been on our mind since ancient times. They've been called messages from the gods, a link to the spirit world, a source of great wisdom and guidance. Research, as well as anecdotal evidence, reveal that dreaming about the future is not an uncommon experience. Surveys have shown that from a third to half of the population say they've experienced precognitive dreams.

Such dreams can warn us of disasters or dangers ahead, or of something positive, such as a new relationship or a boost in income. They are often vivid and sometimes so realistic that we wake up afterward surprised that we were asleep. But since we spend a third of our life sleeping, removed from our daily, conscious life, the dream world is a fertile realm for precognitive dreams.

As testament of our interest in dreams, and the possibility that they can provide a peek at the future, is the longevity of a book on the subject. *Oneirocritica* (The Interpretation of Dreams) by Artemidorus of Dalis was written more than 1,800 years ago and remains in print, a remarkable achievement in the world of publishing.

Artemidorus, who lived in Greece about AD 140, saw virtually all dreams as prophetic. For example, if a slave dreamed of having no teeth, it meant that he would be freed. But Artemidorus also understood that some dream images were metaphors, a common approach to interpreting dreams today. To dream of kissing someone might be a metaphor for "kiss and make up," or it could mean the "kiss of death," or similarly "kiss it good-bye."

Scholars say he almost certainly borrowed from older works, such as Ashurbanipal's dream book. Ashurbanipal, an Assyrian king, lived from 669 to 626 BC and his book, written on clay tablets, tells of the importance of dreams for both royalty and commoners. His book was found in the remnants of an ancient library at Nineveh, and it's believed that it was linked to even earlier books that may have dated all the way back to 5,000 BC.

For his part, Artemidorus defended his prophetic dream interpretations as his own: "I have not relied upon conjectures here, nor have I constructed a system of probabilities. My writing is based on personal experience. I myself have observed, in each occasion, how these dreams have come true."

When you dream about an event, typically it's a version of something that you have already experienced. But in the case of precognitive dreaming, the event takes place after the dream version. In other words, effect precedes the cause.

In late November 2012, Janet, a friend from California, wrote us about a dream she had a month earlier. In it, she was feeling sad, depressed, restless, with an urge to flee, emotions that weren't normal for her. In the dream, missiles rained from the sky. She was with a group of people scrambling over rubble, trying to get around a tall, burning building. People were crying, sobbing. Explosions reverberated around her. She was pleading loudly to any universal force that would listen. *Please tell them to stop! Make them stop before it's too late!*

The dream was so vivid that she thought it must be related to a future event. A few days later, she experienced an earthquake and thought that her emotional state was related to it. But she soon changed her mind. She wrote: "Today I watched the news, which I rarely do, because I find it too depressing. I turned on CNN and watched the horror unfolding in Gaza with the Israeli airstrikes. They reported it being the seventh day of the airstrikes and the possibility of it turning into a full-scale war. That's when the significance of my dream hit me."

Janet's interpretation of her dream is clearly subjective because she wasn't a participant in the disaster. However, the videos of the aftermath of the bombing convinced her that she'd found the source of the dream. Precognitive dreams of disasters are much less subjective when the dreamer is directly involved in the future event. That was the case in the Welsh village of Aberfan, when many residents dreamed or otherwise sensed an upcoming disaster.

Mining Disaster Foreseen

If you've ever heard of Aberfan, it's probably because of the tragedy that struck the town on October 21, 1966, and seized international attention. A slagheap collapsed in the mining village and inundated the Pantglas Junior School with more than 52,000 cubic yards (40,000 m^3) of mud and rubble that filled the classrooms. The dead included 116 children and 28 adults who were either crushed or buried by the sludge.

In the aftermath, many of the residents reported that they had experienced premonitions related to the disaster. The best known among them was that of a ten-year-old girl, Eryl Mai Jones. Two days before the disaster she told her mother that she wasn't afraid of dying, that she would be with her friends, Peter and June.

When her mother asked why she was talking about dying, Eryl said, "I dreamt I went to school and there was no school there. Something black had come down all over it!" Two days later, she was among the deceased, and was buried in a communal grave with her friends, Peter on one side, June on the other.

The local minister first reported the story and Eryl's parents verified it for a psychiatrist, Dr. John Barker, who lived near Aberfan. He collected 76 accounts from locals and others throughout Europe who had experienced premonitions in the days leading up to the landslide. A third of them had shared their accounts with others. Barker published his findings, "Premonitions of the Aberfan Disaster," in the December 1967 issue of the *Journal for Psychical Research*.

One week before the mountain of sludge collapsed, a housewife from Plymouth, England, dreamed that she saw "an old school nestled in a valley and then a Welsh miner. After this I saw an avalanche of coal hurtling down the mountainside. I saw the rescue operations. I had the impression of a little boy who was left behind and saved. I could never forget him."

The next day she told friends at her church social club about the dream. Barker contacted six members of the social club, who confirmed that they'd heard about the dream days before the disaster. When the woman saw news reports of the tragedy on television, she said she recognized the young boy and one of the rescuers from her dream.

Sybil Brown from Brighton had a nightmare about a screaming child in a telephone booth and another child moving toward her with a "black, billowing mass" following him. Suddenly Sybil found herself on a street in the dream and a voice said to her, "The whole family is in the house." She knew something terrible was about to happen, but she was unable to do anything about it. The Aberfan landslide destroyed 20 adjacent houses.

Other premonitions included feelings of depression or uneasiness combined with a sense of something bad about to happen. Some felt choking sensations and a feeling of gasping for breath. A man in the northwest of England reported a dream where he saw the word A-B-E-R-F-A-N spelled out in large, brilliant letters.

Precognitive Dreams about 9/11

Considering the magnitude of the 9/11 disaster, it's not surprising that numerous people reported dreams that foresaw the catastrophic destruction of the World Trade Center. This one was sent to us from Sarah, a marketing executive from Surrey, England, who contacted us in October 2014, after reading *The Synchronicity Highway*. Surprisingly, she had never told anyone about this dream.

"In the early hours of September 11, 2001, I had a dream that was so powerful and had such an impact on me that I went to work and looked online to see if anything 'bad' had happened in the world overnight."

In the dream, she was in a glass-enclosed reception area, waiting for a meeting. She was sitting on a low, boxy, black leather couch with her back to the reception area and faced giant windows. "As I looked out, the lifts were on my left and I could see people walking through the courtyard outside. The day was gorgeous."

"I hadn't been there long when I heard this enormous explosion and suddenly, powdery cement like fine snow covered the lobby and me. I remember standing up like it was an earthquake and half crouching down, not sure if there was going to be another tremor or explosion."

Suddenly, the dream cut to what looked like a scene from the movie *Mad Max.* Some Middle Eastern men were driving a yellow Datsun and one of them was standing up through the sunroof waving an assault rifle, punching the air with it, whooping and shouting in celebration as they drove through a harsh desert landscape. "I was like the camera man or director speeding along beside them, filming. I eventually stopped and they drove off into the setting sun."

When she didn't find any news stories of disasters, she put the dream out of her mind and went about her day. It was just before 2 p.m. in Surrey when a professor she worked for told her what had happened in New York. That was when she understood her dream.

Famous Premonitions

Two of the best known precognitive dreams ever reported came from a sitting president of the United States and a famed humorist.

Abraham Lincoln

In early April 1865, Abraham Lincoln revealed a startling precognitive dream that has become an unforgettable part of his legacy. He told several people, including Ward Hill Lamon, his former law partner, that in the dream he heard strange sounds of mourning in the East Room of the White House.

According to Lamon, Lincoln walked into the room and saw a "catafalque on which rested a corpse wrapped in funeral vestments. Around it were stationed soldiers, who were acting as guards, as a throng of people gazed sadly at the corpse." When Lincoln asked a guard who it was, he was told it was the president. A week later, on April 14, Lincoln was assassinated.

Lincoln apparently was interested in the predictive power of dreams. Proof of his curiosity lies in a letter written in 1863 in which he told his wife, Mary, about a dream he had about their son. Mary and the ten-year-old boy were in Philadelphia at the time. Lincoln wrote that she should put Tad's pistol away as he had an ugly dream about him. This letter was included in *Collected Works of Abraham Lincoln*, published by Rutgers University Press in 1953. No details were provided about the content of the dream, but given Mary Lincoln's interest in dreams and the paranormal, apparently no details were needed.

On the morning of his assassination, members of Lincoln's cabinet recalled that the president told them he'd dreamed of sailing across an unknown body of water at great speed. He also revealed that he'd had the same dream before nearly every major event of the Civil War.

Mark Twain

He was born Samuel Clemens in 1835 and adopted the pen name Mark Twain. More than a century after his death, he remains one of America's most beloved humorists. In spite of his success and buoyant personality, he faced a number of dark times—financial difficulties later in life and the deaths of his daughter and younger brother. Although he always managed to bounce back, he was haunted by the death of his brother, Henry, for the remainder of his life. And a dream foretelling Henry's death was at the heart of his sorrow.

In the late 1850s, Sam and Henry worked together on riverboats plying the Mississippi between Saint Louis and New Orleans. In 1858, during a stay at his sister's house, Sam dreamed he saw Henry's body laid out in a metal casket, dressed in a suit with a huge bouquet of white roses on his chest and a single red rose at the center. The dream was so vivid and realistic that when he woke up he was certain that his brother had died and his casket was in the sitting room. Grief stricken, he left the house and after a short walk realized he'd dreamed of his brother's demise. His sister, upon hearing the dream, urged him to let it go, and he agreed to do so.

A few weeks later, the brothers were in New Orleans together, and headed back to Saint Louis on the *Pennsylvania.* Sam got into an argument, then a fight, with William Brown, the boat's pilot, a man known for his violent temper. The captain sided with Sam, who was transferred to another boat to avoid further conflict.

Before he left, Sam told Henry what he should do if the boiler blew up, a dangerous issue at the time with riverboats. Henry continued on and when the *Pennsylvania* was near Memphis, the boiler exploded, killing several crew members, including Henry who died a few days later in a Memphis hospital. Although most of the men were buried in wooden coffins, a group of Memphis lady volunteers were saddened by Henry's youthful face, which was spared injury, and raised money for a metal casket.

When Sam Clemens entered the 'dead-room' of the Memphis Exchange on June 21, he was startled to see his dream unfolding. Henry was laid out in the metal casket in a borrowed suit. The only element missing were the flowers. As Sam mourned, a lady came in with a bouquet of white roses with a single red one at the center and laid it on Henry's chest.

As Mark Twain, he wrote about his brother's death and thought about his precognitive dream the rest of his life. After the Society for Psychical Research in London was founded in 1882, he was one of the first to join and did so in the hope that investigators could help him understand dream precognition. He always wondered if there was some way he could have used his knowledge to save Henry's life.

Joseph and the Pharaoh

Another famous dream precognition comes from the Bible. Genesis 41 tells the story of Joseph, who grew up in Canaan—modern-day Palestine, Israel and Syria. His father favored him over his ten brothers, who became jealous and sold Joseph into slavery. As an Egyptian slave, he was known for his ability to interpret dreams. After he was imprisoned for defying the amorous wishes of the wife of a high-ranking official, Joseph interpreted the dreams of prison authorities, and eventually did the same for higher officials. One day, the pharaoh called upon him to interpret a dream that puzzled him. The dream featured seven fat cows and kernels of grain, and seven skinny cows without grain.

Joseph told the pharaoh that the dream meant he could expect seven years of abundance followed by seven years of famine. As a result, the pharaoh prepared for the harsh years, elevated Joseph to second in command in Egypt and restored him to his family. There's no clear proof of historical accuracy of the story. But whether it's legend or historical fact, it's probably the best-known tale of precognitive dreaming. It appears in the Hebrew Bible, New Testament and Quran.

While the Joseph story may be apocryphal, you can verify the reality of precognitive dreams through your own experiences. Here are some basics for recalling, recording, interpreting and even requesting dreams that may open doors to your future.

Recalling Dreams

Here one moment, gone the next. Your dreams are like your own personal movies that run every night. Some of us even have multiple "showings" of the same dream. Crawl into bed, close your eyes and wait for the drama to unfold. But what fun is it if you can't remember them in the morning?

Everyone dreams. But not everyone remembers them. Some people have a hard time even remembering traces of their dreams, and so they assume they don't dream at all. Learning to recall dreams is the first step to becoming a dream precog—someone who sees future events in his or her dreams.

- *Before you fall asleep, simply tell yourself several times that you'll rest well and that when you awaken, you'll remember the most important dream or dreams of the night. The best time to make this request is right as you're starting to fall asleep. That's when your mind is most likely to heed your command.*
- *If that works, then tell yourself that you'll remember all of your dreams. Often, you'll remember the last one first, and then work backward. As you recall one dream, it triggers memories of the one before it.*
- *Another technique is to imagine that you're bringing a dream camera to bed with you. Tell yourself that you'll take dream snapshots during the night, which will be available to you in the form of memories when you wake up during the night or in the morning.*
- *You can also set your alarm to go off after you've been sleeping for a few hours. When you're awakened, scan your memory for any dreams. You might actually find yourself half-awake and still in a dream, and unaware that it's a dream . . . at least for a short time. This technique works best, of course, if you're sleeping alone and not disturbing another person. It also disrupts your sleep. So, it's best to try it on a night when you don't have to get up early the next morning.*
- *You can also trigger memories by returning to your favorite position for sleeping. Just relax and ask for your dreams. After a few minutes, roll over to the other side. If that doesn't work and you start to drift off again, sit up or stand so that you're forcing yourself to remain awake until you recall the dreams.*
- *In the morning, remain in the position in which you were sleeping and try to recall as many details of your dream or dreams as possible, even if they seem silly or trivial. Don't judge or dismiss any parts that seem extraneous, embarrassing or negative. Even if you can't remember any dreams at first, ask yourself what you dreamed. Sometimes the request will evoke an image and then another and another.*

Dream Journal

Record your dreams in a journal and mark the ones that you think might be precognitive. Those dreams are usually vivid and realistic. You might even wake up and feel confused or surprised to find that you were dreaming.

Keep a pen and paper or a recorder near your bed. Take notes during the night if you wake up or in the morning. Later in the day you can rewrite and expand upon your dreams in your journal. Give each dream a title and be sure to record the date. Details will come to you as you write. Document all the details, especially how you felt. Were you upset or happy, frightened or empowered? Did you notice colors, numbers, animals? Often the little things, the details, in dreams provide clues to their meaning.

Interpreting Your Dreams

The images in your dreams are usually symbolic and relate to some aspect of your life. If you're uncertain about the meaning of an image, you could look up the symbol in a dream dictionary. While such generic interpretations might provide clues to the meaning, they aren't necessarily accurate. You need to translate the images in a way that fits into your life.

Let's say, for example, that you were faced with a ferocious bear in a dream. It might suggest that you're empowered, a warrior. Shamans consider bears as bearers of healing energy. It might also mean that some aspect of your life is untamed, wild, out of your control. It could even be a pun. Are you bearing a burden, baring your soul, feeling exposed or bare? But if you're about to go camping in the wilderness, in bear country, it could be a premonition of a bear that you meet on the trail!

Likewise, if you dream about losing your wallet, it could signify a concern you have about your identity. That could be especially true if you're in a transitional period of your life, maybe leaving one career for another, or experiencing the breakup of a relationship that leaves you feeling lost. On the other hand, if in your waking life you drop your wallet as you leave your table at a restaurant, then the dream would've been precognitive.

Literal vs. Symbolic

How can you tell if the events in a dream are directly linked to your waking life or are symbols that you need to interpret? Even though dreams are inner experiences and often symbolic, they also may reflect on outer world experiences . . . or events yet to unfold. If the dream is vivid, it could indicate that the images are literal, possibly serving as a warning or a hint of what is to come.

If you're still confused and want to see where the dream was going, you can attempt to re-enter the dream by focusing on the events as you enter a relaxed, drowsy state. You can even ask a character in the dream for an explanation of what the events mean. You might also relate your dream to a friend for advice. But remember the dreamer is the best one to decide whether the events in the dream are symbolic or reflect on past or present waking life experiences . . . or ones to come.

Years ago, when Rob belonged to an online dream group, he began exchanging emails about dreams with a Canadian man. Rob tended to seek out symbolic interpretations while William usually tried to interpret his dreams literally and would see the dream events as precursors to waking life events. If he dreamed of being stabbed in the back, he was certain he would be facing a physical assault in the near future. Meanwhile, Rob would suggest that it was probably someone doing something behind his back to undermine him, possibly at the engineering firm where he worked.

One day, William wrote that he'd dreamed his cabin, which was two hours from his home, had shifted on its foundation and was tilting sideways. The dream was so vivid he had seen his furniture sliding to one side. Now he was worried that something was wrong with his cabin and he was considering taking a day off to go inspect it.

Rob remarked that the dream probably didn't have anything to do with the physical structure of his cabin. If it was his dream, Rob said, he would consider the shifting foundation to be related to some change or instability in his life. But since it was his second house, it probably wasn't a serious matter.

William said that he was considering taking a new job, one that wasn't so stressful, but paid less. He recognized that could be the shifting foundation. However, he was still concerned about the cabin, but decided to wait until the weekend. When Rob next heard from him, William said that a concrete block under one corner of the cabin had crumbled, leaving more than a foot of empty space. Fearing the cabin would start tilting, William had propped up the corner with the jack from his car until he could get someone out to work on the foundation. He was convinced that if he hadn't found the problem, the cabin could've slipped off the foundation.

Interestingly, it's not always an either/or matter. The following dream, reported on a blog by a seventeen-year-old boy named Jerry, was both symbolic and precognitive.

> *"I was driving my car through a strange area. A lot of the trees looked black and the ground was blackened like there'd been a forest fire here. I could even smell the burnt wood. Suddenly, my car started shaking. I gripped the steering wheel and then I heard an explosion. The car swerved just like it would do with a blowout. Then I hit something and it flipped over. I crawled out the window. But I was stuck on the side of the road in the burned out forest and it was getting dark. I noticed one green plant poking up through the black landscape and I couldn't take my eyes off it. That's when I woke up in a sweat. I was really relieved that it was a dream."*

From a symbolic perspective, the dream image of being stuck on the side of the road suggests that Jerry felt "sidelined." His life had been turned upside down by his parent's recent separation. He wasn't able to move ahead. But, in this case, the boy considered the literal meaning of the dream.

He took a look at his car and discovered a gash in the left rear tire that could cause a blowout. The dream alerted him to a problem that he wasn't consciously aware of. So, it was a precognitive dream and through his actions, he succeeded in keeping it from coming true. However, in Jerry's case, the symbolic meaning was every bit as true as the literal meaning of the dream.

But how do you distinguish a precognitive dream from one that is symbolic? Most dream explorers say that precognitive dreams stand out in some way. Possibly the colors are more vibrant, your feelings are stronger and you might confuse the dream with the waking world.

When Trish's younger sister was a freshman in college, Trish was in graduate school at the same university. They saw a lot of each other and were close friends during that time. One Friday night, Trish dreamed she was staying at Mary's apartment off campus, but in the dream it looked vastly different from the actual apartment. The hall was long and narrow and the floor buckled in the middle. Numerous closed doors lined the hallway in the dream, and Trish didn't know which one to open to find whatever she was looking for. She was afraid of opening the wrong door.

She finally stopped in front of a heavy wooden door and touched the knob. It wasn't locked, so Trish pushed it open and stepped inside. It was completely dark and from within that utter blackness, Trish heard Mary shouting her name. She sounded terrified.

Trish bolted out of the dream and for seconds afterward Mary's voice seemed to echo in the bedroom. It spooked Trish. She felt that something bad might happen to her sister. Even though it was late, she called Mary's place. No one answered. Since this was in the days before cell phones, her only recourse was to go back to bed and tell Mary about the dream in the morning.

The next day, she found out that Mary's car had broken down as she and her roommate were on their way home from a party. It was the middle of the night and their only option was to walk to the nearest gas station several miles away to call AAA, something that made both women deeply uneasy, but they didn't have any other choice.

There was nothing in the dream to suggest that Mary's car might break down. But the fact that Trish heard her sister shouting for help in the dream and that she sounded frightened, indicated that whatever was about to happen to Mary wasn't going to be good.

If you never seem to experience precognitive dreams and would like to test your abilities to glimpse future events, you can be proactive and seed your dream life. In other words, you can program a dream about a future event.

Cooking Your Dreams

In the early 1990s, we experienced several changes in our careers that resulted in a search for new publishers. Since we write full-time, this sort of change meant that no income was coming in. We were scrambling.

Our agent was sending out proposals, but no one had made an offer. One of the publishers considering Trish's proposals was Hyperion, a Disney company. Trish felt increasingly anxious about the situation and asked for a dream that would shed some light on the situation. On January 16, 1992, she dreamed she was floating to earth in a hot-air balloon or on a parachute, she wasn't sure which. She realized she was actually looking at a photo taken by a reporter. It was on the front of a magazine and said NIKE in big red letters.

The next morning, Trish did some research on Nike. She was the Greek goddess of victory, known specifically as the Winged Goddess of Victory. In some references, Nike and Athena were supposedly once considered to be one and the same. Trish took this to mean that she would be "victorious" in finding a new publisher, a comforting reassurance. But which publisher?

She looked up Hyperion and discovered that in ancient Greece, he was known as Helios Hyperion, the sun god. Over time, he gradually became identified with Apollo, the god of light. Trish reasoned that since Athena and Apollo were two of the twelve Olympian gods and were allies, she had a good shot at selling her proposal to Hyperion.

Sure enough, Hyperion made an offer five weeks after she had this dream. Even though the dream was metaphorical and complicated and required some research to understand, it qualifies as precognitive. It also illustrates what can happen when we incubate a dream—direct our dreaming self to answer questions posed before falling asleep. This practice dates back to the ancient world.

Dream incubation was practiced in Mesopotamia, Egypt, Greece and Rome. People traveled to temples dedicated to specific gods, where they spent the night in hopes of receiving a dream that would heal, illuminate or resolve a problem. But you don't have to search for a dream temple to incubate your dreams.

The first step in dream incubation is to know when to ask for a dream. The best time is when your desire for an answer to a puzzling question, situation or issue is strongest. The night that Trish requested a dream about who would buy her novel, her anxiety was great.

Formulate a question. Are you concerned about a relationship, a health problem or a career matter or a disruption in your daily life? Make your question simple and direct, but stay away from yes or no questions.

It's vital to take the practice of dream incubation seriously. Don't ask trivial questions. Remember that the ancients journeyed to the dream temples when a serious matter needed to be resolved.

You can also ask broad futuristic questions. *How can I improve my life? What path should I follow? Why do I feel this way? What am I doing wrong?* Pay attention to the symbols that appear, even if they don't seem to relate to your question. Write down your question in your journal before you go to bed. This ritual helps fortify the question in your mind as you fall asleep. Then repeat the question to yourself several times as you start to doze off.

If your dream doesn't seem to provide an answer, let it rest. Your challenge is to find the connective tissue between your question and the dream scenario, and it doesn't always appear immediately. However, after a few minutes or even an hour or two, the connection might suddenly pop into your thoughts in one of those "aha" moments of illumination and understanding. But if you remain stumped, try again. With practice, chances are you will soon begin receiving answers to your questions from your dreaming self.

When Robert Moss finished writing *Conscious Dreaming: A Spiritual Path for Everyday Life*, his first book on the subject, he asked for a dream on how to get it published. When he woke up the next morning, he remembered a dream that at first seemed unrelated. He was in his car pulling into an Esso station to fill up. He also noticed that his car jerked ahead when he tried to stop it. Then he had a difficult time fitting the nozzle into the gas tank. The gas came out slowly, but he felt satisfied when the tank was full. Moss noted that Freudian dream analysts would probably find the dream symbolic of sexual issues.

But he had asked about his book and attempted to interpret the dream in that context. He figured that the Esso station must represent something from the past, since that name brand no longer existed. In the past, he had written best-selling spy novels for large advances, had had a *brand*, but now he was discovering that books on dreaming were not in the same league. The way the car had jerked ahead when he pulled up to the pump suggested to him that the engine was overcharged.

Moss realized that his agent, who was holding out for an ample advance, was overcharging. Since he had to use finesse in the dream to get the nozzle inserted, he told his agent to work with the editor who was interested in the book. It was published less than a year later and the editor arranged an interview with a book critic, who oddly enough took Moss to see a movie before the interview. It was a rerelease of an old movie starring Catherine Deneuve and in the climactic scene the male protagonist achieved his longtime dream of owning an Esso gas station.

In *The Boy Who Died and Came Back: Adventures of a Dream Archaeologist in the Multiverse*, Moss writes:

> *"I value the scout who goes out every night, in dreaming, to identify challenges and opportunities that lie ahead of me and to explore the consequences of making different choices at certain crossroads that are still in my future. Every morning, he brings me memories of the future. He not only shows me things that will*

happen; he shows me things that may or may not happen, depending on whether I pay attention to his travel reports and take proper action. To my certain knowledge, he has enabled me to escape probable death on the road on at least three occasions."

Prophetic Death Dreams

Years ago, we saw author Anne Rice speak at the Miami Book Fair, where she told the heartbreaking story of how she'd come to write *Interview with a Vampire.*

She had dreamed that her young daughter was dying of a blood disease and not long afterward, the girl was diagnosed with leukemia. The dream was precognitive, perhaps a way of preparing Rice for a tragedy no parent should have to endure. After the girl died, Rice used her grief creatively and wrote *Vampire* in a feverish frenzy, completing it within just three weeks, as though it were a kind of purging.

In the late 1970s, Trish dreamed that she and John, a friend from college, were sitting on a grassy hillside overlooking a valley. She wasn't sure what they were doing there or how they'd come to be there, but that didn't seem to matter in the dream. They talked about friends they'd known in college and all the crazy things they used to do. Suddenly, John turned to her and said, "It's time for me to move on. But don't worry about me. I'll be in touch."

The next morning, Trish remembered the dream and figured it meant John would be showing up soon. He was nomadic in that way, taking off when the urge hit him, hitching around the country and dropping in on friends who were always delighted to see him. Several times that day, she thought about calling their mutual friend, Linda, who usually knew where he was. But that evening, Linda called Trish in tears. John had been killed in a car accident the night before.

The dream was precognitive in the sense that Trish didn't know John had died. But it may also be an example of spirit communication, where John was already dead and visited Trish to let her know it was time for him to "move on."

Dreaming the Future in the Lab

Most stories about precognitive dreams that matched future events are at best anecdotal, a term that in the world of science is equivalent to "proof of nothing." Even if you have recorded a precognitive dream and told others about it prior to the event occurring in waking life, it still remains anecdotal in the eyes of science unless you can reproduce it at will under laboratory conditions.

A British man who repeatedly dreams about future events was aware of that fact, so he found a scientist willing to test him under laboratory conditions.

In 1994, Chris Robinson published a book in which he recounts his journey from television repairman to undercover agent for Scotland Yard and British Intelligence. He made the leap as a result of his apparent ability to dream about future events.

In fact, the book claims that Robinson was able to predict serious crimes, terrorist acts and natural disasters through messages received while he slept. Robinson recorded many of his precognitive dreams in diaries and demonstrated his precognitive dream ability on more than a dozen television shows.

His precognitive dreaming talents apparently emerged as he recovered from a serious heart ailment. In 1961, at age ten, Robinson underwent cardiac surgery and afterward began dreaming about future events, and the dreams continued into adulthood. In one instance, he dreamed of a crash at an air show and then traveled to the show where he witnessed the crash. In the dream, the pilots had survived by parachuting out of their planes, and that's what happened at the actual air show. He had called police to warn them and although they had doubted him, the air show incident led to a working relationship with law enforcement agencies in the United Kingdom.

In 2001, Gary Schwartz, PhD, a professor of psychology, medicine and surgery at the University of Arizona and director of the university's Human Energy Systems Laboratory, took an interest in Robinson's abilities after the Brit volunteered to serve as a test subject for precognitive dreaming. Before Schwartz made the commitment, he contacted two police officials from different agencies, who confirmed Robinson's long-standing collaboration on cases and their satisfaction with the information he provided.

Schwartz created an experiment with strict controls to determine whether Robinson was able to see future events in his dreams, specifically whether he could dream details about ten different locations that he would be taken to, one location per day for ten consecutive days. Schwartz selected 20 locations, wrote descriptions of them and enclosed them in sealed envelopes. He shuffled the blank envelopes and sent them to a second experimenter, a trained magician who was enlisted to eliminate the possibility of fraud. The second experimenter then sent the envelopes to a third participant who was unknown to Schwartz or Robinson. That person shuffled the envelopes and numbered them 1 through 20. Envelopes 1 through 10 served as the experimental locations. Envelopes 11 through 20 were placed in a separate large envelope and served as the control locations.

Robinson arrived in Tucson and began the experiment on August 2, 2001. The procedure was the same for each of the ten days. Every evening before falling asleep, Robinson would ask for a dream that would show him where he would be taken the following morning. In addition, he had asked for dreams about each of the targets on the same day of the month over three preceding months. In other words, he could draw on elements of three earlier dreams as well as his fresh dream the night before the target was revealed.

He recorded his dream in the morning in a notebook. Schwartz videotaped the written material, then Robinson read the entry and summarized the information and themes or patterns that he recognized.

The primary theme in Robinson's dream on his first night was "holes, lots of holes." He also saw a "basin empty of water." Schwartz called the second experimenter, but didn't tell him anything about Robinson's dream. The second experimenter contacted the third person involved, who then opened the envelope for the day in front of a video camera that recorded it. That person contacted the second experimenter and told him the target, which was then relayed to Schwartz.

Schwartz accompanied Robinson to the selected location—the Sonoran Desert Museum. The outdoor museum looks out onto an expansive basin that had once been the floor of an ocean. The museum's exhibits of animals all involve large holes in the ground. One section has prairie dogs with hundreds of holes in the ground. The museum was the only target that included the theme of an empty basin and a lot of holes.

It continued like this over the next nine days. The dream theme each day was more recognizable as the target location than any of the other nine locations.

On Day 2, for example, the primary themes of Robinson's dream were "shops and workshops . . . fabricating things . . . metal." Robinson was taken to an artist colony called Tubac, to a specific shop that featured metal sculptures. It had a workshop in the back. None of the other nine locations had this combination of specific themes.

On Day 3, the primary themes were "heads, lots of heads . . . belts, leather, jeans." He was taken to the Tucson Mall; Schwartz parked in front of Dillard's, where he usually parked. Upon entering Dillard's, the first sales counter they approached had a large selection of mannequin heads for sale. Schwartz also purchased a pair of jeans in the store as a reminder. None of the other nine locations had this pattern of themes.

On Day 4, the primary themes were "suns, mirrors, LCDs, telescopes, Mount Olympus, airplanes, hangars, a pitched propeller." Robinson was driven to Kitt Peak National Observatory, located on a mountaintop, to the world's largest solar telescope. Schwartz and Robinson ate lunch at a nearby airport restaurant with hangars that had a large pitched propeller in front.

On Day 7, the primary themes of Robinson's dream included "dust, dust everywhere, including on the floor in a building, a court room, and a train robbery." Robinson was taken to an old theme park in the Tucson area that is also used as a movie set. Dust covered everything, including the floor of a room. A large train that has been used in more than a hundred movies involving train robberies was also part of the theme park. And the older part of Tucson includes a courtroom.

In his written report on the testing, Schwartz concluded: "The present findings, when viewed in their entirety, cannot be explained using conventional mechanisms such as fraud, guessing or selective searching for information to fit each location. Instead, the data are consistent with CR's claim that he has precognitive dream abilities."

Even though Robinson was focusing on his daily targets, he still dreamed about other future events. The night before the first target was revealed, Robinson dreamed of a bomb blast in London. The next day, CNN reported a bombing in London. On August 5, his third day in Tucson, Robinson had a nightmare involving planes crashing into large buildings in New York City and killing thousands of people. The disaster dreams continued when he returned to England. He recorded them, drew pictures of the buildings and told his police contacts about the dreams. A few days before 9/11, he posted a letter to the US Embassy in London in which he warned of a serious threat to US safety.

Six months later, Robinson was tested in Washington, DC, by the US Secret Service, which had taken an interest in his abilities. In these experiments, Robinson was asked to predict major events that would make headlines. Although the results remain secret, Robinson says that with every attempt, he succeeded in identifying upcoming news events.

In spite of Christopher Robinson's apparent overwhelming success in the precognition dream experiments devised by Gary Schwartz, the professor was unable to get his research paper published in a journal for nearly a decade. Finally, in January 2011, Schwartz's study appeared in the *Journal of Spirituality and Paranormal Studies.*

His paper had previously been rejected by a parapsychology journal on the grounds that one aspect of the method to collect data was not completely double-blind, and that "selective attention/perceptual priming" could explain the results; "I attempted to explain to the reviewers that the patterns of findings obtained in the experiment ruled out this experimental limitation as a plausible explanation for the totality of the findings. In other words, the design limitation was inconsequential in light of the actual findings. However, the reviewers chose to ignore the findings and instead focused on the limitations."

The response to Schwartz's paper was an example of the adage: "Extraordinary claims require extraordinary evidence." That comment, originally penned by paranormal skeptic Marcello Truzzi, was made famous by Carl Sagan when he explained why mainstream science didn't readily accept laboratory evidence of precognition, telepathy and other psychic abilities.

Schwartz's study of precognition in the laboratory was patterned after experiments at the Dream Laboratory at Maimonides Medical Center in the early 1960s. Researchers Montague Ullman, Stanley Krippner and Charles Honorton found evidence that accurate precognitive information can be obtained in dreams. In the study, volunteers spent eight consecutive nights in the dream laboratory. Each night they were asked to dream about a picture that would be chosen at random the next day. The researchers had hoped to get one success out of eight, but some volunteers scored as high as five hits out of eight.

One volunteer dreamed of a large concrete building where a patient dressed like a doctor was trying to escape but had only reached "as far as the archway." The painting chosen the next day was *Van Gogh's Hospital Corridor at St. Rémy*, a watercolor that shows a single patient standing at the end of a bleak corridor as he exits through a door beneath an archway.

The Mystery of Time

How can we possibly dream something that hasn't happened yet? If we think of time as linear—a single line of time with events from the past affecting the present, and events in the present affecting some yet-to-happen future—then it would seem that precognition is impossible unless you believe the future is predestined. Then we appear to be robots moving along a fixed, preset path of life.

However, precognition comes into sharper focus when we think of all time as *now*—the past, present and future interwoven and influencing one another. If we think of all time as accessible at this moment in time, then we have the ability to influence all time, the past as well as the future.

From our ordinary daily perspective, where we are seemingly locked into linear time, that may sound befuddling. Yet, our dreams open us to the true underlying nature of time. For instance, a precognitive dream today might not come to pass as a waking event for years.

That was the case for Angie, who dreamed about a man she would marry years before she met him. In the first dream in 2008, she was in a market to buy bread: "The clerk told me not to buy bread from the front of the store, because it was stale. She directed me to the back of the store for fresher bread. A bald-headed man who spoke with an accent told me that I would have to wait, that the bread had to be kneaded and baked. So, I waited. In the dream, my mother told me that the kneading of bread means that I had to be patient. Very patient."

On March 26, 2013, Angie met the bald-headed man who spoke with an accent. He'd pulled in behind her at the garage where she'd taken her car and they started talking while they waited. He introduced himself as Eduardo and said he was from Brazil. He mentioned that he owned a business that distributed bread around the country.

As they talked, Angie remembered the dream from five years earlier. *Bald, accent, bread.* She also realized that five years ago to the day she met Eduardo she had received her first passport. At the time, she was still with her ex-husband, Patrick, and he was annoyed by her obtaining a passport. "Why do you need a passport?" he had asked.

"I don't know. Maybe we're going overseas." But that didn't happen. A few months later, they got divorced.

Her relationship with Eduardo developed and in July they flew to Brazil, where she met his family. And she'd finally used her passport. In the fall of 2015, they were married.

Angie's second precognitive dream occurred on that same night in 2008. She and her then-husband Patrick were in a parking lot about to drive somewhere and they were late. Two young Mexican women came up to the car window and asked Patrick for directions. He told Angie he was going to help them. When she pointed out they were already late, he got out anyway and talked to the women. Angie drove off and left him behind.

The dream turned out not only to be symbolic of their future breakup, but a similar scenario happened five years later on the day their divorce became final. When Angie and Patrick left the courtroom, they walked downstairs and signed papers, then walked outside. As they headed to their cars, two young Mexican women stopped Patrick and asked for help: "They were the same women from my dream, young with long dark hair. Patrick asked me to wait and said he would be right back. I kept on walking and left him behind, just like in my dream."

The "Eternal Now"

John William Dunne, an aeronautical engineer, who came of age at the turn of the 20th century, was so baffled by a series of dream premonitions that he undertook experiments with time. For a man so fully embedded in the mainstream science of his day, he came up with a startling conclusion. In his book, *An Experiment with Time*, published in 1927, Dunne suggests that time isn't linear as we experience it in the daily world. A more accurate sense of time can be perceived in dreams when past, present and future unfold simultaneously. Dunne's conclusion in his experiment was that all time exists as an "eternal now."

Dunne didn't hesitate to use his own dreams in his book. He recalled a dream when he was a soldier in the field in southern Africa during the Boer War in 1902. The dream involved the eruption of a volcano on an unidentified island. He saw jets of steam surrounding the mountain and knew it was going to blow up. The only way to save the 4,000 residents was to bring ships. He consulted French authorities on a neighboring island, but they ignored his plea. Not surprising, since he couldn't pinpoint the island in question.

But when a copy of the *Daily Telegraph* from London arrived in the field, Dunne discovered the name of the island. Mount Pelée, a volcano on the French island of Martinique in the West Indies, had erupted. Saint-Pierre, the commercial capital, was buried in ash, the island was devastated and 30,000 people had been killed.

Dunne was stunned by the accuracy of his dream, though the number of deaths was far greater. At the time, it was estimated that 40,000 had died. So, he noted his dream of 4,000 people in peril was missing a zero.

"Neutral" Premonitions

Precognitive dreams about death and disasters tend to be the ones we remember most vividly. But many dreams about the future are more neutral.

In the 1970s, artist Adele Aldridge discovered that John C. Lilly—author, physician, neuroscientist and dolphin researcher—was going to be giving a talk at Wainwright House in Rye, New York, not far from where she lived. One of his books had just been published and he was on a lecture tour. Adele hadn't yet read the book but was aware of his research and wanted to hear him talk.

On the night before the lecture, Adele dreamed she attended and was surprised at the way Lilly was dressed: "He was wearing a jumpsuit instead of the usual suit or sport coat of the time. I thought that very odd. He was dressed like an auto mechanic, and I couldn't figure out the symbolism of the jumpsuit."

In her waking life, she didn't have any idea what Lilly looked like, but when she arrived at the lecture, he was the spitting image of the man she'd seen in her dream—and he was wearing a jumpsuit: "I've never seen another man before or since who wore a jumpsuit as his clothing of choice."

Even though Adele's precognitive dream was nothing earth-shaking, all such dreams connect us to what Carl Jung called the numinous, the interconnectedness of all life, and to something so vast and profound that our consciousness is forever changed. In essence, precognitive dreams allow us to escape the time-bound limitations of the daily world and open us to higher knowledge of a timeless realm.

Altered States

There is no such thing as "now," independent of a system of reference.

—Lincoln Barnett

In the early 1990s, Vicki DeLaurentis lived in the suburbs of Philadelphia and attended a day-long spiritual retreat with past-life therapist and author Carol Bowman. At one point, Bowman shifted gears and instead of leading another hypnotic regression session, she progressed the group into the future. Vicki, who is highly intuitive, saw the Twin Towers burning and collapsing. However, she didn't have any idea when this would happen and for years tried to figure out the timing.

In 1997, Vicki and her husband and family moved to Long Island and she began to worry about what she'd seen in Carol's workshop. Her husband was employed in the oil business and his traders worked in the World Trade Center. Fast-forward four years. Vicki's husband had a meeting in the WTC scheduled for September 11, and he and Vicki planned to have dinner that evening at Windows on the World, the restaurant at the top of the WTC. Vicki felt uneasy about it. She's afraid of heights and remembered what she'd seen that day in Carol's workshop.

A week before 9/11, her husband's meeting was postponed until September 12; "If the original meeting hadn't been changed, my husband would have been in the Twin Towers on the day the planes flew into them."

Why did her altered state—achieved through a group hypnosis—enable her to see the burning Twin Towers? She could have tuned in on any number of mass events in the future. It wasn't as if she'd seen any time frame or uncovered any of the specifics related to this event that would help her to prepare for it. Perhaps she saw that specific event because her husband would be working in the Twin Towers in the future and might be inside one of the buildings on the day they burned.

In any altered state of consciousness, the usual ego barriers drop away and precognition is more likely to occur. In Vicki's case, it was a group hypnosis, but meditation, shamanic journeying, remote viewing, even intense creative focus and emotional or physical crisis can invite precognition into our lives.

Hypnosis

Nobody knows exactly what hypnosis is or how it works, but generally speaking it's the induction of a state of altered consciousness in which a person becomes highly responsive to suggestion and sometimes loses the power of voluntary action. Some people are incredibly susceptible to hypnotism and can move their consciousness and bodies into realms that far exceed normal abilities. Studies have shown that the tricks of stage hypnotists can be duplicated in laboratory conditions.

For example, a Russian study from the 1950s found that some subjects, located at a distance from a hypnotist, could experience what the hypnotist was experiencing. The subjects were able to taste what the hypnotist tasted, hear the ticking of a watch held to the hypnotist's ear and feel pain when a hypnotist pricked his skin with a pin. In a test on the Science Channel program *Curiosity*, four hypnotized individuals were placed in 35°F (1.7°C) ice water after being told it was warm and comfortable. Two subjects immediately snapped out of their trance, one lasted eighteen seconds, and the other one made it for two minutes. That subject seemed relaxed and his heart rate actually slowed down.

Considering such abilities, it's not surprising that on the frontiers of science and spirituality, hypnotism is a means of recalling past lives and exploring future lives or future events. In therapy, hypnosis is typically used to recover suppressed memories or to create behavior modification, such as helping people to stop smoking or lose weight. But in one case, a therapist hypnotized a client to the future as a means of making her aware of the ultimate results of her current behavior. The case was described by Pallavi Velugu, a past-life regression therapist and clinical hypnotherapist, who wrote about it on her website.

Her client, a 27-year-old woman she calls "Sandra," was from Trinidad, married, with a three-year-old daughter. However, Sandra was in love with another man and was wondering whether to continue living with her husband or get a divorce and live with her lover. She was unable to make a choice between the two men.

"During the session she easily went into deep hypnosis and I took her a few years into the future of her current life. She was thirty-two years old, dressed in a beautiful red dress, in a comfortable house, along with her daughter and her lover, and also her lover's son. They seemed to be a happy family with the children in school, her lover at work and with her managing the home."

Then Velugu moved Sandra a few more years into the future: "This time she felt afraid because she saw herself all alone in the same house, but without her lover or the children. Her lover had left her along with his son, and her daughter had returned to her father. Ten years into her future, Sandra found herself alone, without a job, without a family and without any support."

Sandra didn't want to go any further, so Velugu brought her out of the trance and back to the present. Sandra realized she had a choice either to continue living the comfortable life with her husband and daughter or pursue a questionable future with her lover; "Going through a progression session made her aware of a possible heartbreak and regret ten years down the line."

Velugu doesn't say what Sandra decided, but it's clear that her future was in her own hands. But with other progressions, the future seemed more fixed.

In *The Future is Now*, Arthur W. Osborn relates a startling story of a hypnotic progression involving the French actress Irene Muza. After being hypnotized and asked whether she could see her future, Muza replied, "My career will be short: I dare not say what my end will be: it will be terrible."

The experimenter was disturbed by what he heard and decided not to tell Muza what she had said. He gave her a posthypnotic suggestion to forget everything she had experienced during the hypnosis. He ended the session and Muza had no memory of what she had said about her demise. Even if she had remembered, it's doubtful that she would've been able to avoid what later happened.

A few months after the session, her hairdresser accidentally spilled some mineral spirits on a lighted stove. Muza's hair and clothing were set on fire, and within seconds she was engulfed in flames. She died in a hospital a few hours later and the future she'd seen for herself had come true.

Some hypnotic progressions move far into the future into what seems to be future lives.

The Dome

One evening in the late 1980s, we got together with a friend, Renie Wiley, in Fort Lauderdale, who offered to hypnotically progress us into the future. Renie was an artist and a psychic, not a professional hypnotist, but had practiced hypnosis on family and friends. She had a soothing voice and an infallible relaxation technique.

She didn't specify any particular year, but said we should go to a life in the future that is somehow connected to our current lives. Once she had gone through the relaxation process, she began to take us deeper and deeper, almost to the edge of sleep.

"What do you see?" she finally asked.

Trish suddenly saw herself as a bald woman. She was at least 6½ or 7 feet (about 2 m) tall and lived in a domed city. She began to describe what she was seeing.

"Why are the people living in domes?" Renie asked.

"It's safer in the dome," Trish replied. "Outside, the air is bad, it's a wilderness."

"Do all people live in domes?"

"Only the lucky ones. We aren't many. There are only a few other domes."

It went on like this for several minutes, with Renie asking questions and Trish answering. Afterward, Trish felt deeply unsettled by this progression. It had felt real; she had sensed the texture and reality of this young woman's life.

Years later, Trish was reminded of the hypnotic progression when she read an article about the creation of large-scale domes. In the aftermath of the devastating tropical storm Sandy that struck the Northeast in October 2011, Texas, a state that has experienced its share of devastating hurricanes, decided to build 28 domes that will double as high school gymnasiums and emergency shelters during the hurricane season. The Federal Emergency Management Agency is paying for about 75 percent of the cost for the projects. Nationwide, more than $683 million had been awarded by FEMA for domes in eighteen states.

Is the construction of these domes the beginning of what Trish saw during that progression 25 years ago? Or is it just a fluke, a random coincidence? The Texas domes are about 20,000 square feet (1,860 sq m) apiece, enough to accommodate refugees in a storm, but only a fraction of the size she saw under hypnosis, massive things that enclosed entire cities. We probably won't see any such structures in our lifetimes, but our children or grandchildren might experience it.

Yet if we live in a multiverse, if the many worlds theory of quantum physics is correct, then there are other paths that are unfolding simultaneously. In other words, alternate versions of ourselves might be simultaneously experiencing worlds that vary slightly from our own to worlds that have evolved in dramatically different ways. Maybe we can dream ourselves into one of those alternate paths, especially the ones with universal peace, goodwill, a stable, sustainable environment, a place where all people are entitled to the same basic rights.

A few months after that group hypnotic experience with Renie, *Mass Dreams of the Future* by Helen Wambaugh and Chet B. Snow was published, a book we hadn't heard of. Wambaugh, a past-life regressionist for 30 years, had discovered that she could progress people into their future lives. In 1980, she began a painstaking project in France and the United States, whereby she progressed 2,500 people to the year 2100. She passed away before the project was completed, but Snow, a civilian employee of the US Air Force, archivist and military historian, finished the work and published the findings.

Most of the individuals who were progressed agreed that the population of the earth in 2100 was vastly diminished. The futures they experienced fell into four distinct categories: a future that was sterile and joyless, where most people lived in space stations and ate synthetic food; a future in which people lived in harmony with nature and with each other; a postnuclear future of survivalists; and a future in which people lived in underground cities enclosed by domes. The latter scenario seemed close to what Trish had experienced.

Snow explained the four different scenarios as probabilities, potential futures that we're creating through our collective consciousness. As he wrote in *Mass Dreams*, "If we are continually shaping our future physical reality by today's collective thoughts and actions, then the time to wake up to the alternative we have created is now. The choices between the kind of Earth represented by each of the types are clear. Which do we want for our grandchildren? And what do we perhaps want to return to ourselves someday?"

It's not surprising that precognitive visions of a distant future—decades or centuries away—reveal a variety of results. So many variables come into play that the differences in possible futures could be enormous and the "correct one" difficult to pinpoint. Yet, in the Wambaugh-Snow study, the one consistent and startling factor is that by 2100 the planet's population is considerably smaller.

In an article published in 2001, twelve years after the publication of his book with Wambaugh, Snow returned to the question posed by the subtitle: Do we face an apocalypse or a global spiritual awakening? The choice is ours.

> *"All of the four future civilization types outlined in my book are currently distinguishable, albeit still in somewhat embryonic form. Only the reason behind the massive decline in world population that both our dreamers and indigenous seers foretell for our current century has yet to be identified in a clear and unambiguous fashion. And, even there, there's no lack of potential causes, ranging from a massive outbreak of an Ebola-like virus or other plague, to a solar flare, asteroid strike (or even a near-miss) or the cumulative effects of over a century of fossil fuel burning, provoking severe global warming."*

He concluded: "And the ultimate response that we found in the mid-1980s still remains true because the ultimate choice between these . . . widely-touted future archetypes is still ours to make today. Let us choose wisely, with humility and compassion. Our children's future, and just possibly our own, depends on what we choose now."

Edgar Cayce

Edgar Cayce, who entered a self-induced trance state, was known for his predictions of Earth's changes, including a shifting of the poles. He pointed to the years 1958 to 1999 as key. There was no dramatic, earth-altering pole shift during those years that resulted in coastal cities inundated with flood waters. However, considering the hazards of climate change that we face, Cayce's predictions could be correct in effect, but with the wrong time frame.

One questioner asked Cayce in 1936: "What great change or the beginning of what change, if any, is to take place on the earth in the year AD 2000–2001?" From his altered state, he responded, "When there is a shifting of the poles. Or a new cycle begins." Of course, a broader, symbolic definition of "shifting poles" could encompass the shift in the world that took place after the terrorist attack that destroyed the World Trade Center.

Even more uncanny was a prediction made more than a century before the 9/11 catastrophe. During the late 19th century, members of the Golden Dawn, an occult group, were inspired by the Great Pyramid of Egypt, which they considered a prophecy in stone. They meditated on the pyramid, receiving visions and messages that they compared to biblical prophecies. As a collective consciousness, they arrived at the year 2001 at a point of crucial change in the world. Henry James Forman, author of *The Story of Prophecy*, published in 1936, wrote "In September, 2001, mankind, pyramidologists believe, will have reached another stage in its growth, another civilization—perhaps a theocratic world-state—and all things will be made new."

While the language of the prophecy isn't precise, it's easy to recognize the theme of a new state of world affairs that developed after September 11, 2001, and the role of religion in those changes. From close within, 9/11 seems detrimental to humanity, but maybe the lessons learned were necessary for us to advance on our path as a species.

Hypnosis/Meditation

You might wonder about the difference between hypnosis and meditation, and which is a superior method for glimpsing future events. These two practices have much in common and a few differences. Let's take a brief look before moving into the question of their uses for precognition.

Meditation involves relaxation and focus that can help you improve your life by reducing stress and improving your sense of well-being. It's often associated with spiritual development. Hypnosis is more directed toward the past, helping people reprogram negative patterns of behavior and break bad habits through positive and inspiring thoughts and feelings.

Where hypnosis focuses on dealing with past issues, meditation is more directed at living in the present moment. Researchers have found both practices can make us feel better by allowing us to gain better control over our thoughts and emotions. By dealing with the past we can create positive futures.

Regarding precognition, it should be noted that peering into the future is not a primary directive of either practice. However, it can be pursued by both approaches, and when that effort is made the differences between the two practices fall away.

The following is a series of activities related to precognition. They can be considered either self-hypnosis or a form of meditation. The intent is to determine which sense—feeling, seeing or hearing—works best for you. For each activity, take several minutes to enter into a relaxed state. To avoid confusion and overlap, do the sessions on separate occasions, rather than one after another. Before you start, have a question in mind, something related to your future. For example, you might ask, "What changes can I expect over the next six months related to my finances?"

Get Relaxed

Find a comfortable chair, cushion or couch where you can sit or lie down. Begin by taking several long, slow, deep breaths. Gradually shift to gentle breathing. Slowly scan your body from the bottom of your feet to the crown of your head. As you go, feel each body part relaxing. Feel your entire body relax.

If you have trouble relaxing, you might begin by focusing on your skin as you scan your body, then all of your muscles, tendons and ligaments. Next, move to your bones, your skull, all the bones in your neck and your shoulders and down your arms to your wrists and hands, where most of the bones in your body are located. Scan your spine, rib cage and move all the way down to your sacrum, your hip bones, femurs, knees, shins, to your ankles and all the bones in your feet.

Now slow your breath even more and imagine slowing the flow of your blood from your heart through your arteries, capillaries and back through your veins to your heart. Relax all of your internal organs and your glands. Relax your nervous system. Say to yourself: *Relax, relax, relax.* To further your relaxation, you might slowly count from one to ten, then reverse it, ten to one.

Seeing the Future

Now phrase your question in terms of vision, such as: "What do I see happening related to . . ." In your relaxed state, with eyes closed, notice how your vision seems directed toward your brow or "third eye." Look for images to appear like a movie in your mind's eye. Even if the images don't seem to relate to your question, don't dismiss them as meaningless. Look for anything symbolic, as if your vision were a dream, and see how you can interpret it.

Sensing the Future

With your question in mind, phrase it in terms of bodily sensations. In other words, "What do I feel happening related to . . ." Become aware of the area between your solar plexus and your belly. What is your gut feeling about the matter?

Notice any sensations or emotions that you experience. Is it a feeling of joy or foreboding, anger or fear? Is it a positive or negative feeling? If you feel nothing, what kind of nothing is it? Does it indicate something hidden, a lack of something or "nothing good"? If what you perceive through your feelings is something that you don't like, what can you do to change the circumstances?

Hearing the Future

Keeping your question in mind, relate it to hearing. For example, "What do I hear related to . . ." Relax and close your eyes. Filter out any outside sounds, such as traffic. Imagine a voice whispering a message. Look for ways to apply the answer to your question, even if it doesn't seem related.

Ultimately, you might use all three senses as you move into a deeply relaxed state and seek answers about the future. Surprisingly, when you're in an altered state, it's even possible for your senses to become jumbled. In other words, you might "see" sounds and "hear" colors. In such circumstances, the brain temporarily assigns incoming information in a slightly different way, creating sensory overlap. Whether such a condition aids or interferes with the ability to glimpse the future is an open question.

Shamanic Journeys

When Arizona sculptor and artist Lauren Raines was going through a divorce, she heard about a shamanic practitioner in Crownsville, Maryland, who was also an energy healer and herbalist. Raines was at a point in her life when she was open to anything, and so she went to him for a soul-retrieval. That's a shamanic practice directed at recovering a soul that has become trapped, disconnected or lost through some sort of trauma. Depending on the circumstances, a divorce can certainly qualify as a trauma.

"He was very businesslike and without knowing anything about me, put on his drums tape and headset, had me lie down next to him, and we tranced together. At the end of the session he blew soul fragments back into my body, and we talked about what he 'saw.' We talked about cutting the cords from my ex-husband and my former community, because I'd moved away."

He concluded the session by telling her: "You'll know it's all over when you see a magenta flower that looks like a cosmos, and a terra-cotta angel."

Eight months later, Lauren crossed the country to the West Coast with her cat and all her possessions loaded into her van. She was determined to move back to Berkeley and start a new life. She had decided she would sleep in her van if necessary until she found somewhere to live: "I began my adventure as soon as I arrived with a visit to a coffeehouse I last visited 20 years earlier. Almost immediately I was greeted by a friend from long ago, who bought me a cup of coffee and offered me a place to stay. I didn't have to spend a single night in my van. When I walked into his living room, there was a huge photograph of a magenta cosmos flower hanging above his fireplace!"

A few months after that, Lauren answered an ad for a roommate: "I walked into a house that had an altar and in the center of it was a terra-cotta angel. Needless to say, just like that, my new life began and I ended up working with the very people I most wanted to work with, never having had to even try! The shaman was right in his prediction."

The shaman gave Lauren two very specific bits of information, markers that would signal her transition period was finished. The uniqueness of the two items—the magenta cosmos flower and the terra-cotta angel—enhances the believability in the shaman's power to foresee future events. But how was it possible?

"Shamans are inspired visionaries who are able to access information through their invisible allies for the benefit of themselves, their families, and their communities. This process is known as divination, and it is usually accomplished through ceremony and ritual," wrote Sandra Ingerman and Hank Wesselman in *Awakening to the Spirit World.* "Through their relationship with these transpersonal forces, shamans are able to retrieve lost power and restore it to its original owners . . ."

So, through the trance state that the shaman and Lauren entered together, he was able to retrieve power that Lauren had lost and was allowed to see the most probable path her future would take.

Native cultures throughout history have held the belief that our waking state of mind limits our ability to perceive reality. A broader, truer perspective, shamans say, can be achieved through altered states and dreams.

Shamanism has been called the world's oldest religion, dating back tens of thousands of years. It's not a religion in the traditional sense, because faith and belief aren't required. Rather, it's the oldest *healing* system, and was part of all indigenous cultures. It's about direct contact with the spiritual realms, not only by the shaman, but also by those seeking help and healing.

Through their experiences, shamans believe that everything that exists in this world is alive and has a spirit—even the earth, rocks and trees. Shamans say these spiritual energies are all interconnected in a web of life. So, anything that happens to one form of life affects the entire web.

Shamanic meditations are usually referred to as journeys, and often these journeys go into a higher world, a middle world or a lower world. In addition, going outside of time is a central premise of shamanism, according to Michael Harner, renowned Western shaman and author of *The Way of the Shaman.* Many shamans have had near-death experiences as a result of illness or dramatic incidents, such as being struck by lightning. As a result, their lives were radically altered. In essence, they underwent a powerful shamanic initiation in which spiritual forces literally devour the body and mind, ego and emotions. Even though most of us will never undergo such dramatic "awakenings," we can participate in shamanic practices and meditations.

Entering the spirit world or moving into a future reality are both common shamanic practices. Usually the method of entry is through a trance induced by repetitive drumming that leads you into a different state of awareness. Here's a method you might try for such a journey to the future. However, if you're unfamiliar with shamanism, first take some time to learn more about the practice through related books and Internet sites.

Entering the Journey

You'll need to have a recording of shamanic drumming ready on whatever device you use for playing music. There are numerous Internet sites where you can download such drumming. You could also do the drumming yourself if you have a drum available and are familiar with the shamanic beat. You might also want to cover your eyes with a blindfold to cut out the light.

Find a comfortable place to sit or lie down where you won't be disturbed. Begin by taking several deep breaths and slowly relaxing your body. As you enter a meditative state, set your intention. Maybe you would like to gain insight about your life and its direction by journeying to a future version of yourself and asking for guidance. Alternatively, you might move ahead to a particular time in the future, possibly to a future life. Another possibility would be to simply set your intention to journey to the future without any stipulated time frame, and let the adventure unfold.

Surround yourself with a protective white or gold light that completely envelops your body. You can also drape yourself with an image of reflective, mirrorlike armor that covers your body from head to toe. When you're fully relaxed and ready, turn on the drumming to initiate your journey.

Along the way, you may encounter beings. They could be spirits, power animals or mythical beings. Any of them could serve as a teacher. You might also encounter yourself in a future life. Interact with the beings unless you feel malevolent energy—and then just move on. Ask questions, anything that comes to mind that will help you understand where you are and what sort of reality you're experiencing. You might simply ask for guidance.

When the drumming begins to slow down, thank the being or beings you have contacted, and direct yourself to return to the place where you began. Take a couple of deep breaths, grounding yourself before you get up and go about your day.

Remote Viewing

Remote viewing (RV), in essence, is an updated term for clairvoyance, the ability to "see" at a distance. The term was popularized in the mid-1990s, after the US Army and CIA's psychic spying program became public. The remote viewers in that program, known as Stargate, were given targets ranging from secret Soviet Union military installations to the surface of Mars.

Men Who Stare at Goats is a 2009 film that pokes fun at the army's seventeen-year program to gather information through the use of psychic spies. The idea of mixing the military with New Age ideas was the trigger for the comedy.

However, during the 1980s and early '90s, Stargate was no joke. It was created as a reaction to the exploration of psychic warfare by the Soviet Union.

In the early 1970s, thanks in large part to Sheila Ostrander and Lynn Schroeder's book *Psychic Discoveries Behind the Iron Curtain*, high-ranking American military and intelligence officers worried about what the Russians might be uncovering in their psychic research. As a result, a secret project aimed at psychic spying was created. Harold Puthoff and Russell Targ, researchers at the Stanford Research Institute in California, were asked to test the psi waters. The Stargate program developed out of their research.

From 1978 until Stargate's public disclosure in 1995, the American intelligence and military communities used psychic abilities for intelligence gathering purposes. They developed a form of clairvoyance, known as remote viewing, which deals with the ability to see something at a distance.

As Joe McMoneagle, known as Remote Viewer #001, explained in a recent interview with us, remote viewing follows a strict protocol. Typically, the target would be identified in a sealed envelope and all the remote viewers would see was a set of numbers on the outside of the envelope; "Remote viewing is being psychic under very strict controls, specifically a protocol that ensures the remote viewer or psychic does not know anything at all about the target they are viewing. Clairvoyance is being psychic, but within which there are no controls at all."

A remote viewer will pick up more than just information about the target, McMoneagle explained. "They will get pertinent noises, tastes, smells, feelings and sometimes actually hear things that are pertinent." In other words, the remote viewer is immersed in the sensory world of whatever he is viewing.

The key factor is getting the subject into an altered state through deep relaxation.

While in that state of awareness, time is nonlinear; past, present and future exist simultaneously. That's why remote viewers sometimes target future events. The remote viewer is handed an envelope about a possible future event and reads it as he would any other target. He isn't told that the event lies in the future.

At the Stanford Research Institute, Puthoff and Targ would send someone out to a site unknown by the subject, who would then remote view the location. Test subjects were able to "see" what the other person involved in the experiment was seeing. In addition, Puthoff and Targ found that test subjects were able to psychically describe a location that experimenters would be visiting in the future, even before the location had been selected.

In one such example, Hella Hammid, a photographer and talented psychic, was asked to describe where Puthoff would be in 30 minutes. She said she could see him entering "a black iron triangle" that was "bigger than a man." While she didn't know its precise location, she could hear a rhythmic squeaking sound occurring "about once a second."

Ten minutes before making that description, Puthoff had set off on a half-hour drive in the Menlo Park and Palo Alto areas. After 30 minutes and well after Hammid had described his near-future location, Puthoff selected one of ten sealed envelopes containing different target locations. Inside the envelope was the address of a small park about 6 miles (9.6 km) from the laboratory.

He drove to the park, where he found a children's swing set—the black iron triangle. He walked over to it, sat down and the swing squeaked rhythmically as it moved back and forth. Hammid had made a direct hit with psychically seeing and hearing significant elements related to Puthoff's location.

Dutch psychic Gerard Croiset devised one of the most unusual and astonishing precognitive remote viewing experiments, known as the chair test. He apparently had the ability to describe whoever would sit in a particular chair at upcoming public events. The event could take place anywhere in the world as long as there was no prereserved seating. Croiset stipulated that the event had to take place within 26 days.

In one experiment, Croiset, who was in Utrecht, Holland, said that the person who would sit in a particular chair at a conference in Denver, Colorado, would be a man 5 feet 9 inches (175 cm) tall, who brushed his black hair straight back, had a gold tooth in his lower jaw and a scar on his big toe, worked in both science and industry and sometimes got his lab coat stained by a greenish chemical. Two weeks later, on January 23, 1969, the meeting took place in an auditorium and the person who sat down in the selected chair fit Croiset's description in every respect—except that he was 5 foot 9¾ (177 cm).

Croiset performed the chair test with repeated success over a 25-year period. During that time, numerous investigators in Europe and America tested his abilities. Usually he would be able to accurately describe the person's gender, facial features, dress, occupation and even background details on the individual.

But sometimes he was wrong and that could relate to free will. Maybe the person who Croiset saw sitting in the chair changed his mind. Maybe he decided not to attend the event or simply chose another chair. Scientists were baffled by Croiset's successes, but skeptics maintained that it could be a clever trick and claimed there was room for cheating.

You might not be able to duplicate Croiset's uncanny ability to foresee who will sit in a chair on the other side of the world, but there are some introductory steps you can take to discover your potential as a remote viewer. Both activities that follow are derived from the laboratory testing program used at the Stanford Research Institute and are good ones for your first attempt at remote viewing. Each activity also has a second part, a chance to try precognitive remote viewing.

You need at least one friend, but two are preferable—one to hide the object and one to interview you. If you have only one helper, eliminate the interviewer.

RV Activity 1—Describing an Object

Enter a relaxed state and take several deep, slow breaths. Take as long as needed to clear your mind and settle down. Meanwhile, your assistant will put an object in a box, bag or envelope and place it in another room. Your mission is to describe the object, then attempt to identify it. The best objects are things that have several sensory details. A piece of sandpaper, for instance, would have color, texture and sound associated with it. A tomato would have scent, color, texture and shape. Your friend should stay with the object so as not to give you any clues to its identity.

After relaxing and moving into a meditative state, begin to watch for unbidden images, words, scents and feelings to manifest. Take about ten minutes to gather your impressions, writing them down or drawing a picture of the perceived object. If you don't get any inklings about the object after a couple of minutes, try any of these methods:

- *Tell yourself to move into the future and see the object in the palm of your hand after your friend has given it to you.*
- *Look into the past before the object was placed in a bag or other container. Use all of your senses: see it, feel it, smell it, taste it. Don't try to guess what it is. Let your sensory impressions accumulate.*

Meanwhile, if a second friend is on hand to interview you, he or she should ask questions that guide you in new ways of experiencing the object. For example, if you are describing a round, red object, the interviewer might ask you to describe its texture. Is it smooth or hard? You might also be asked to look at the object from a different angle. Make sure that the interviewer doesn't know the identity of the object. You don't want leading questions that will taint the results.

When you feel you've gotten as much as you can, end the session by asking to see the object. Hold it in your hands. Feel and sense all of its qualities. Make a mental note of which characteristics came through clearly and which ones were muted or missing altogether. Notice whether you got sidetracked by the tendency to overanalyze. Don't skip this final step. It's important feedback in the process of learning the skill.

Precognitive RV

Once you've practiced describing a hidden object, you can sample precognitive remote viewing. This time your assistant should select six objects, which are numbered 1 through 6 and kept together out of sight. As you move into your altered state, you will describe the object that your assistant will select. Follow the same procedures as you did in Activity 1.

When you have written your description of the object and completed your session, your assistant will pick one the objects. The best way to make the selection is through a random process, such as picking one of six raffle tickets, numbered 1 through 6, from a paper bag. You could also download a free random number generator from the Internet to a cell phone, set it for numbers 1 through 6, then make your digital pick. Your assistant can be present with you or at another location. But, as in Activity 1, it's a good idea to be able to see and feel the object that you described and make comparisons.

RV Activity 2—Describing a Location

This exercise is similar to the first one, except this time you're going to attempt to describe a location rather than an object. You begin your remote viewing at the same time that your helper arrives at the location.

Ask a friend to go to a specific place of his or her choice. Make sure that it's not an obvious place, such as a national monument located nearby or a coffee shop where the two of you meet regularly. Your friend should arrive at a specific time and spend about fifteen minutes there. He or she should look around, focusing on tall things or angular objects, soft and sharp things. Your friend should be aware of sounds, smells and movement. He or she should look, but avoid making any effort to send you any information.

As the appointed time approaches, relax and quiet your mind, preferably in your usual place for meditation. Breathe deeply and slowly. Then, as the time frame begins, jot down your impressions of the location as they come to you. You might want to have another friend, who doesn't know where the helper has gone, ask you questions. Describe all the qualities that you sense, the shapes and sizes, the colors and textures, the scents and movement.

See whether you can examine the site from several angles. Try to hover above it. Look, but don't analyze. If you want, sketch the scene to complement your written comments about it. When the time is up, your friend should call or text you with the location and a description. Visit the place as soon as you can and look for things that resemble the images you saw.

Don't be surprised if you get information that is totally irrelevant. That's just your mind's chatter getting in the way or your attempt to analyze rather than *see*. With practice, you'll be able to separate the good information from the rest. If you take turns being the viewer with your friends, you'll soon see how others tend to analyze and how that process distorts the original impression.

Precognitive RV

After some practice describing a hidden location, you can move on to precognitive remote viewing. This time your assistant should select six locations, write the name or address on a sheet of paper, then number them 1 through 6. As you move into your altered state, you will describe the location that your assistant will go to before he or she has picked the site. Follow the same procedures as you did in Activity 1.

When you have written your description of the location and completed your session by a designated time, your assistant will pick one of the locations. Like the first exercise, it's best to make the selection through a random process, either by numbered stubs of paper mixed in a bag or through a downloaded random number generator. As in Activity 2, it's a good idea to visit the location that you described.

Keep a record or journal of your various experiments. Your hits will help bolster self-confidence. Once you become proficient at these activities, set up new challenges for yourself. You might, for instance, take time before you go to bed to envision tomorrow's headlines on your favorite news site or to see the winning numbers for the next lottery!

Painting the Future

Imagination is the living power and prime agent of all human perception.

—Samuel Taylor Coleridge

In the September 21, 1997, episode of *The Simpsons,* Lisa holds up a magazine that has a large 911 and New York City map on the cover. The 11 is created by the Twin Towers and the 9 is actually part of a headline of the magazine's cover story, about a $9 bus fare to New York. Seen together, the magazine titles say, *New York 911.* Was this a random coincidence or was the illustrator tapping into the future?

In 1972, Regency Press published a novel called *Black Abductor* by Harrison James, the pseudonym for James Rusk Jr. The story centered on a terrorist group led by a black man who kidnapped a college student named Patricia. Her father was wealthy, well known and had right-wing sympathies.

In the novel, Patricia was kidnapped near the campus and her boyfriend, who was with her at the time, was badly beaten by the abductors. For a time, he was even a suspect in the case. The fictional Patricia initially resisted her captors but soon subscribed to their ideology and became a champion of their cause. The terrorists sent Polaroid photos to her father and described what they'd done as America's "first political kidnapping." They predicted that they would eventually be surrounded by police, tear-gassed and wiped out.

In 1974, two years after this book was published, Patricia Hearst—college student and daughter of wealthy, right-wing Randolph Hearst, was abducted from her apartment near her campus. Her kidnappers were members of the Symbionese Liberation Army, a terrorist group led by a black man. Her boyfriend, Steven Weed, who was with her at the time, was badly beaten and became a suspect in the case. Patricia Hearst, like the fictional Patricia, became a sympathizer of her abductors' cause. She eventually robbed a bank with her abductors and was photographed carrying an M1 carbine.

The FBI apparently had read the novel and author James Rusk became a suspect in the case. Patricia's real abductors were eventually surrounded by the police, tear-gassed and killed, just as the fictional kidnappers had predicted they would be.

So, were the terrorists familiar with the novel? Or was this an instance where an author sensed the future and tapped into it so deeply that he uncovered stunning details that were identical to those that would unravel two years later?

Artists and Writers

When artists and writers and other creative individuals are in the throes of their passions, they often tap into what Jung called the collective unconscious, a primal sea, a psychic repository of our history as a species. Here, past, present and potential futures exist as one.

This inner space is what author Stephen King, writing in *The Craft*, calls "dreaming awake." It's what he's referring to when he says that in the middle of his writing day, the world vanishes. He merges with whatever he is writing. Elizabeth Gilbert, author of *Big Magic: Creative Living Beyond Fear*, believes that "creativity is a force of enchantment—not entirely human in its origins" and that ideas are "a disembodied, energetic life-form . . . driven by a single impulse: to be made manifest." But the individual must be open and receptive to the idea before the magic can slip through. "The idea, sensing your openness, will start to do its work on you."

Many of the paintings by visionary New York artist Alex Grey are based on his visions. "Just as I imagine musicians hear music constantly in their heads, painters see visions," he says. One of his most famous paintings, *Gaia*, was based on a vision he had in 1988, on the day his daughter was born, and it was both "hopeful and terrifying."

A massive tree rises in the center of the painting, its trunk vivid and alive with people, faces and esoteric images. To the left of the tree is the world of nature as it existed before the Industrial Revolution—elephants, deer, birds, a lion and other wildlife, with pristine mountains rising in the distance, topped by a clear blue, unpolluted sky.

On the right side of the tree, branches are burning, the polluted sky is a dirty gray, smoke spews from smokestacks and from a nuclear plant containment building, and power lines riddle both sides of a highway. The New York skyline rises against the horizon, with the Twin Towers eerily visible. A pair of commercial jets are visible in the sky near the towers.

At the base of the tree, on the right, stand two men—one in black clothing reminiscent of a terrorist and a second man who bears an uncanny resemblance to George W. Bush. At Bush's side, a penis the size of an adult rises from the ground. As Grey puts it in a YouTube video, "a dick." Dick Cheney.

Grey's vision enabled him to dip into the collective soup of the future, to tap into the mass event thirteen years before it happened and a dozen years before Bush was elected to the presidency. The fact that the painting depicts such specific details about 9/11 is a testament to Grey's immersion in his art. In that place where such deep creativity occurs, time dissolves.

"Bohm's assertion that every human consciousness has its source in the implicate implies that we all possess the ability to see the future," writes Michael Talbot in *The Holographic Universe: The Revolutionary Theory of Reality.*

We each have different ways of doing it, though, and creativity is just one method. Sometimes, the connection between a creative endeavor and precognition isn't evident until long after it occurs. Take Edgar Allan Poe. His unfinished sea-adventure novel, *The Narrative of Arthur Gordon Pym*, illustrates just how far into the future the big magic of creativity can take you.

In Poe's novel, three men and a sixteen-year-old boy are adrift at sea in a lifeboat after being shipwrecked. A lifeboat is a very narrow atmosphere for a novel, but since it was Poe who wrote this, we're already *expectant*, right? We know it's going to be over-the-top but believable, strange, scary, with a plot that twists like a pretzel.

So, on this lifeboat, the men are desperate, hungry and on the brink of starvation, and decide to draw lots to determine which of them will be sacrificed to the greater good—killed and eaten so the others can survive. The cabin boy, Richard Parker, picks the short straw and is promptly stabbed and consumed. Certainly a grim little tale, but not unexpected for Poe.

On July 25, 1884, forty-seven years after Poe stopped working on the novel, a seventeen-year-old cabin boy named Richard Parker was killed and eaten in a similar incident.

In real life, Richard Parker was on his first voyage of the high seas. He had boarded the *Mignonette* in Southampton, England, and headed toward Australia. But in the South Atlantic, the ship was struck by a hurricane and sank. The survivors scrambled into a lifeboat with just a few provisions, and nineteen days out were in danger of starving to death. They talked about drawing lots to select a victim who would be consumed by the others, but settled on Parker who was delirious from drinking seawater.

The group in the lifeboat survived for 35 days on Parker's carcass. They were then rescued by the SS *Montezuma*, aptly named after the cannibal king of the Aztecs, one of those in your face synchronicities that sometimes accompany precognitions.

How was Poe able to sense the particulars of a desperate situation that lay nearly fifty years in his own future? And how could he possibly have known the full name of the actual man who was cannibalized? Perhaps Poe, like Leonardo da Vinci, was a master precog. But because he was a storyteller rather than an inventor, his consciousness tuned in on a spectacularly gruesome tale in the future rather than on future contraptions like flying machines and cars. Or, as Elizabeth Gilbert would say, the magic slipped through.

Why didn't he ever finish his novel?

Writers abandon novels for all sorts of reasons—the plot doesn't work, the characters aren't quite right, the twists aren't there, the agent or editor says, "Forget it" or the idea turned out *not* to be as great as you thought. But do novelists ever abandon an idea because *it scares them?*

Well, yes.

Dual Hurricanes

On August 14, 1992, Trish mailed off a novel, *Storm Surge*, to her editor at Hyperion. It revolved around a category 5 hurricane named Alphonso that slams into South Florida, flattens neighborhoods and devastates the coast. On the same day that she mailed the novel—in those days we didn't email manuscripts—a tropical wave moved off the coast of Africa that, ten days later, would become one of the most powerful hurricanes on record. The wave had completely escaped Trish's notice. The Internet was still in its infancy, smartphones and apps lay nearly 20 years in the future and we relied on TV for our weather news.

By August 24, about the time that Trish's editor was reading the novel, that tropical wave had become Hurricane Andrew. At one point, its winds were estimated to be in excess of 200 miles (322 km) per hour. It slammed into Homestead, Florida, as a category 5 hurricane with a central pressure just below 922 millibars and flattened the city.

The precognition is striking in several regards. In fiction and real life, both hurricanes were the first named storms of the season and began with an *A*. They were category 5 storms and were tightly compacted rather than sprawling masses that covered the entire state. In the novel, Miami and Miami Beach were devastated; in actuality, Andrew struck farther south of Miami. The parallels disturbed Trish enough so that for the next decade she didn't write another novel that dealt with a hurricane.

Then in 2004, another hurricane idea knocked at Trish's door. *What if* a sociopath breaks his girlfriend out of the county jail on the fictional island of Tango Key as a category 5 hurricane approaches the island? *What if* he and his girlfriend and another woman who also escapes take refuge in the home of the protagonist during the storm?

The series features Mira Morales, a psychic and bookstore owner; her daughter Annie; her fey grandmother Nadine; and her lover, FBI agent Wayne Sheppard. Tango Key was the perfect setting for this kind of story—an island 12 miles (19 km) west of Key West, floating like a green pearl in the middle of the Gulf of Mexico and the Atlantic. But Trish, remembering what had happened the last time she'd written about a hurricane, was hesitant about opening this door.

Then she reasoned that kind of precognition couldn't happen twice, could it? Of course not. Besides, Tango Key was a fictional place. It existed only in Trish's imagination. She hurled open the door and off she and the idea went.

She wrote *Category Five* and emailed it to her editor. It was scheduled for publication in October 2005. On August 29, 2005, Hurricane Katrina slammed into New Orleans as a category 3 hurricane with winds of up to 125 miles (201 km) per hour. At its peak not long before landfall, it was a category 5 storm with winds of up to 175 miles (282 km) per hour. Its central pressure at landfall was 920 millibars, which ranked third lowest at the time for a landfall hurricane in the United States. Only Hurricane Camille of 1969—900 millibars—and the Labor Day hurricane of 1935—892 millibars—beat it. However, in October of the same year, Hurricane Wilma—another category 5 storm—became the strongest hurricane ever recorded, with a central pressure of 882 millibars—but not when she struck the United States.

It was the storm surge, not the hurricane, which proved to be the nemesis for New Orleans. Its levees were breeched, 80 percent of the city flooded and more than three million people were left without electricity. In short, Hurricane Katrina hurled New Orleans back into the Dark Ages.

What followed, of course, were the tragic images of people stranded on rooftops, in the Superdome, survivors being rescued by choppers and entire neighborhoods under water.

On Tango Key, Hurricane Danielle struck with a central pressure of 919 millibars—below Andrew's—and its 20-foot (6-m) storm surge destroyed the entire southern portion of the island. The 12-mile (19-km) bridge that connects the island to Key West fell apart halfway across, stranding all the inhabitants. Tango's electrical infrastructure was obliterated and for the next two months the residents, without electrical power or running water, struggled to rebuild their lives within the context of this new normal.

As the media images of Katrina's devastation began rolling in, Trish felt a kind of elemental horror about her novel and how it seemed to attract similar synchronicities she'd experienced with *Storm Surge* and Hurricane Andrew. On Wednesday, August 31, her daughter's 16th birthday, she got a call from her publisher's publicist. The media, the publicist said, was hungry for information about Katrina and hurricanes in general. Since *Category Five* was about the kind of devastation New Orleans was experiencing, would she be willing to do radio shows as a hurricane expert?

When you're asked to do this by the publicist of the company that has published your novel, you don't say no. You say, "Sure, of course, great—as a novelist writing about hurricanes"—and then frantically gather your information and hope you don't come off sounding like a complete idiot.

In the next several days, Trish was on so many radio shows that it began to feel like a part-time job. Some of the hosts were hostile about her theories that the frenzied construction along the US coastlines and the eradication of mangroves, nature's natural buffers against hurricanes, had contributed to the massive destruction along the Gulf Coast. Other hosts laughed when she mentioned climate change and derided her for saying that humanity was even partially to blame. And some agreed with her.

At the end of that frenzied period, Trish told Rob she would never again use hurricanes in a novel because the parallels in these two novels to real-life hurricanes *scared* her. Even though ideas that include hurricanes have knocked around in her head in the ten years since *Category Five*, she has stayed away from them. For writers and artists and other creatively driven individuals, future violent events seem to be easier to tune into than, say, your uncle's wedding to his future wife.

In his book, *The Sense of Being Stared At and Other Unexplained Powers of the Human Mind*, British biologist Rupert Sheldrake notes that in his database of 312 cases of precognitions, 76 percent of them concern dangers, disasters or deaths. This coincides with data gathered by the Society for Psychical Research between the 1880s and the 1930s, which found that 174 out of 290 cases—60 percent—concerned deaths or accidents.

"It is unlikely that selective memory alone can account for this predominance of dangers, deaths and disasters in reported cases of premonition," Sheldrake writes. "There are strong evolutionary reasons for this bias. In people, as in animals, natural selection must have favored the ability to sense impending disasters."

Paranormal and Precognition in Comic Books

Since 1944, nearly 60 films have been made or are scheduled for production through 2019 that are based on characters and properties of Marvel Comics. Many of these films involve superheroes who have become as well known as the actors who portray them. Superheroes, naturally, have supernatural abilities of one kind or another: X-ray vision, the power of flight, healing powers, clairvoyance, telepathy, memory manipulation, animal communication, teleportation, invisibility, shape shifting and precognition.

Jeffrey L. Kripal, author of *Mutants and Mystics: Science Fiction, Superhero Comics, and the Paranormal,* theorizes that these illustrators and writers draw upon their personal paranormal experiences for some of their material. Take prolific comic book writer Doug Moench.

In the 1970s, he wrote and worked on *Planet of the Apes* for Marvel Comics. It was Marvel's longest-lived series and featured original Ape stories as well as adaptations of the various movies. In 1975, it ran eleven issues that included color versions of the adaptation of the first two films, which Moench wrote.

On one particular day, Moench had just completed writing a scene for a *Planet of the Apes* comic book about a black-hooded gorilla named Brutus. In the scene, Brutus invaded the hero's home, grabbed the man's partner by the neck and held a gun to her head so as to manipulate the hero.

Typical bad guy stuff. But what followed was anything but typical. Just as Moench completed writing the scene, he heard his wife calling for him from the other side of the house. Her voice sounded strange. He walked across the house and when he entered the living room, there stood a man in a black hood who had one arm around his wife's neck and clutched a gun that he was holding to her head.

"It was exactly what I had written . . . it was so immediate in relation to the writing and such an exact duplicate of what I had written, that it became an instant altered state," Moench told Kripal.

In the aftermath, the experience made it difficult for Moench to write. He was frightened that whatever he wrote might actually happen. "It really does make you wonder," Moench said. "Are you seeing the future? Are you creating a reality? Should you give up writing forever after something like this happens? I don't know."

Moench didn't give up writing, but as Kripal notes, the black-hooded intruder became his obsession for months, then years.

What's intriguing about Moench's experience is how quickly the real-life situation occurred after he had written the scene. Was the black-hooded intruder already in the house when he began writing the scene? If it took him only a few minutes to write the scene, then the experience would qualify as clairvoyance rather than precognition. But if the scene took him several hours to write, then it's likely that it was an example of precognition.

What we don't know is how this entire scenario turned out. Was Moench's wife injured? Did he rush the intruder? Was the intruder arrested?

Kripal believes that the paranormal often needs the pop-cultural form to appear at all: "The truth needs the trick, the fact, the fantasy. It is almost as if the left brain will not let the right brain speak (which it can't anyway, since language is generally a left-brain function), so the right brain turns to image and story to say what it has to say (without saying it.)."

Perhaps, as writer and researcher Lynn McTaggart suggests in her book *The Intention Experiment: Using Your Thoughts to Change Your Life and the World*, the future "already exists in some nebulous state that we actualize in the present." Or, as Moench asked, was he, through the act of writing the scene, *creating a reality?* Maybe so. Quantum physics tells us that subatomic particles exist in a state of potential until they are observed or thought about. If, as Bohm suggested, consciousness rises from the implicate order, if it operates at what McTaggart calls the "quantum frequency level," then we can impact moments other than the present through intense focus, as during the creative process, visualization, meditation and any number of other ways.

Nancy Pickard

In 2006, *New York Times* bestselling novelist Nancy Pickard published *The Virgin of Small Plains.* The story takes place during a blizzard in Kansas in 1987 and centers around the discovery of the naked body of a teenage girl and the dark secrets surrounding her murder.

In 2011, five years after the novel was published, scenes from it unfolded right in front of her with such specificity that she later wrote us about it, how spooked she felt, and how this kind of thing has happened to her several times before:

"This happened in Abilene, Kansas, but before I tell you what happened there, I'll tell you what happens in the book. In *The Virgin of Small Plains*, our heroine goes with *three* women friends to a restaurant for *lunch* in the small town. As they travel there, they're aware of *severe storm warnings.* At the restaurant, while they're seated at a *round wooden table*, one of them *looks out the windows* and notices that the sky has turned seriously *ominous.* She tells the others, and they all get up and *troop to the windows to look.*

"At that moment, a *tornado warning siren blares.* The women hurry to the *restaurant basement* with the rest of the customers, *except for* our heroine, who hangs back to *stare at the boiling clouds.*"

Now here is the precognitive part of this. Nancy and *three friends* were en route to Abilene to have *lunch* at the Kirby House, a popular spot. They're aware that *severe storm warnings* have been issued. At the restaurant, they're seated at a *round wooden table.* Nancy *looks out the window* and notices that the sky has turned seriously *ominous.*

In the Midwest, on the open plains, this kind of sky means thick, sagging, dirty gray clouds, fractured light that looks like diseased tissue, the kind of scene you look at and immediately know in your bones that it means tornado weather. In real life, Nancy mentions the sky to her friends and they all *hurry to the windows* to look. At that moment, a *tornado warning siren blares.*

Everyone *except for* Nancy hastens to the *restaurant basement* with the rest of the customers. Nancy hangs back *to stare at the boiling clouds.* And then it hits her and she exclaims, "Wow, this is just like in my book!"

Notice the words in italics in both the fictional and real-life versions of the story. The details don't just dovetail; they're identical. In real life five years after the book was published, Nancy becomes the heroine in her novel. She does exactly what her character does.

A skeptic might argue that Nancy imbued her protagonist with elements of herself, so yes, of course it makes sense that the fictional character would act like she would. But what about the external conditions? A trip for lunch to another town with three female friends, the round table at which they sit, the storm warnings en route, the glance out the window at the scary sky, the tornado warning sirens and everyone but the heroine makes it into the basement. The difference between Nancy's precognition and Poe's is that hers was personal.

Poe wasn't ever in a lifeboat, wasn't a victim who chose the short straw, wasn't cannibalized. But Nancy experienced the same external conditions that her character had, the same circumstances and atmosphere, almost as if she had drawn the circumstances into her experience by writing about it.

This wasn't the first time this kind of precognition had happened. In 2007, she wrote a novel called *Dead Crazy* that featured, as Nancy explains it, "God knows why, a victim who was an old woman who collected porcelain pigs, plastic pigs, pigs made of every craft material."

In the book, the woman's body was found in her bathtub, with pigs floating around her. Nancy still wonders why she even thought this was "an attractive idea." About three years after the book's publication, she opened the local paper to read of an old woman who had been murdered. "She collected porcelain pigs. Her body was found in her bathtub. At least there were no pigs in there with her!"

The third instance in which Nancy's fiction proved to be precognitive also came from *The Virgin of Small Plains.* In the book, a large red parrot escapes during the previously mentioned tornado. His current owner, Abby, is heartsick about losing him and puts up signs all over town. The parrot's original owner was Abby's teenage love, Mitch. In the novel, Mitch shows up in town after an absence of sixteen years, drops by his parents' home, and the large red parrot just happens to fly back into the yard while Mitch is there.

Mitch is delighted to be reunited with his parrot and finds an old cage in the basement where he puts him. "When I wrote that scene, I thought that nobody would ever believe it," Nancy says.

But several months after the book was published, a friend's cockatiel escaped and flew away. Nancy's friend, like Abby in the novel, was heartbroken about it. Nancy and her friend put up posters all over town, just as Abby had in the novel. "A week passed, the temperature was dropping, we were sure the bird was a goner in more ways than one."

On the day the bird flew away, it apparently headed straight for Kansas City, Missouri, where it landed in the backyard of people who keep cockatiels. They had an old cage and put the bird inside, just as in the book. They also saw one of the lost bird posters and called to tell Nancy's friend that they had the bird. The story ended happily, just as it did in the book.

"And what is the moral of that story to me, as a writer? It's that I can trust my instincts about what is 'true,'" Nancy says. "Just because something is a wild coincidence doesn't mean it can't happen."

Richard Brautigan: Telepath or Precog?

In 1961, the world was in transition. We were emerging from the post-WWII era and entering an age of space exploration and the Cold War. Segregation was in full swing, blacks didn't have the right to vote and the civil rights movement was picking up steam. The US severed diplomatic ties with Cuba, John F. Kennedy was inaugurated as the 35th president, and soon afterward he launched the Bay of Pigs invasion.

The conflict in Southeast Asia was brewing and the Berlin Wall went up, separating East and West Germany. The Soviet Union launched the first manned spacecraft with Yuri Alekseyevich Gagarin on board and the United States sent Alan Shepard into space.

A gallon of gas cost 27 cents, the cost of an average home was $12,500, eggs cost 30 cents a dozen and the average annual income was $5,315. In other words, 1961 bears little resemblance to the second decade of the 21st century. The hippie counterculture movement with its drugs, free love and antiwar protests still lay years in the future.

During this transitional period, an aspiring writer, his partner and their daughter left their Greenwich Street apartment in San Francisco and drove east. Their decade-old station wagon, purchased with a $350 tax refund, was loaded with camping gear, books and a manual typewriter that had been loaned by the writer's barber. They were married in Nevada and eventually ended up in southern Idaho, where the writer fished for trout.

When he wasn't fishing, Richard Brautigan wrote. He finished two books that summer—*Trout Fishing in America* and *A Confederate General from Big Sur. Trout* was actually Brautigan's first novel, but *Confederate* was published first and didn't have much critical or commercial success. When *Trout* was published in 1967, however, Brautigan was hurtled to international fame and hailed as the writer who best represented the emerging counterculture revolution.

Trout Fishing in America became the vehicle through which Brautigan sensed the future that had begun to unfold the year the book was published. As one reviewer from *The Observer* of London noted, "Streets ahead of Burroughs or Kerouac."

In the *New American Review*, John Clayton wrote about *Trout* in a piece called *Richard Brautigan: The Politics of Woodstock*:

> *"Brautigan is talking (over a bottle of cheap wine that gets passed around) to the WE of a subculture—a subculture I'm a part of. He is creating for us a mental space called Trout Fishing in America where we can all live in freedom. He's not preaching about it to us: he assumes we're already there, or just about there. But I'm also in an unfree America, not by mental choice but by condition. And the politics of imagination is finally not enough for me. It's not enough for us . . .*
>
> *I want to live in the liberated mental space that Brautigan creates. I am aware, however, of the institutions that make it difficult for me to live there and that make it impossible for most people in the world. Brautigan's value is in giving us a pastoral vision which can water our spirits as we struggle—the happy knowledge that there is another place to breathe in; his danger, and the danger of the style of youth culture generally, is that we will forget the struggle."*

It's unlikely that Brautigan, pounding away on his manual typewriter in a campground in southern Idaho in 1961, tried to peer into the future intentionally. His wild imagination and powerful creative drive did it for him, diving headfirst into the collective essence of the counterculture revolution that brought in sweeping and dramatic change to every facet of American life.

Poets

Poets are a special breed, able to capture an emotion, thought or situation in a few words or with a particular phrase that resonates so deeply within us that everything else melts away. Poetry requires the writer to enter an altered state of consciousness that is often so extreme the artist is swept up in the creation, lost inside of it and merges with whatever he or she has created.

Anne Sexton was that kind of poet, who came of age in the fifties and sixties and tackled taboos in a way that few other female writers had at the time. Abortion, menstruation, incest, adultery, sexuality, masturbation, drug addiction, depression, suicide and death. These days, such topics are the stuff of TV talk shows, but in Sexton's era, propriety didn't look kindly on open discussions of this kind.

After the birth of her first daughter, she suffered from postpartum depression, and in 1954, had her first breakdown. The second breakdown occurred a year later, and after a suicide attempt, she was hospitalized. At Glenside Hospital, she met Dr. Martin Orne, the psychiatrist who became her longtime therapist. He encouraged her to write poetry as a kind of therapy. (Orne would later become well known for his work as an expert witness for Patricia Hearst and for his pivotal testimony that led to the Hillside Strangler's pleading guilty.)

Sexton's first published book, *To Bedlam and Part Way Back*, brought confession poetry to a whole new level. She continued writing while she battled what was later diagnosed as bipolar disorder. Her work was tremendously popular during her lifetime and even though critics often attacked her poetry for its confessional and taboo themes, she won numerous awards, received a Guggenheim Fellowship, grants from the Ford Foundation, honorary degrees and became the first woman to receive Harvard's Phi Beta Kappa award. She also held professorships at Colgate University and Boston University and won the Pulitzer Prize in 1967 for her third book of poems, *Live or Die*.

Just in these lines of Sexton's poetry, you can see the themes:

But suicides have a special language.
Like carpenters they want to know which tools.
They never ask why build.

Twice I have so simply declared myself,
have possessed the enemy, eaten the enemy,
have taken on his craft, his magic.

In 1974, Houghton Mifflin published *The Death Notebooks*, the last book of her poetry published while she was alive. On October 4 of that year, a month before her 46th birthday, Sexton had lunch with poet Maxine Kumin to revise galleys of Sexton's *The Awful Rowing Toward God*, scheduled for publication in March 1975. When she returned home, she put on her mother's old fur coat, removed all her rings, poured herself a glass of vodka and locked herself in the garage. Then she started the engine of her car and killed herself by carbon monoxide poisoning.

You might say that because of her mental history, previous attempted suicides and the themes of her poetry, Anne Sexton was destined to commit suicide. The fact that her last published work was *The Death Notebooks* certainly qualifies as a tragic synchronicity; she initially wanted the volume published posthumously. But was *The Death Notebooks* precognitive? Perhaps. It was in this volume she wrote: "For God was as large as a sunlamp and laughed his heat at us and therefore we did not cringe at the death hole."

In the October 27, 1974, edition of the *New York Times*, author Erica Jong wrote that for Anne Sexton the writing of poetry wasn't just some literary exercise; "It was a kind of essential, life-giving stay against confusion—and the silence that 'is death.'" The epigraph for *The Death Notebooks* is a quote from Hemingway that goes: "Look, you con man, make a living out of your death." Anne Sexton could not die until she put the whole story of her death into poetry. This was her "living," and she made it last as long as she could.

Precognition Meets Technology

In 2001, *Psychosomatic Medicine* published an article by James Pennebaker, professor of psychology at the University of Texas, who conducted a study that showed how a poet's words can foreshadow their suicides. It sounds like a tool along the lines of *Minority Report*, doesn't it?

In the movie, three precognitive women predicted crimes before they happened. In Pennebaker's study, the tool was a computer analysis of 156 poems written by nine British, American and Russian poets who killed themselves. The analysis found stark differences in words and language patterns compared with the work of nine poets who died naturally.

Among the suicidal poets who were studied were Anne Sexton, Sylvia Plath, John Berryman, Hart Crane, Sergei Esenin, Adam L. Gordon, Randall Jarrell, Vladimir Mayakovsky and Sara Teasdale.

Their work was compared with 135 poems written by Lawrence Ferlinghetti, Boris Pasternak, Matthew Arnold, Joyce Kilmer, Robert Lowell, Adrienne Rich, Denise Levertov, Osip Mandelstam and Edna St. Vincent Millay. Pennebaker's findings are intriguing.

Suicidal poets, Pennebaker said, used words that indicated detachment from other people and a preoccupation with themselves. Such words as *I*, *me* and *my* were used more frequently by suicidal poets than by nonsuicidal poets. "The words we use, especially those that often appear to be the unimportant words, say a lot about who we are, what we are thinking and how we approach the world," Pennebaker noted in the article. "People who are suicidal or depressed use 'I' at much, much higher rates and there is also a corresponding drop in references to other people."

Just as the precogs in *Minority Report* pinpoint strong probabilities of a crime that will be committed based on the patterns of violence and emotions in the images they pick up, Pennebaker found that suicidal poets generally reduced their use of such words as *talk, share* and *listen* as they approached their death. Nonsuicidal poets, he found, generally increased their use of those words as they got older. The potential suicides used words associated with death more frequently than did the second group, but there wasn't much difference in the use of words such as *hate* and *love.*

Pennebaker also noted that suicide is more prevalent among poets than other writers or the general population; "Poets are more prone to depression. No one would call poets a particularly bubbly, chipper group."

He believes these *patterns of language* used by poets who eventually killed themselves could be "linguistic predicators of suicide" in poets who are still with us. "We are not saying that if you use *I* a lot, then you will commit suicide. It is simply a marker of greater risk."

The danger in technology using "predictors" for any sort of behavior is that people change, grow and evolve. Our emotional life is as ephemeral and ever-changing as the ocean. The priorities we had at fifteen, the emotions we experienced, the way we understood the world and ourselves within it bears little resemblance to what we experience at thirty. Or fifty.

The poets in this study who were suicides lived in times and cultures that no longer exist. In today's world, if you're a depressed poet, you probably tweet about it, start a closed Facebook group, Instagram it or publish a YouTube video. You write a free e-book that is downloaded two million times and you're offered a six-figure publishing contract and suddenly have a renewed interest in life. In other words, the Internet offers an almost instantaneous *community.* An intriguing study would be the words that poets use now, sixteen years after Pennebaker's article was published.

Since 2001, the world has changed drastically. If you would like the specifics, just Google (there's one of the changes!): "How has the world changed between 2001 and 2016?" You can bet that today's poets are among the first who have reacted and are shaping those changes.

Musicians Sense the Future

John Lennon

Musicians who write their own lyrics are also poets and in the world of music, sensing the future is sometimes tied to a musician's own death. Granted, it's not information that most of us want to know. But perhaps foreknowledge like this is enfolded into the texture of profound creativity and acts as a sort of ticking clock that brings an intensity and urgency to the musician's art. This certainly seemed to be the case with John Lennon.

By the time Lennon retired from music in 1975 and unwrapped himself from his own myth and fame to care for his young son, Sean, it's likely that most people on the planet knew who he was. He and his wife, Yoko Ono, had reconciled twelve months earlier after a year-long split and Lennon apparently wanted to focus on being a husband and father.

In 1980, however, he returned to the studio to record a number of songs that eventually became the *Double Fantasy* album. Lennon was so prolific during this period that some of the songs weren't completed and didn't make it onto the album, which was released on November 17, 1980, in both the United States and the United Kingdom. Less than a month later, on December 8, Lennon was shot and killed by Mark David Chapman outside the Dakota apartment building.

The unfinished songs eventually found their way to an album called *Milk & Honey* and included "Borrowed Time," inspired by a sailing trip he'd taken that same year from Newport, Rhode Island, to Bermuda. According to a memoir by Frederic Seaman, Lennon's personal assistant during the last year of his life, the yacht encountered a violent storm en route, and because the crew got seasick, Lennon had to take over the yacht's navigation. He found the experience both terrifying and exhilarating and it prompted him to think about the fragility of life and his own mortality.

In Bermuda, Lennon heard the line "living on borrowed time" from legendary Jamaican reggae musician Bunny Wailer's "Hallelujah Time" and decided to write lyrics around it. The final version of the song that appeared on the *Milk & Honey* album included a line that in light of Lennon's death, was eerily prescient: "Living on borrowed time without a thought for tomorrow."

As Lennon himself once said, "Laurel and Hardy, that's John and Yoko. And we stand a better chance under that guise because all the serious people like Martin Luther King and Kennedy and Gandhi got shot."

Jimi Hendrix

Incredibly, Hendrix's professional career spanned only four years. But in those four years, following his appearance at the Monterrey Pop Festival in 1967, his prowess as a musician exploded across the music scene of the late 1960s.

In 1968, his third album, *Electric Ladyland*, hit the top of the charts in the United States, and in 1969, he was the headline act at Woodstock. At the peak of his career, he was the highest-paid entertainer in the world. The Music Hall of Fame described him as "arguably the best instrumentalist in the history of rock music" and *Rolling Stone* ranked him as the greatest guitarist of all time.

Whew. All this in just four years? But if you were fortunate enough to see him perform live, if you have watched him on YouTube, listened to his music and lyrics, you can't deny the astounding power of his talent.

The lyrics from "All Along the Watchtower," a song written by Bob Dylan, were owned by Hendrix when he sang it. The words seemed to rise from Hendrix's soul and may tell us a great deal about why he became a member of the 27 Club. Hendrix, like Janis Joplin, Brian Jones, Jim Morrison, Kurt Cobain, Amy Winehouse and an assortment of other musicians, died at the age of 27. And he apparently had a precognitive sense about his own death five years before it occurred.

On September 18, 1965, two years before he released his mind-blowing debut album *Are You Experienced*, Hendrix recorded a song with Curtis Knight called "The Ballad of Jimi" that predicted his death. It never appeared on an album, but the song was dedicated to "the memory of Jimi," and the self-mythologizing song clearly shows that Hendrix had sensed his personal future. He actually sings about himself as if he were already dead and he refers to his time as five years.

There are plenty of speculations and conspiracy theories about Hendrix's death in London. But according to the autopsy, he died shortly after midnight on September 18, 1970, from an overdose of barbiturates and by asphyxiating on his own vomit. In other words, he died five years to the day that he predicted his own death in the recording of "The Ballad of Jimi."

John Hart Young, a musician and producer at Oneness Records, pointed out another instance in which Hendrix predicted his own death: "I always thought that his exquisite, final album, *The Cry of Love*, was the heart-rending precognitive lyrical and musical announcement of his impending departure from planet Earth. The words themselves tell us that he's going to go."

Lynyrd Skynyrd

In 1974, Lynyrd Skynyrd released its second album, *Second Helping*, and it featured the band's biggest hit single, "Sweet Home Alabama." It's one of those songs that makes you want to *move.* You shoot to your feet, your body sways, your hands clap, the energy suffuses you and suddenly, you're transported.

On October 17, 1977, three years after *Second Helping*, the band released *Street Survivors.* The cover showed the band engulfed in flames, a startling and—as it turned out—prescient image. Three days later, on October 20, the band took a Convair CV-300 from Greenville, South Carolina, bound for Baton Rouge, Louisiana, and it crashed outside of Gillsburg, Mississippi. The passengers had been told that one of the plane's engines had developed problems and were warned to brace for impact. Ronnie Van Zant, the lead vocalist and lyricist and one of the founding members of the band, was killed on impact when the plane crashed into a tree. Five other people also died—two band members, the assistant road manager, the pilot and copilot.

But the high strangeness didn't stop there. One of the songs on this album, "That Smell," is downright creepy in light of the plane crash. Even though the lyrics address drug usage, there's another undercurrent in the refrain "The smell of death surrounds you."

And when you watch the band perform this song on YouTube, Ronnie Van Zant invariably spins his hand in the air as he sings, "The smell of death surrounds you."

Apparently Van Zant had confided in a number of friends and family members that he would never live to see 30. He was 29.

Big Magic and the Pentagon

A month after 9/11, the Pentagon commissioned several dozen writers and directors to brainstorm with advisers and officials about possible future terrorist attacks. Pentagon officials apparently had realized that several blockbusters—*The Siege, Die Hard, The Peacemaker*—indicated the extent of Hollywood's research into such scenarios as hijacking, bombs in New York, manhunts for Muslim extremists and even the use of planes as guided missiles aimed at Washington. So, why not brainstorm with creative types, such as screenwriters and directors, for possible future terrorist scenarios?

Steve de Souza, screenwriter for *Die Hard I* and *II*, was one of the participants and spoke to BBC's *One Panorama* about it. The sessions, he said, covered three days and were held in an "anonymous" building in L.A. No armed guards or uniformed generals were present, but de Souza said they communicated with a high-ranking official through an optical link: "That was the closest it got to an underground bunker thing. We were in an utterly ordinary office building, but we had somebody on a screen talking to us like Captain Kirk."

The participants had been sent intelligent briefings of material that had been declassified, so they learned about what had been found in the al-Qaeda camp concerning biological and chemical warfare. They were told that Pentagon officials were looking for "left-field, off the wall ideas" and the participants were encouraged to say the craziest thing that came to mind.

"So, if we got one new idea or one new vulnerability that we thought of, that the Pentagon would not think of, then we accomplished something," said de Souza.

The problem with Hollywood's visions, of course, is the same problem that exists in many precognitions—a lack of specifics, the *when*, *where* and *how*. Yet Jimi Hendrix predicted his own death five years to the day in the recording of "The Ballad of Jimi." And Nancy Pickard's experience included eleven identical details to a scene she'd written five years earlier. So, specifics are possible when we allow our imagination to roam free.

Whether we understand it or not, our imagination knows things that matter. It has the power to reshape not only our life, but the world.

Professional Precogs

All around the world we find people who believe in the ability of some human beings to foresee the future. Shamans, seers, prophets, oracles or soothsayers are found in most . . . traditional societies, and even in modern industrial societies, fortune tellers and clairvoyants still flourish. No doubt some of them are fraudulent. But there are far too many convincing examples of human premonition to dismiss this entire area of experience out of hand.

—Rupert Sheldrake

Forty-five minutes north of Disney World lies another world altogether, the spiritualist community of Cassadaga. As soon as you turn off I-4, memories of Mickey Mouse and Epcot, Universal and MGM, give way to a hilly pine forest where a mysterious presence infuses the air. You feel that nothing is what it appears to be.

If you're not paying attention, you might miss the small green sign on I-4 that reads CASSADAGA. Even when you enter the name on a GPS using Google maps, the nearby city of Lake Helen comes up unless you have a specific Cassadaga street address. It's as if people who are supposed to find their way here, do so.

Established in 1894, it's the most unusual town in Florida, a community where nearly every resident is a medium who specializes in contact with spirits. Outside the border of the Cassadaga Spiritualist Camp, as it is known, reside other mediums and psychics attracted to the mystical energy or vortex of this hamlet, which looks and feels like a place from another era. Most visitors come here for a taste of professional precognition, readings from the mediums and psychics.

The town includes a Mediterranean-style hotel built in the 1920s, a spiritualist church, a café, small grocery store and post office. Several New Age shops offer books, crystals and other esoteric paraphernalia and, of course . . . psychic readings. On weekends, the small town fills with enough tourists to wake the dead—so to speak—and the two-story Cassadaga Hotel is often fully booked. The rooms are modest and slightly spooky in their own right. Visitors won't find a television in the room, but there may be a ghost prowling the hallways at night.

The hotel dates back to the heyday of spiritualism, when the rich and the famous arrived for the séances and for readings with the mediums. Along the right side of the hotel stretches a wide porch with picnic tables and rocking chairs. Sometimes in the evening, when the light plays tricks with perception, some of the empty chairs rock, creaking softly in the quiet. And your imagination slams into overdrive. Are there spirits in in those chairs, enjoying the evening? Playing cards with their companions and sipping mint julep tea in the afterlife? You never know for sure. Perhaps that's part of the lure and mystique of the town.

Visitors meander along the narrow streets, passing old wood-framed houses with front porches and white picket fences. Some of the houses appear in need of repairs, but all of them have *personalities*. Many of the houses feature hanging signs with the name of the resident medium, usually referred to as "reverend."

Both Spirit and Colby Lakes border an expansive park with hiking trails just outside the residential streets and not far from Colby Temple, where spiritualist services are held. The park offers a trip through time with photos and historical information about the spiritualist community appearing on small framed placards bordering the main paved trail.

A Spiritualist Service in Cassadaga

On one Sunday in September 2012, more than 100 people were in attendance at a service at Colby Temple. Most were local residents and members of the spiritualist church. A handful of visitors were also in attendance, including a few who had joined an orb photography tour the night before.

For those unfamiliar with the tenets of spiritualism, a pamphlet explained that spiritualism's main focus is to "promote an individual's personal experience with God," adding that "any attempt to personalize the idea of God only limits the totality of that Intelligence, which is the reason that Spiritualists sometimes refer to that idea of God as *Infinite Intelligence* or *Infinite Spirit.*" According to the philosophy of spiritualism, "all religions can produce enlightenment, and believe that Jesus, as well as all other saviors and prophets, was a real person."

The pamphlet goes on to say that spiritualism includes the belief of survival of the personality after death, and that such survival can be proved through mediumship; "Belief in the survival of the personality also removes grieving when it is realized that our loved ones are still around us from time to time, are able to communicate with us . . . from the spirit realm."

The spiritualist service that day began with the deceptive flavor of a Southern Baptist service, with the singing of several old gospel songs from a hymnal led by a woman playing an organ. After a couple of songs and announcements, another woman, a spiritualist reverend who was acting as moderator, called for all the healers at the service to assemble at the back of the room. Nine men and women took their place behind empty chairs, then those who wanted a healing were told to line up along the side wall and wait their turn.

While the healers were working, holding their hands several inches from the heads of those in the healing seats, the reverend led the rest of those assembled into a relaxed, meditative state with a guided visualization that focused on a serene, bucolic setting. No fire and brimstone here; no male figure leading the congregation; and instead of a life-size crucifix, the backdrop on the stage was a pair of large paintings of sunflowers.

As the healers finished, the moderator introduced a guest lecturer, another female spiritualist reverend named Diane. She gave a humorous talk that emphasized positive thinking and finding joy in everyday life. After another song, she returned to the pulpit and began what makes the spiritualist way unique among church services. Instead of giving communion or reading Bible verses, Diane offered spot readings to people in the audience, each one lasting a few minutes. She talked about relationships, health issues, travel and other upcoming events in each person's life. It was difficult to judge how accurate these were, but there was no shortage of raised hands when she finished with one reading and moved to the next.

The Camp and the Noncamp

The town is composed of two distinct areas. The actual spiritualist camp covers 35 acres (142 sq m) and lies to the south of 430A, behind and west of the hotel. It's owned by the Southern Cassadaga Spiritualist Camp Meeting Association, which certifies the mediums who live and work in the camp.

Across the street from the camp, other mediums and psychics live and work in various neighborhoods. They haven't been certified by the spiritualist association, so the implication is that they are opportunists, less skilled and talented than the certified mediums. Even in spiritual communities, bureaucracy abounds!

A medium, regardless of whether he or she lives inside or outside of the spiritualist camp or elsewhere, acts as an intermediary between the living and the dead. When you consult one of these individuals, the medium delivers messages from your departed loved ones. And sometimes, these spirits have plenty to say about your future.

Today, fewer than 50 mediums live in the camp. If you count the practicing psychics and mediums who aren't certified by the spiritualist association—but live near Cassadaga—there are probably 100 individuals who do readings, but they aren't all mediums. They use various tools.

Some are psychometrists who read a personal object—a piece of jewelry, a watch, cell phone—to sense your future. Others are clairaudient (hearing of sounds or music not audible to the normal ear), clairsentient (sensing a past, present or future physical or emotional state) or clairvoyant (perceiving events or things in the future, beyond normal sensory ability). There are also card readers, astrologers, tea leaf readers or other people who have particular divination tools that enable them to delve into your past, present and future.

In the early days of Cassadaga, séances were marked by great fanfare and drama. Flamboyance was at its height: materialization of spirits, apports (paranormal transference of objects) and physical manifestations. Trumpets and cabinets were among the tools, but charges of fraud resulted in the new rules requiring readers to avoid any mediumistic tools.

The Medium and the Spirit Guide

The roots of Cassadaga go back to 1874 when, during a late summer séance in Lake Mills, Iowa, George Colby, a 27-year-old medium from Pike, New York, received a message from an Indian spirit named Seneca. According to some, Colby reportedly said that Seneca manifested in physical form and instructed him to immediately leave Iowa and make contact with T. D. Giddings, a medium in Eau Claire, Wisconsin.

The two men, according to Colby's account, were to conduct another séance through which Seneca would spiritually commune with them. When they did so, they entered a trancelike state and were told that, "A congress of spirits had selected Florida for the establishment of a great spiritualist center, and that Colby had been chosen to lead in its creation."

In a series of spiritual sessions that followed, Colby continued receiving directions from his spirit guide, Seneca. He was told that the proposed location of this new spiritual center would be "near Blue Springs, Florida, on high pine hills overlooking a chain of silvery lakes." It wasn't long before Colby and the entire Giddings family headed for Florida.

They boarded a steamboat in Jacksonville, and on the night of November 1, 1875, landed at Blue Springs, then a remote settlement of a couple of clapboard structures on the St. Johns River. Because of limited accommodations at Blue Springs, the Colby party resided temporarily in palmetto huts to await further instructions from Seneca. Then, late one night in the faint light of a kerosene lamp, they were contacted by Seneca with orders to "Go east, to the outskirts of the village and find the seven hills, this will be the place."

The next morning, traveling by mule and wagon, they headed from Blue Springs along a rutted sandy road that cut eastward through palmettos and slash pines. Near the town of present-day Lake Helen, they found seven pine-covered hills and saw the silvery lakes mentioned by Seneca. Colby and Giddings agreed that this was the spot where they were to build a new spiritual center.

For many years, the Colby and Giddings homesteads were frequented by mediums from the Cassadaga Free Lakes Association, of Cassadaga, New York, where they had attended summer spiritualist camp meetings. But it wasn't until October 1894 that a group of these mediums established the charter for the Southern Cassadaga Spiritualist Camp Meeting Association.

By 1895, Cassadaga was becoming a winter retreat for spiritualists. In the early 1900s, advertisements in northern newspapers invited mediums to permanently relocate to the growing spiritualist camp. By the 1920s, Cassadaga had become a regular settlement and a center of spiritualism, and the hotel was built to accommodate the increasing number of visitors and mediums. George Colby died on July 27, 1933, his spirit-guided vision of a new center for spiritualism a reality.

The Making of a Medium

Hazel West Burley is a soft-spoken, diminutive and pretty woman who invariably answers her door with a quick smile. "Hi, may I help you?"

Her pink house lies past Spirit Lake, at the end of a lane in the spiritualist camp. She leads us along a screened porch to the door to her office, a narrow room with a couch, a chair and a small coffee table. The wall against which the couch sits is glass and overlooks an outside patio bright and festive with flowers. The wall in front of us is filled with books from floor to ceiling: old books and books about the esoteric weirdness. Many of these treasures were published when Cassadaga was in its infancy.

Hazel has lived in Cassadaga longer than any other medium. She has resided there for so long that her identity is inseparable from the town's identity. For years she was married to another spiritualist, Art, who passed away in 2006. Hazel has two children from her first marriage and a grandson, Sean, on whom she dotes. But it's obvious that her life *is* her work.

Hazel ended up in Cassadaga because of a dream she had in 1963, when she was living on Merritt Island on Florida's Treasure Coast. She and her first husband, Hugh, were students. In the dream, she was shown a deep cavern with people climbing the walls, scrambling to get out. She understood that she would never lose her soul or spirit as these people had. Then she was in a palace where exquisite art covered the walls and beautiful organ music played. An elderly man in a wheelchair was in the palace and he asked her to help him with a book. Hazel told him she would be delighted to do so but first, she had to do two things.

When she had this dream, Hazel had never heard of Cassadaga. She was clueless about the identity of the man in the wheelchair. But she knew the dream addressed what would become her life's work: "I had been asking for guidance about what to do with my life. Although I was happily married, I sensed there was something else I was going to do."

Seven months after Hazel had this dream, a friend took her to Cassadaga to have a reading with one of the mediums, Anne Gehman. Sometime in the future, Anne would become famous enough so that in 2009, Hay House published a book about her, *The Priest and the Medium: The Amazing True Story of Psychic Medium B. Anne Gehman and Her Husband, Former Jesuit Priest Wayne Knoll, Ph.D.*, by Suzanne R. Giesemann. But in the early 1960s, Anne Gehman was just another medium who lived in Cassadaga.

"After I had the reading, I understood all the strange experiences I'd had throughout my life—voices, dreams, the knowing," Hazel recalled.

Gehman became Hazel's first teacher, and every several months over the course of the next year, Hazel returned to Cassadaga to study with her. A year after that first meeting, Anne urged Hazel to meet her at a spiritualist community in Wisconsin. Even though there were 1,000 reasons not to go, Hazel went. There, she met the elderly, white-haired gentleman in the wheelchair who had appeared in her dream. His name was Wilbur Hull and he was one of Cassadaga's finest mediums: "He was thirty-five years older than me, a very private person, and I was too intimidated to tell him about my dream. But we became good friends."

In the spring of 1968, Hazel returned to Cassadaga to study with Hull. The first time she walked into his home, she recognized it as the palace in her dream five years earlier. Art covered the walls. Organ music drifted through the rooms. During her stay, Hull asked her to help him with a book. "Just like in my dream," she said.

Hull had muscular dystrophy and although he could move his upper body, he needed legs for research: "I had legs. I remembered from the dream that I had two things I had to do before I helped Wilbur with the book, but didn't have any idea what those two things were." Even though a gynecologist had told Hazel she couldn't have children, she had a recurring vision of a little girl and a boy. "I knew they were 'the two things' I had to do before I could help Wilbur with his book."

Hazel told Hull about her dream and on the last night of Hazel's visit, he went into a trance and his guides spoke directly to Hazel. They described how she had been guided to Cassadaga, how certain events and meetings had been arranged for her to arrive at that precise place, at that precise time. "That night, I asked for healing so I could have children. Wilbur's guides told me it was improbable but not impossible and that they would do everything they could to heal me."

Less than a week later, she got pregnant with her daughter, Dionne.

In 1974, Hazel's marriage ended. She was living in Atlanta by then and her husband realized she didn't belong there, that her destiny lay in Cassadaga. He urged her to follow that dream. "We split without so much as a harsh word. By then, I had my two children, a boy and a girl, and I knew it was time."

She traveled to Cassadaga to look for a place to live. Since nothing was available in the camp at the time, Hazel made an offer on a place outside the camp. She wasn't crazy about the house, but it was at least near to other mediums she knew. That evening she stopped by Hull's and he went into trance. His guides told her she would have an opportunity to buy the house she really wanted.

Hazel thought they were referring to the place she'd just made an offer on. That was around ten o'clock at night. The next morning, Anne Gehman and her husband called Wilbur and told him their home was for sale and was he or anyone else interested? Hull asked Anne when she and her husband had decided to sell and she told him it was around ten o'clock the previous night, at exactly the time that Wilbur's guides were telling Hazel she would have the opportunity to buy the house she wanted.

A year later, Hazel moved to Cassadaga, into the very house where she'd had her first reading with Anne. She had left a 5,000-square-foot (465-sq-m) home north of Atlanta for a cottage in the Florida Hills. "Spirit told me to not look at the wood, the mortar. The house in Cassadaga is made of the vibration that holds it together. It's created out of the love and spirituality that you put into it and which others bring to it."

A number of precognitions had paved Hazel's way to Cassadaga and she, in turn, often senses the future of her clients. Sometimes she hears inner voices and other times she receives images, pictures, impressions. But mostly, she's clairsentient (sensing of emotions). Quite often her guides will give her information on people who show up unexpectedly several days later. Sometimes, she makes notes—the person's name, the particulars—but usually she just files it in the back of her head and when she hears the person's name, the rest of the information falls into place.

"I don't just give predictions. I try to help people understand how they can use their free will to create the life they want. In most instances, we create the life we want through our thoughts and actions, and those in Spirit get behind our efforts. My readings are always a teaching in helping people to help themselves."

We met Hazel more than 26 years ago when Trish was about four months pregnant with Megan. Trish had had an amniocentesis several weeks earlier, so we knew our baby's gender. We sat in her cozy office and Hazel asked us to write down our names and something about ourselves on separate sheets of paper. She uses handwriting to attune herself to the client, it's her tool, the trigger that opens her up psychically: "To me, handwriting is the picture of the soul."

She ran her fingertips over what we'd written and began to talk. Most of that reading was about our unborn daughter and, in retrospect, Hazel nailed some specific details about Megan.

Very artistic and imaginative. I see incredibly vivid colors around her.

Megan majored in art in college. She now teaches classes several nights a week for Paint Nite, a Boston-based company that sponsors painting classes in bar-restaurants in large metropolitan areas across the United States and in several foreign countries. She also paints pet portraits in vivid colors, with exquisite attention to detail. Hand her a photo of Fido and she'll turn it into a work of art.

Joyful.

For her, the glass is always full, brimming to capacity.

Athletic. I see her engaged in all sorts of sports.

She windsurfs and taught it part-time when she was in college. She rock climbs, runs, does yoga and hits the gym. She water-skis and played on a kickball team. She has skydived. She samples all of it. She's fearless.

She's surrounded by animals.

Megan interned at a dolphin facility in the Florida Keys when she was sixteen, volunteered at an animal sanctuary in Ecuador, interned with Disney's Epcot Center in their dolphin area and has a dog-walking business.

She'll be a writer.

At this point, Hazel didn't know what we did professionally. We had published a lot of magazine articles and several books in the six years we'd been married and were pursuing careers as writers.

Megan started a novel when she was sixteen and in ten years, the characters have changed and gotten older, just as she has. The plot has evolved. Writing, she says, is what she wants to do . . . along with everything else!

How was Hazel, who had never met us before, able to hit such specifics about our daughter, who was barely larger than a comma? This is an example of the kind of precognition that matters most to us as individuals. It doesn't change the world, doesn't predict disaster, doesn't tell us who will be president after the next election or whether the stock market will fall or rise in the morning. Instead, it provides the broad arc, a pattern in time and space for the life of someone who hasn't drawn her first breath. Who doesn't have a Social Security number.

Hazel advises people to seek a medium's help at a time when they're relaxed. "Excessive skepticism, arguing, or wanting things done your way often leads to failure," she says. "The true value of a reading is not always measured in prophecy. Prediction is possible, but you have the free will to make changes. Mediumship is not fortune telling. During a reading, be fair. Do not attempt to confuse the medium. Let them know when they are correct."

She believes we're are all psychic and mediumistic, some of us more than others. This work, she says, requires "focus and discipline. And it requires love of the world. You must have the ability and willingness to enter into another person's world, their life, to feel their pain, to go through with them what they're going through."

Tips on Choosing a Professional Precog

A recommendation from someone else is the best way to choose a professional precog. It saves you time and money. Don't bother with the Internet psychic sites or the 800 numbers. Word of mouth is an ideal reference and that's true regardless of the kind of psychic you're selecting.

No psychic should ever tell you how to live your life, whom you should marry, what job you should take or leave or apply for. The psychic may have a personal agenda or hope to make more money by keeping you engaged and building a dependency. Don't fall for such tactics.

If a psychic says you have a lot of negative energy around you or that a spirit has attached itself to you and that you would benefit from additional cleansing and healing work—at a hefty fee—don't buy into it. Avoid such bait-and-switch tactics. The same is true when a psychic promises to make someone fall in love with you or to repair a damaged relationship. Counseling is appropriate, manipulation is not.

If a psychic says you must not tell anyone else what he or she is doing for you, then the psychic is more interested in protecting his own interests and keeping you engaged.

This happened to a friend when she and Trish were traveling in California. They were in a neighborhood in L.A. and, on impulse, went into a New Age shop where a woman was doing readings. During the course of the friend's reading, the psychic told her that if she wanted to keep the man she was in love with, she needed to pay extra for a spell that would bind him to her. The psychic added that if the friend told Trish about the price she was paying, the spell wouldn't work.

Allow your intuition to guide you in the choice of a psychic. If you resonate with the person, if the energy feels right to you, then it's more likely you won't be scammed. Always weigh the psychic's information against your own intuition and feelings. After all, you are the expert on your own life.

Don't provide a lot of information about yourself before or during the reading. Legitimate psychics tune in on your energy and will not want any information that engages their rational mind and distracts them from their intuition. On the other hand, don't build a psychic barrier around yourself, either.

One woman who consulted a psychic in Cassadaga removed her jewelry before the reading because she thought it might provide too much information about her spiritual leanings. Then, she sat throughout the reading with her arms folded across her chest, completely closed off physically, emotionally and psychically. She offered absolutely no feedback. For any psychic, this would be the equivalent of trying to read a block of cement.

If psychics ask if something they say resonates for you, give a definitive yes or no, just as Hazel suggests—but no further information. Feedback helps them determine whether they're tuning into your energy or into the energy of someone in your environment. Within yourself, be open and receptive emotionally.

Before you have a reading, jot down your questions. This helps fix them in your own mind. A good psychic will not ask whether you have any questions until the last part of the reading, and usually will answer most of your questions before you've asked them. Record the reading or take notes so that you'll remember the details.

Sometimes, you have to connect the dots in the information that a psychic provides. Let's say you're told that within a year, you'll have enough money to buy a second home, a refuge in the mountains or by the beach. Rather than taking this statement at face value, ask specifically how it's going to come about. Often, this kind of questioning cuts open a new vein of precognitive information that enables you to piece together the broad strokes of this story about your future.

Psychics are often inaccurate about timing. Good psychics, regardless of the tools they use to read you, must immerse themselves in the collective river of no time to be able to read you at all. They must allow themselves to be drawn into the energy matrix of information that surrounds you and your life. This is no easy task and makes the accurate timing of future events quite tricky.

"The present is an inscape, something that is inexhaustible in its very nature," writes theoretical physicist F. David Peat in *Pathways of Chance*. "It is only from within the present that one can explore those tendencies and patterns that may lead into the future."

These patterns that Peat mentions may be the same type of probability pattern that psychics work with, a pattern no different than what's created when you toss I Ching coins, lay out tarot cards or do any kind of divination. When a psychic tunes in on you, he or she *sees the events and situations that are the most probable for you at the moment of the reading.* If you dislike what you hear, take steps to change the circumstances in your life that pertain to the issue. *Nothing in a reading is preordained.*

The best readings—and the most powerful synchronicities—often occur when your life is in transition and you really need answers and guidance. Then, it's as if everything about you floats right there at the surface of your consciousness and for a psychic, it's like skimming cream off milk.

You don't have to pay an outrageous sum to get a good reading. Edgar Cayce, even at the height of his fame, kept his fees reasonable. Just because a psychic charges a thousand bucks for a reading doesn't mean the information you receive is any better than that of a psychic who charges $50. Well-known psychics, especially those who appear on television frequently, are likely to charge high fees. John Edward, for instance, charges $850 for a private reading. This price takes it out of the realm of most people with families, a mortgage and car payments.

John Edward

In Gary E. Schwartz's book, *The Afterlife Experiments: Breakthrough Scientific Evidence of Life After Death*, there's a chapter called "Is There Such a Thing as Precognition?" He writes about an experiment that was filmed by HBO in 1999. It's complex and involves several mediums, including John Edward, Suzane Northrop, Anne Gehman (yes, that Gehman from Cassadaga), George Anderson and Laurie Campbell. There were two sitters—the people the mediums read—and the most interesting reading was the one John Edward did for Pat Price, a teacher.

All sorts of controls were put in place for the filming. The mediums were separated from the sitters at all times, except during the actual reading. Even then, they were separated by a screen so they couldn't see each other. This prevented the medium from picking up any facial cues. The medium and the sitter were fitted with electrodes that would measure their brain waves and electrocardiograms. The only thing the sitter was permitted to say—aside from a brief hello at the beginning—was a simple yes or no to whatever the medium asked.

When Edward read Pat Price, he began by explaining how he worked, that he would receive a series of impressions, pictures, words. "Things that make no sense to me come through in my mind." He said he would describe what he saw, heard and felt and would ask her to confirm and verify it with a yes or no.

Every psychic has a method for interpreting the information he or she picks up and Edward was no exception. When he referred to someone being "above" you, it meant it was someone older—a parental figure, father, grandparent, uncle. If he referred to someone at your "side," then it was a husband, wife, brother or sister, or a friend. A male figure at your side would be a brother-in-law, half brother, stepbrother. Someone "below" you would be people younger than you—children, nieces, nephews, grandchildren.

The first thing Edward pegged was a male figure at Pat's side—a husband or brother who had passed on. When he asked Pat if she understood that, she replied yes. Schwartz notes he was puzzled about that because Pat's husband was alive and sitting in a nearby room.

"John continued talking about what he thought was a deceased husband," Schwartz writes. "Yet, apparently without realizing it, he was no longer talking about her husband, but about her son; these statements made more sense because the son had indeed passed over."

At the end of the reading, Pat requested more information about her husband. Edward said: "Prior to leaving his body he shows me a male figure who is not of clear mind, the physical body is still running, but the soul is not in it. So, I see this being like if the soul is the driver of a car, the car would be the body, the car was running, but the driver was not in it."

Only then did Pat tell Edward that her husband was still alive, but Edward maintained that his first impressions were valid. After the filming, Schwartz asked Pat Price why she went along with Edward's statement that her husband, Mike, was dead. She admitted that a month before the HBO filming, she'd had a nightmare that Mike had died in a car accident, that his white car had crashed into a tree. She felt that Edward's statements might be a confirmation of the dream. It scared her.

Years earlier, she explained, Mike had been mugged and nearly killed. Ever since, he'd suffered from chronic head and neck pain, and was now experiencing blackouts, occasional paralysis in the back of his neck and was losing his coordination as well. Mike and Pat had considered the possibility that he might die, but they hadn't mentioned it to anyone.

Schwartz considered the possibility that what Edward saw was "an instance of psychic precognition," that he'd seen the future and not realized it. This was confirmed several months later when Mike Price's white vehicle veered off the road, crashed into a tree and he was killed.

In his autobiography *Memories, Dreams, Reflections*, Carl Jung wrote: "There are indications that at least a part of the psyche is not subject to the laws of space and time. This indicates that our concepts of space and time, and therefore of causality also, are incomplete. A complete picture of the world would require the addition of still another dimension; only then could the totality of phenomena be given a unified explanation."

Or, as Michael Talbot wrote in *The Holographic Universe: The Revolutionary Theory of Reality*, "Bohm's assertion that every human consciousness has its source in the implicate implies that we all possess the ability to access the future."

Cops and Psychics

Renie Wiley, Dennie Gooding and Christy Luna

One afternoon in May 1984, eight-year-old Christy Luna walked to a store near her home in Greenacres, Florida, in Palm Beach County, to buy cat food. She never returned. The police suspected foul play, but over the ensuing months, they failed to find any leads. They finally asked Renie Wiley, a professional psychic and artist, for any insights she could provide.

Renie, who lived in Cooper City, Florida, had worked frequently with cops over the years, and agreed to meet the investigators at the Greenacres Police Department. She asked them to bring any toys or stuffed animals that Christy had played with and several articles of the girl's clothing. Renie was an empath who tuned in psychically on energy fields by handling objects that belonged to an individual or through clothing the person had worn. Renie also requested the presence of Christy's mother so she could confirm any information she picked up. Renie knew we were interested in observing her when she worked with cops and invited us to join her.

So, one night in late 1984, we accompanied Renie to the Greenacres Police Department. Greenacres is a suburb of West Palm Beach with fewer than 40,000 residents. Back in 1984, the population was a fraction of that figure and as we drove through the pounding rain, we felt we were headed into the middle of nowhere.

But as that same rain beat down against the roof and windows of the police station, it created an almost hypnotic environment in the room where we gathered. We were introduced to Christy's mother, then Renie went over to the area where a couple of Christy's stuffed toys and several articles of her clothing had been placed. She slipped off her shoes and twisted her bare feet several times against the floor, grounding herself. Then her breathing altered and slowed as she entered an altered state. She sat down on the floor and picked up a little bear.

It was a battered bear, worn, well loved. Renie held it to her chest, shut her eyes and rocked back and forth, humming to herself. Even though Renie was a tall, large-boned woman, her body at that moment seemed small and childlike.

She started whimpering, then crying and sobbing, and her body hunched over the teddy bear, as though she were struggling to avoid blows, to protect herself. "The mother's boyfriend used to beat up on her," Renie said softly. "She's deaf in one ear because of it."

The deafness and other details about the girl's health were later confirmed by Christy's mother.

With Christy's mother in the room, it's likely that Renie held back some of what she'd felt when she'd clutched the teddy bear. But as soon as the three of us were in our car, with a cop following us to wherever Renie would lead us, she said, "The mother's boyfriend killed her, then took her body somewhere and buried it. I hope I can get a handle on where he buried her."

"Why did he kill her?" Rob asked.

"She came between him and Christie's mother. She was in the way. He has rage issues."

"*In the way?*" Trish blurted. "That's a reason to kill a kid?"

Renie, seated in the front passenger seat, glanced back at Trish. "Hey, he's a nutcase, okay? A sociopath, a sick man."

The rain that had sounded so hypnotic inside the station now blew horizontally across the road as Rob drove around Greenacres, through the wet darkness, following Renie's directions. *Turn here, turn there, just ahead.* We passed the house where Christy had lived and the store where she was headed when she disappeared. We finally arrived at a wooded area surrounded by a high barbed-wire fence. The cop pulled up alongside us. Renie felt that Christy's body was buried somewhere in the woods and that the mother's boyfriend definitely had killed her.

This entire episode was a fascinating example of how a psychic works, but nothing in this story was precognitive—until *24 years* later, long after Renie had passed away.

In the early spring of 2009, several friends were headed into town for a visit—past-life therapist and author Carol Bowman and Julie Scully, a TV writer. Then we got a call from another friend, Nancy "Scooter" McMoneagle, now president of the Monroe Institute, who said she would be in our area that same weekend with Dennie Gooding, a psychic from Los Angeles.

We had met Dennie a couple of years earlier through a Canadian astrologer who had recommended her as a psychic. Rob had a reading with her, and we were eager to meet her in person. She said she had been hired by a Palm Beach County sheriff's detective to look into a possible homicide case. The detective knew Scooter, who had recommended Dennie for the job. So, we planned a party.

When you get this many people together who have common beliefs—that we are more than our physical bodies, that the paranormal isn't weird or scary, that linear time is an illusion—then synchronicity and precognition flourish.

The day before the gathering, we were going through some old books, weeding out what we no longer needed. A check fell out of one of them. It was dated 1986, made out to us for $50 as a repayment on a loan and was signed by Renie Wiley. We exclaimed about how strange it was that the check had been inside the book all these years, and we wondered if Renie was trying to contact us. In all the years since she'd passed away, we'd never experienced any contact with her. And we didn't have any recollection of our lending her $50 or of her paying it back. It never occurred to us that the check might be a huge precognitive clue.

On the night of the festivities, Dennie told us she'd been hired to work with a detective in the cold cases division. When she began describing the case and mentioned Greenacres, Trish suddenly interrupted her.

"Is this the Christy Luna case?"

Dennie's eyes widened with shock. "Yes. How . . . ?"

"You're not going to believe this." Rob walked over to the drawer where we'd put Renie's check, brought it out and told the story of our involvement in the case through Renie.

Finding that check was an example of precognition—seemingly initiated from the "other side"—but we didn't recognize it as such until later that evening when Dennie began describing the case she'd been hired to investigate.

Neither of us remember sticking Renie's check inside a book. In fact, in 1986, we were just starting out as writers, money was tight, and it's likely we would have cashed the check as soon as we'd gotten it.

We realized we were the inadvertent connection in a series of events that led to a startling synchronicity and precognition. And it all revolved around the unsolved disappearance of Christy Luna and two professional psychics who didn't know each other, were separated by nearly a quarter of century and worked on the case.

Interestingly, Dennie led the detective to the same wooded field where Renie had directed us all those years ago. Dennie said the body was buried somewhere in the undeveloped land. The body has never been found and the boyfriend never charged.

Alternate Futures?

When a professional psychic tunes in on future events in your life—or when you experience a precognition about something in your future—is that future set in stone?

Throughout history, there have been numerous instances of people who experienced precognitions about their own deaths and avoided the circumstances and situations they'd glimpsed and lived to talk about them. Take any man-made or natural disaster—and there have been an abundance of both since the 21st century started—and you'll find these kinds of stories. Some are documented and many are anecdotal, but they suggest that the future isn't fixed and can be changed.

"For those pondering the puzzle of precognition, the Pribram-Bohm holographic mind theory seems to offer the greatest hope yet for progress toward the sought-for solution," writes David Loye in *The Sphinx and the Rainbow: Brain, Mind, and Future Vision.*

Loye contends that the sticky problem of how information can be transmitted psychically is eliminated with the holographic theory. In a hologram, each part contains the information of the whole, so "if we are each parts of a larger whole . . . if our minds and bodies are, in effect, holograms within the larger hologram of the universe, then there is no transmission problem, because the information is already within us!"

Loye believes there are many different holograms drifting around within the primal waters of what Bohm calls the implicate or enfolded order. When we experience a precognition or a psychic tunes in on a future event in our lives and we then act to change the outcome, what we've actually done is moved from one hologram to another.

This idea is similar to the many-worlds interpretation of quantum physics, which says that we live within a web of infinite timelines. If an action you take has more than one possible outcome, then when you act or choose not to act, the universe splits off. The 1998 movie *Sliding Doors* plays with this idea. Gwyneth Paltrow is a young woman in London whose love life and career—and everything else—depends on whether she catches a train. We see the ramifications of both possibilities.

Frequency, a 2000 movie with Dennis Quaid, also plays with the many-worlds idea. An anomalous radio signal links a father and son across 30 years and enables the son to save his father's life. This interference creates a new timeline with unforeseen consequences.

So, if a professional psychic sees you on a road trip where you're stranded on a dark road in the pouring rain because of a flat tire or with steam pouring out from under the hood of your car, you can change that outcome. You take your car to a mechanic and have it checked out thoroughly. You buy new tires. You make sure that on your road trip, you drive only during the daylight hours.

The action you've taken causes reality to split off. In one reality, you may still get stranded on a dark road, but in another you arrive safely at your destination. Perhaps in a third reality, you get stranded during the day because you run out of gas or your vehicle develops some other problem. At some point, it all begins to sound like an episode from *The Twilight Zone.* But suppose it's an accurate depiction of the nature of reality?

In 2011, an indie production company released a movie called *Another Earth.* It's about the discovery of a second Earth that proves to be identical to this one, right down to the 7 billion souls who inhabit it. It focuses on the story of a brilliant young woman whose passion is astronomy. On the day she learns she has been admitted to MIT, she celebrates with one drink too many and on the way home, hears about the discovery of Earth 2 on the radio. She inadvertently crashes into another car at the intersection and kills the driver's wife and son and puts him in a coma.

The story follows her through prison and her release four years later. By now, scientists have communicated with their counterparts on Earth 2. They have learned that until Earth and its twin became aware of each other, everything between the two was identical. But now, certain small details have begun to deviate. And there it is, that moment, reality splitting off. Alternate worlds, alternate futures.

"Are the vagaries of life truly random or do we play a role in literally sculpting our own destiny?" asks Michael Talbot.

Hollywood does a great job of depicting these ideas in visual stories. But they really hit home when they happen to you.

Your Alternate Futures

We discuss these ideas in greater length in the last two chapters, but for now, think back through pivotal moments in your own life when decisions you made may have created an alternate future. Sometimes, those moments are obvious—you married this person instead of that one, moved or didn't move, changed schools or jobs or stayed where you were. Other times, those significant moments are more subtle and nuanced.

In one of Jane Roberts's early books, she and her husband, Rob, saw a couple dancing whom they recognized as themselves. But this couple seemed unhappy, older, beaten down. Jane realized it was how they would look if they had never discovered the Seth material.

"The 'you' that you presently conceive yourself to be represents the emergence into physical experience of but one probable state of your being," says Seth in the couple's *The Nature of Personal Reality.* "When your ideas about yourself change, so does your experience."

Millie Gemondo

We first heard about Millie from our accountant, Tom, who is from the same West Virginia town where Millie has lived most of her life. Even though he isn't a guy who ordinarily consults psychics, he called Millie amazing. So, in the summer of 1992, Trish scheduled a phone reading with Millie. We set it up for the evening of August 24, 1992, not knowing at the time, of course, that a category 5 hurricane named Andrew would target South Florida on that same day.

It was early in the evening. Our house was boarded up, but not much had happened outside. Trish and Millie connected by phone and the reading began. Millie's tool to get into the zone is a regular deck of playing cards. But in the years since that first reading, we have observed her in person as she reads for us or others, and not long after she draws that first card, she doesn't even see the deck. She's seeing an image or feeling something in her body or hearing what eludes the rest of us. The gist of that night's reading was that the hurricane wouldn't touch us, but the damage "farther south" would be considerable, historical.

She nailed it.

From then on, we had periodic readings with Millie and she visited us several times in Florida. She and Trish coauthored a book on animal totems. They frequently traded readings—Millie with her deck of cards, Trish with her tarot cards.

In the late 1990s, Millie warned Trish that Rob should be especially careful while windsurfing. She saw some sort of injury to his foot. Since a number of Millie's predictions over the years had come true, Trish passed the warning on to Rob, who promptly forgot it. A month later, Rob was windsurfing at a local lake, came into shore, leaped off the board and onto a broken beer bottle. He ended up in ER, where he got nineteen stitches. The sole of his foot was sliced open to within a quarter-inch (6-mm) of the bone.

When Trish's mother was in an Alzheimer's unit, Millie happened to be in town and they went to visit Rose Marie, who was agitated that evening. She insisted that her youngest brother and oldest sister, both of them dead for years, had visited and that none of the staff believed her.

"Is your brother's name . . . Dick?" Millie asked.

Rose Marie sat up straighter in her bed, suddenly attentive. "Yes. Dick, my baby brother."

"He's still here. He says to ignore what the staff says. He and Pat are with you a lot."

Pat was Rose Marie's oldest sister. Trish had never told Millie their names.

After they left the facility and were on their way to the car, Trish asked Millie how long her mother would survive in a state like this, her memory like chopped liver. "At least another year," Millie said.

And she was right. Rose Marie died about a year later.

In the late spring of 2009, Millie and Trish were exchanging readings and Millie told Trish that Rob needed to pay attention to his feet. She kept seeing his left foot injured, in some sort of bootlike cast. "From another windsurfing accident?" Trish asked.

Millie replied that she wasn't seeing the cause, just the left foot in the boot-cast.

In late June of that year, he was riding his mountain bike on an off-road trail, the kind of biking where you climb or hop over obstacles—log piles, tree stumps and aboveground networks of roots. Rob slipped on the wet terrain and broke his left foot.

Millie has registered so many precognitive hits over the decades we've known her that when she speaks these days, we listen closely. We take notes. And yes, because of her, we have taken what Loye calls "hololeaps," where you jump from one hologram of possibility to another and avoid mistakes, pain and disaster.

Predicting Death

Among most professional psychics, predicting death is a big no-no unless the client asks. Even then, it's uncomfortable terrain that psychics hope to avoid.

"I see only possibilities," Millie says. "The actual time, place and circumstances of death are dependent on the soul's itinerary."

But a French Canadian psychic we met in early 2000 apparently didn't know the rules. We had recommended her to a friend who had never before consulted a psychic. She was interested in the paranormal and, in fact, went on to coauthor *Power Tarot* with Trish. But she was also extremely wary about getting a reading. Perhaps her own psychic abilities had alerted her to what might happen. As soon as she sat down for the reading, the psychic blurted, "Your husband will die within a year and your son-in-law will die a few months later. And that is all I have to say. No charge." With that, she got up and left.

Our friend sat there, stunned and upset. Unfortunately, the psychic's prediction came true, within the time frame she had stipulated.

Why had the psychic acted in such a blunt and rude manner? She had talked to Trish about coauthoring a book with her about her work as a psychic. But as she began the reading, perhaps she realized that the book Trish would write would be coauthored by the woman seated across from her. She left with tears in her eyes, for herself, not the woman who would lose the two important men in her life.

These two examples illustrate the vast differences in how a psychic delivers precognitive information. If you plan to consult a psychic about your future, do your homework first. Is the person reputable? Do you know anyone who has consulted the psychic? Have the psychic's predictions panned out? Also, examine your own reasons for wanting to consult a psychic. Is it for entertainment? Or are you at a place in your life when information about what's coming up will help you to make important decisions?

Yet, let's look at this from the psychic's point of view. It seems there are times when such information should be imparted. In Chapter 1, we related the story of a psychic who was urged by her spirit guides to tell her client that her husband of 25 years, who was healthy, would die in a few months. She silently argued with them, because she never predicted deaths. But they insisted and she reluctantly passed along the message, adding that afterward her life would improve. The client later told the psychic that the reading had saved her life. She'd been contemplating suicide because she couldn't tolerate life with her husband any longer. As predicted, her husband died of a stroke months later.

Psychometry

Harry Price was a British psychic investigator and author who during the course of his career exposed several fraudulent spiritualist mediums. But in his investigations, many of them documented in his book, *Fifty Years of Psychical Research*, he encountered some psychics he deemed to be the real thing. One of these was well-known French psychometrist and clairvoyant Jeanne Laplace.

On July 7, 1928, Price met with her in Paris to conduct an experiment. They met at the home of Dr. Eugene Osty, whose sister-in-law knew shorthand and took notes about the session. Price was asked to give Jeanne a document, photograph or something similar. Price notes in his book that Jeanne didn't go into trance, as many mediums do, and didn't have any spirit guides. She just chatted with him.

Price had a number of letters in his pocket and chose one at random and handed it to her. It was from Dr. Robin John Tillyard, an entomologist in Canberra who worked for the Australian government. At the time, he was traveling and the letter, dated June 6, 1928, had been mailed from Canada. It was folded, the blank sheet outward. "The inside was not visible and there was nothing to indicate whether it was a written, typed, or printed document," Price wrote.

Jeanne didn't even glance at it. She held the letter between her palms and reeled off 53 impressions, which were written down verbatim and numbered. "Out of the fifty-three, forty-two were correct or reasonably correct," Price writes. "I could verify some of them myself, and Dr. Tillyard confirmed the rest." Some of her correct hits: the letter was typewritten; the writer was a doctor or a scientist; that he wasn't in good health; that arteriosclerosis was indicated. Then, in the 30th impression, Jeanne moved into the precognitive part of the reading.

The person who had written the letter wouldn't have a long life and didn't have very many years to live. At the time, Tillyard was 47. Jeanne went on to say, "The writer will die through a railroad or automobile accident; wheels or rail are bad for him." She said he would have a tragic death, "congestion of the brain and will fall on railway or under car."

Neither Jeanne nor Price knew that in 1913, fifteen years before this reading took place, Tillyard was badly injured in a railway accident and suffered a concussion, broken arm and back injuries that laid him up for two years. Some years later, he was in two different car accidents and sustained injuries as well. In retrospect, Price felt that Jeanne had sensed Tillyard's previous accidents.

When Price told Tillyard about Jeanne's predictions, his remark was, "These things never come true."

But Price was so impressed with Jeanne's comments on Tillyard that he wrote an article on the predictions. It was published in September 1928, in a magazine called *Psychic Research*, the official journal of the American Society for Psychical Research.

On January 13, 1937, eight years and seven months after the prediction, Tillyard was killed in a car accident. He, his daughter and a female friend were driving between Canberra and Sydney when Tillyard's car skidded and overturned. When they were found, Tillyard was terribly injured, paralyzed and his head had gone through the windshield, causing a concussion. He died the next day.

Price, who had made a name for himself as a psychic debunker, considered this case to be one of the best examples of a fulfilled prediction because it had been so carefully documented.

Psychometry, the ability to psychically pick up information from an object, has been used in numerous books, films, TV shows and comic books. One of the best depictions of this skill comes from Stephen King, in his novel *The Dead Zone*.

The protagonist, Johnny Smith, was injured in an accident that plunged him into a coma for nearly five years. When he awakens, he discovers he has the ability to psychically read objects. He uses the ability to help cops solve crimes. Fairly simple premise, but with King at the helm, you are drawn into the *process*, what ordinary life is actually like for a psychic with this skill. Can you shake a stranger's hand without being drawn into the dark corners of that person's life? Can you walk into a friend's house and touch a plate, a glass, a fork, without seeing that person's secrets?

In our explorations, we have met one impressive psychometrist, Kathy Adams. She lives and works across the street from the Cassadaga Hotel, in that part of town where psychics and mediums aren't certified by the spiritualist camp board. She's a vivacious, pretty woman in her late 40s or early 50s. She used to work part-time as an emergency room nurse, on Mondays, the day she closed up shop in Cassadaga. But that ended when the full-moon crazies in the ER started getting violent. Now her part-time gig is buying houses, renovating them and selling them. When she's not doing that, she's open for business in town and can read virtually any object.

The common wisdom with psychometry is that metal best retains a person's energy, the stuff someone like Kathy reads. A piece of jewelry, car keys, a cell phone. But let's say that for years you've carried around a small wooden box that belonged to your grandmother or some ancestor even further back. Or maybe you've been carrying around a glass vial of holy water as a means of protection against something. Pass either one to Kathy. Metal, wood, glass, paper, liquid, plastic, cardboard. If you've handled it, she can read it.

She has made accurate predictions for us, although nothing quite as dramatic as what Jeanne predicted when Harry Price conducted his experiment. In the fall of 2015, she saw our daughter starting a new business in the spring of 2016, and it looks as if that business is now on track to reality.

Kathy also saw us working on a joint project that involves a series of nonfiction books that span several years. One possibility came to mind. For ten years, after famed astrologer Sydney Omarr died, we wrote a series of astrology books under his banner. That ended in 2014. We then decided to do the series on our own for 2016, as *Genie in the Stars*. At the time of the reading, we'd already embarked on the project. We're planning the series for 2017 as well, and with success, will probably continue it.

Kathy Adams glimpsed the series in the blueprint of our future. But as with any blueprint, we can revise it or alter the details. We could also shift to another blueprint, if there was one that we preferred.

And so can you.

Rescripting the Future

The fact that the future can occasionally be foreseen does not exclude freedom in general but only in this particular case. Freedom could become doubtful only if everything could be foreseen.

—Carl Jung

Precognitive experiences can be startling and dramatic, particularly when they're about a tragic event. Other times they are more of a nudge from the unconscious mind rather than a full-blown scene from a disaster movie. But precognition invariably begs the question: Is the future set in stone like yesterday's headlines? For that matter, if time is an illusion, are those headlines from yesterday unchangeable?

Mass Events

If you dream that a large-scale disaster is imminent—the crash of a jetliner, for instance—chances are, you're not going to be able to do anything about it. Even if you know the airline, the flight number and the time of the event, it's unlikely that the airline will ground a plane on the basis of your dream. However, if you've got a ticket for that flight, you can change flights or cancel your plans. In other words, you may not be able to prevent a future disaster, but you can alter your involvement in it.

In 1950, *Life* magazine featured a story about a church fire in Beatrice, Nebraska, that proved to be a stunning example of unconscious precognition and extraordinary synchronicity. A church choir was due to practice at 7:20 p.m. on March 1. There were fifteen people in the choir and all of them, for perfectly legitimate reasons, were late for practice.

The minister and his family were late because they were doing the laundry; another person had car trouble; someone else was finishing homework. Due to a flaw in the church's heating system, the church exploded at 7:25 p.m. The odds of all fifteen choir members missing the opening of practice were later calculated at one in a million.

Unconscious precognitions could also have played a role in why so many passengers canceled or didn't show for flights that crashed into the World Trade Center. According to American Airlines records, 164 reservations had been made for flight 11 departing from Boston on September 11, 2001. But 65 people canceled their reservation prior to departure and an additional 17 were no-shows. Similarly, 116 reservations had been made on flight 77 that left from Dulles Airport in Washington, DC, that same day, yet 54 people canceled and 3 of the remaining 62 ticketholders never boarded.

Some people who worked at the World Trade Center were delayed and late for work; others decided to stay home. Tardiness and absenteeism in the WTC probably weren't anything unusual, but some people actively sensed the dangers on that day.

A notable example is the case of a Wall Street executive who twice sensed danger at the World Trade Center. One morning in 1993, Barrett Naylor stepped off a train in New York's Grand Central Station, and had a strong feeling that he should turn around and go home. He listened to his inner voice and avoided the bombing of the WTC. Naylor experienced a similar premonition eight years later. On September 11, 2001, his inner voice again urged him to go home, and he did. Naylor says he regrets not having shared that message with others because it might have saved lives.

Such incidents, when a disaster was consciously avoided because of a precognition, show that individuals can alter their futures. But those personally involved in the tragedies are not the only ones who have precognitive experiences related to such events.

Seeing from Afar

On the morning of September 11, 2001, around 6:30 a.m., Michelle—who lives in Charlottesville, Virginia—became preoccupied with The Tower card from the tarot. In most decks, this card depicts a burning tower that has been struck by lightning and people are plunging from the windows into the dark, moiling abyss and chaos below—in other words, an archetypal image of the Twin Towers on 9/11.

"For some reason, the image of the card popped into my head, and at the time I had trouble making the connection because it had nothing to do with what was going on around me. At that point, I decided to take heed of the meaning of the card and prepare myself for something major and possibly traumatic."

Michelle arrived at her friend's house and told her she felt this overwhelming sense that something tragic was going to happen and that it was going to be significant not only for her, but for many other people: "It wasn't until I saw the news at 9:30 a.m. and the fall of the first tower that I was able to make the connection to what my experience truly foretold."

Even though she was far from Lower Manhattan and had no relationship with anyone who worked at the World Trade Center or was traveling on the airplanes involved, Michelle's sudden obsession with The Tower card seemed related to events that were unfolding that morning. She was one of numerous people who had dreams or other experiences seemingly foretelling the 9/11 attack, even though they weren't directly involved. But it's doubtful that any of them could have prevented the near-future disaster.

Louisa Rhine has gathered thousands of reports of premonitions. She said that if you feel that a premonition is a valid warning, then you should take reasonable steps to prevent it. However, she added there's no foolproof method of determining if your premonition is accurate. For that reason, she advised against reporting premonitions of tragic events to authorities. She noted that such large-scale events often involve so many people that it's difficult to do anything to change the circumstances. She also pointed out that authorities often deal with delusional people and are unlikely to take your premonition seriously.

Then there's the possibility that by taking action you're actually fulfilling the precognition. One case from the Rhine Research Center involved an Oregon woman who woke up terrified that her three-year-old son was in danger of being killed in a car accident. She decided to take him to her mother's house a few miles away, where he would be safe and she wouldn't have to take him with her during the day. When they arrived at her mother's, she felt so relieved she burst into tears.

However, a while later a policeman banged at the door, holding her seriously injured son in his arms. The child had left the house unnoticed and was playing in the yard when a driver lost control of his car and ran over him. The incident itself apparently couldn't be avoided; it involved another person, the driver, over whom the mother had no control. But because her sense of the future didn't involve the specifics—such as where this car accident would occur—she inadvertently played into the future she'd sensed by taking her son to a place where she believed he would be safe.

Much more common, though, are instances where a precognitive experience leads to action that alters the person's future. The Rhine Research Center analyzed 433 premonition cases and found that when attempts were made to intervene, the experiencers were successful twice as often as not.

Dale Graff, author of *Tracks in the Psychic Wilderness: An Exploration of ESP, Remote Viewing, Precognitive Dreaming and Synchronicity*, dreamed of an upcoming tragic event in his life and changed the circumstances, possibly preventing life-threatening injuries. Graff, a scientist, managed the army's psychic spying program, Stargate, that existed in secret for 25 years. For decades, he balanced his left-brain work as a physicist and aeronautical engineer by recording his dreams in a journal.

In this particular dream, he saw his wife's white station wagon in the driveway and noticed a cylindrical object on the floor in the backseat. One end was glowing bright red, then exploded, enveloping the car in flames. Graff was jolted awake by the dramatic dream. Because of his experience with dream work, he recognized the dream as precognitive. The next morning he inspected the vehicle closely, but found nothing suspicious. Playing it safe, he took the car to his mechanic for a general maintenance checkup.

Later, when he arrived to pick up the car, he was shown a small cylindrical object, the fuel pump, and was told that he had been driving a time bomb! One end of the pump was charred and the insulation on the connecting wires had burned off from an electrical short. The pump was located inside the gas tank and could have caused an explosion.

Graff was astonished. The fuel pump looked like the cylinder he'd dreamed about. The dream and his willingness to act on it probably saved his wife's life. But what mechanism is at play allowing for such precognitive experiences to impact future events?

How Does Sensing the Future Work?

Rather than "seeing" actual future events, people who sense the future may be anticipating events that might unfold. That's a concept expressed by physicist David Bohm in a conversation with author Michael Talbot. Bohm was quoted as saying: "When people dream of accidents correctly and do not take the plane or ship, it is not the actual future that they were seeing. It was merely something in the present which is implicate and moving toward making that future. In fact, the future they saw differed from the actual future because they altered it. Therefore I think it's more plausible to say, if these phenomena exist, there's an anticipation of the future in the implicate order in the present."

Bohm referred to the implicate or hidden order as nonlocal reality and our everyday world at local reality. In *Synchronicity: The Inner Path of Leadership*, Joseph Jaworski describes the impact that a chance meeting with Bohm had on his dream of creating a training program for visionary leadership that focused on serving others. During a four-hour conversation with the physicist, Bohm told him, "You cannot think of existence as local . . . Your self is actually the whole of mankind. That's the idea of implicate order—that everything is enfolded in everything. The entire past is enfolded in each of us in a very subtle way. If you reach deeply into yourself, you are reaching into the very essence of mankind."

Think about that for a moment. It means that any time you're engaged in something that prompts you to look within, to delve into your own psyche, your own consciousness, you're diving into that primal soup, that collective, where we're all connected.

Free Will or Destiny?

If you've had a precognitive experience and accept the reality of precognition, you naturally start to wonder whether events are predetermined or whether we have free will. Perhaps some mass events are meant to happen and there's little we can do to change their course.

Before the arrival of Europeans to North America, Native American shamans, according to legends, predicted the arrival of invaders from the east who would destroy their culture and usurp their land. Those prophecies, handed down generation after generation, were thought to be inevitable, that it was the end of a cycle, that powerful historical and cosmic forces were involved. In other words, there was no way of preventing the invasion. And the shamans were correct.

Clearly that historical event, a catastrophic invasion for the native population of the Americas, seems as if it were etched in stone. It's hard to imagine any other possible outcome after Europeans discovered a great land across the sea. While there was plenty of room to share with indigenous people, the shamans had foreseen repression and conquest, not a sharing of land. And that's what happened.

But suppose this invasion was just one possible scenario? Perhaps events could have occurred in any number of ways and what the shamans were seeing was the *most likely* scenario. If the collective consciousness of the people involved had been focused differently, then perhaps the invasion wouldn't have happened and some alternate historical timeline would have been created. Sounds like science fiction, right?

Maybe not.

The Mandela Effect

In 2010, blogger Fiona Bloom was puzzled by an experience she had at Dragon Con, a multigenre conference that includes science fiction and fantasy writers, game developers, comic book writers and artists and fans. In other words, creative types. She realized that other people had a completely different memory than she did about when Nelson Mandela had died. She believed—*remembered*—that he had died in prison in the 1980s. She recalled the news clips of his funeral, the mourning in the country, rioting in the cities, even Winnie Mandela's speech. Then, she discovered he was actually alive.

Bloom went on to discover other widely held alternative memories that included *Star Trek* episodes that never existed and the death of Billy Graham. In 2012, another blogger, Reece, who also happened to be a physicist, described a similar dichotomy about the spelling of the old cartoon *The Berenstain Bears.* However, many people remember the name as *The Berenstein Bears*. That's how we remember the name from when our daughter was much younger and used to watch the cartoon. But the spelling is actually *The Berenstain Bears,* and the book covers going back to the 1980s *bare* that out. It seems we were just misreading the name. However, Reece provides a theory of the universe that would account for both names being true.

> *"I propose that the universe is a 4-dimensional complex manifold. If you don't se habla math jargon, that means I propose the 3 space dimensions and the 1 time dimensions are actually in themselves complex, meaning they take values of the form a + ib, part 'real' and part 'imaginary.' Within this 4D manifold, there are sixteen hexadectants (like quadrants, but 16 of them), corresponding to whether we consider only the real or imaginary part of each of the four dimensions. In our particular hexadectant, the three space dimensions are real, and the time dimension is imaginary."*

Reece seems to be referring to string theory, where multiple realities—parallel universes—are sandwiched together alongside ours. There's even a YouTube video about the *Bears*, in which the narrator notes how he went back into cartoon archives and found that the spelling changed sometime between April and August 5, 2001—from three weeks to five months before 9/11, when the world did change. Yet, there's plenty of evidence to the contrary that the name has always been Berenstain in spite of popular perception.

We first heard about The Mandela Effect from Sharee Geo, who cohosts a radio show on Truth Frequency Radio, where we were guests. Before our scheduled appearance, she e-mailed us suggestions about what we might discuss.

Synchronicity and meditation are both hot topics on the show. However, we've gone even a little further lately with ideas about a holographic reality that uses synchronicity to reinforce reality, along with phenomena like the Mandela Effect—the idea that something has happened to our "timeline" sometime in the past that is now changing small things in our present reality/timeline.

It's easy to dismiss the Mandela Effect as examples of misidentification and false memories. However, we experienced something like The Mandela Effect when we were house hunting in early 1999. One of the houses we looked at was in Jupiter, Florida, 25 miles (40 km) north of where we live now. The house and the property, about 2 acres (8,000 sq m), were terrific. We loved the place. It had two master bedrooms, one on each side of the pool, with a kitchen that opened to a spacious family room with a great fireplace. We recalled that the owner was a pilot. But it was just out of our price range.

Six or eight months later, on another house-hunting Sunday, we ran across the house again and eagerly went by for a look. Same street, same location, same distinctive gravel driveway, but the house was disappointingly different. Everything we had liked about it was missing. No pool bracketed by master bedrooms, no fireplace. It just wasn't the same house.

The many-worlds theory of quantum physics contends that for every decision we make, the path we didn't choose shoots off on its own and we—our parallel selves—live it out. Is it possible that these other lives sometimes bleed into what we call our present reality? Is this phenomenon what Seth was referring to when he said, "The 'you' that you presently conceive yourself to be represents the emergence into physical experience of but one probable state of your being. When your ideas about yourself change, so does your experience."

Could the Mandela Effect be tangible evidence of these parallel lives?

When we wrote a blog post about the Mandela Effect, Mike Perry, a blogger in the United Kingdom, recounted an incident that happened to him and his wife, Karin. They had gone to a literature and musical festival at their grandson's school. Sammy had been chosen by his class to recite a poem about a mouse. The children had to go onstage, one at a time, recite their poem, and then leave the stage after the applause stopped. Mike wrote, "Sammy did his bit, remembered the words but Karin and I saw the end differently. She is adamant that when he left the stage he did a bow to the audience. I'm adamant that he didn't. So I wonder how we saw something different as we were both paying full attention? It does seem that a similar effect can happen even with small events."

Author Cynthia Sue Larson collects stories like this for her newsletter, "Reality Shifts," and also wrote about it in her book, *Reality Shifts: When Consciousness Changes the Physical World.* Her stories range from people remembering that Jane Goodall died (as of early 2016, she hasn't) to Larry Hagman's being alive (he died in 2012) to more personal accounts that Larson believes are an indication that physical reality is actually changing.

Who's in Charge?

Free will versus destiny is something David R. Hamilton, author of *The Contagious Power of Thinking: How Your Thoughts Can Influence the World,* has wrestled with for years: "There were things that I felt strongly were meant to be in my life: like going to the university I attended and also doing my PhD in the research group I ended up in, to even not getting the job I wanted in the pharmaceutical industry, but instead getting one that exposed me to evidence of the placebo effect. This facilitated my route into writing books about the power of the mind, which I believe is my 'destiny.'"

Since psychics portend to tell our future, do they believe the future is predetermined? How else can they know what's coming up in our life? It's an issue that has puzzled some psychics, including Erin Pavlina, author of *The Astral Projection Guidebook: Mastering the Art of Astral Travel.* "For the past several months, I've been trying to understand and determine if we are all living scripted lives that we cannot change or if we have free will and the ability to completely change our fates," she writes on her website. "It didn't seem to me that both could be right at the same time."

Finally, she said she asked her guides, who provided an explanation. They told her that before we are born, our higher self confers with more advanced spirits who help plan the next life. Major life events will be established—selecting your parents and any siblings, your career and a life plan. She added: "Imagine there is a maze in front of you and it represents your life. At one opening is your birth and way across the maze is another opening that is your death. Inside the twisting corridors of the maze, our higher self and these other spirits place major life events. Think of it like placing cheese in a maze for a rat to run around in. Those events are placed there on purpose. This is the predestined aspect of your life. How you end up arriving at each of those events is where free will comes into play."

Trish, who has written a number of astrology books, disagrees. She views a natal chart as a *blueprint of potential*—nothing more, nothing less. We choose our time, date and place of birth and the circumstances into which we're born—parents, siblings, all of it—that will facilitate our achieving our potential at every level. We have complete free will to fulfill that potential or not. The only "destined" aspect in a natal chart is represented by a point called a vertex. Its sign and house placement point to an agreement made before we were born to experience a particular relationship or event. But even with this, free will dominates. We can choose to keep that appointment or not.

Connie Cannon, a retired nurse and a psychic, believes that certain experiences in an individual's life are intractable and will happen. She views such experiences as free will by the soul prior to birth, which isn't exactly the same as conscious free will.

"The soul designs the blueprint for the upcoming life and draws experiences into the design with permanent ink. Those experiences are not subject to change. The decision was made by the soul's free will while the plan was being drawn." She notes that most experiences are "penciled in," allowing the individual free will within the boundaries of the plan.

Connie feels the same is true regarding mass events: "I tend to think that the Holocaust, the Twin Towers disaster and other global catastrophes are etched in stone because they carry a definitive purpose for humanity. The Paris attacks, the Boston bombing? I don't know if they could've been prevented. Probably not."

If she's right, then these events are decided by what Carl Jung called the collective unconscious of mankind with the purpose of raising human awareness. "Group karma," she says, "seems to be an absolutely viable universal law, and is applicable when there are huge and often heinous events that shift the world view of the entire human species."

Connie compares the reasoning behind such events to a youngster who puts his fingers on a hot stove burner. Hopefully, the child learns that fire hurts and won't touch the stove again; "Negative situations have the ability to bring positive results, and the eventual purposes may be very positive if we are able to release the negative and attempt to understand that Universal Consciousness creates certain vast, massive events toward that end."

It's a difficult concept to grasp, especially when these events seem so heinous. But if individual souls create situations to resolve individual issues, do humans as a species also create situations and issues that require collective resolution?

Maybe.

And maybe not.

Maybe that's not how it works at all.

Entanglement

Chris Mackey, an Australian clinical psychologist and author of *Synchronicity: Empower Your Life with the Gift of Coincidence*, notes that it's been a century since the core findings of quantum physics began to emerge and we still don't understand all the implications. "As some scientists have argued, the universe is not just stranger than we imagine—it's stranger than we *can* imagine. This should remind us of the importance of not dismissing extremely surprising, seemingly irrational notions too readily. We should by now know enough to welcome the weird into our world rather than unreflectingly reject it." Mackey believes that the scientific evidence for entanglement may support the existence of precognition, telepathy and other paranormal phenomena.

Entanglement, what Einstein described as "spooky action at a distance," was first put forward more than 50 years ago by Irish physicist John Stewart Bell.

According to David Kaiser, a professor of physics at MIT, in November 1964, Bell submitted "a short, quirky article to a fly-by-night journal," *Physics, Physique, Fizika.* Even though the journal folded several years later, his paper "became a blockbuster" and today is one of the most frequently cited physics articles of all time. The article was about entanglement.

Fifty years after Bell submitted that article, Kaiser wrote a piece for the *New York Times* called "Is Quantum Entanglement Real?"

"Entanglement concerns the behavior of tiny particles, such as electrons, that have interacted in the past and then moved apart," writes Kaiser. "Tickle one particle here, by measuring one of its properties—its position, momentum or 'spin'—and its partner should dance, instantaneously, no matter how far away the second particle has traveled."

That word *instantaneously* is key to the quantum weirdness of Bell's claim. If the particles are separated by a zillion miles of space, the only way one particle can affect the behavior of the other is if they're moving faster than the speed of light, which Einstein deemed impossible.

Yet, in his article, Bell demonstrated that "quantum theory *requires* entanglement; the strange connectedness is an inescapable feature of the equations." Kaiser notes that Bell's theorem didn't illustrate that nature behaves like this. It only showed that the physicists' equations did. But in the 1970s, several courageous physicists conducted a series of experiments that appeared to show that Bell was correct. And they did this, Kaiser says, "in the face of critics who felt such 'philosophical' research was fit only for crackpots."

Kaiser and his colleagues are conducting their own experiments, a project they describe in an article in *Physical Review Letters:* "If, as we expect, the usual predictions from quantum theory are borne out in this experiment, we will have constrained various alternative theories as much as physically possible in our universe. If not, that would point toward a profoundly new physics."

But for Chris Mackey, the verdict is already in: "If physical objects can be instantaneously connected at any distance, then why can't the same be true of people's minds? There seems to be a clear overlap between entanglement and psychic propinquity."

Paradigm Shift

Normal science, the activity in which most scientists inevitably spend most all their time, is predicated on the assumption that the scientific community knows what the world is like. Normal science often suppresses fundamental novelties because they are necessarily subversive of its basic commitments. As a puzzle-solving activity, normal science does not aim at novelties of fact or theory and, when successful, finds none.

—Thomas Kuhn, *The Structure of Scientific Revolutions*

If you Google the phrase "paradigm shift" or "new paradigm," you'll find more than a million potential links. If anything, the terms are overused. Just as Carl Jung coined the term synchronicity, Thomas Kuhn coined "paradigm shift" in *The Structure of Scientific Revolutions*, a book about the history of science. *The Guardian* newspaper of London called Kuhn "the man who changed the way the world looks at science."

Kuhn, who was a philosopher, contended that change in science rarely comes from mainstream scientists, who tend to prove what is already accepted as true "normal science." Change comes from outliers, who disrupt the orderly affairs.

While that might not sound like much of a startling idea today, it was in 1962 when Kuhn's book was published. Prior to his book, it was thought that science evolved by the gradual addition of new truths that supported the established truths, and that especially did not undermine mainstream science.

Today, the outliers are such scientists as David Bohm and Rupert Sheldrake, who are exploring the frontiers of the mind and consciousness and who aren't bound to the materialistic view. They are explorers of a deeper collective consciousness, of Source energy, of the ability of humans to extend awareness beyond the six senses. And they are viewed with suspicion or worse by mainstream science.

Rather than innovators, they are considered misguided scientists enmeshed in nonscientific belief systems. In fact, scientists who question the predominant materialistic view and flirt with the spirit world are considered potential charlatans. The journal *Nature* published an infamous editorial about Sheldrake's first book, *A New Science of Life*, which describes his theory of "morphic resonance." "This infuriating tract . . . is the best candidate for burning there has been for many years," wrote Sir John Maddox for *Nature*.

Three decades later, the video of Sheldrake's talk at a TEDx event, in which he criticized mainstream science, was removed from the group's main website when radical materialistic bloggers condemned it. Interestingly, before the "banning" of the talk in 2013, the video had received 35,000 views. After the ban, it was viewed more than a half-million times, revealing how many people are seeking a larger picture than scientific materialism provides.

The Skeptical Inquirer, a publication associated with debunking all that is paranormal, is on the frontlines of the so-called old paradigm of science that embraces materialism and reductionism. Ironically, if the results of a survey sponsored by the magazine are any indication of current trends, they're fighting a losing cause. The survey from 2006 found that seniors and grad students were more likely than freshmen to believe in precognition, telepathy and other aspects of the paranormal, including ghosts and astrology. Other surveys conducted in recent years by the Gallup Poll and the Pew Research Center found similar results. Americans, especially younger ones, are increasingly open-minded to the paranormal.

As Kuhn wrote in his revolutionary scientific tome, change comes when the old guard die off and younger scientists with more open minds and fresh perspectives step in. He pointed out that the paradigm shifts have happened over and over again throughout the history of science.

In other words, Sheldrake, Bohm and other visionaries are in good company with the likes of three other previous outliers who rocked science.

Galileo

In 1609, the intrepid Italian astronomer began a serious observation and study of Jupiter and in January 1610, he discovered the four largest moons that orbit Jupiter: Io, Europa, Ganymede and Callisto. His discovery proved to be a critical curve ball for the geocentric scientific theories at the time that said all planets orbited Earth. It laid the foundation for the heliocentric model of the solar system: that all planets orbit the sun. Ultimately, Galileo's discovery also proved to be his nemesis. The Catholic Church contended that scripture was absolute about the sun moving around the Earth, and that Earth was, in fact, the center of the universe. The Church deemed Galileo's beliefs as heretical. In 1633, he was forced to recant his own scientific discoveries as "cursed." It caused him profound anguish but saved him from being burned at the stake. From 1633 to his death in 1642, he lived under house arrest.

The really appalling part of this story is that it took the Catholic Church 350 years to admit that Galileo was right—the planets do revolve around the sun.

Gregor Mendel

In the mid-1800s, the scientific consensus in biology was that all characteristics were passed to the next generation through "blending inheritance"—an idiosyncratic term that means the traits from each parent are averaged together. Then, along came Gregor Mendel who, through his work on pea plants, figured out that genes come in pairs and are inherited as separate units, one from each parent.

Mendel also tracked parental genes and their appearance in the offspring as dominant or recessive genes and recognized the mathematical patterns of inheritance from one generation to another. His laws of heredity can be broken down into three separate areas: that each inherited trait is defined by a gene pair; that genes for different traits are sorted so the inheritance of one trait isn't dependent on the inheritance of another; and that an organism with alternate forms of a gene expresses the form that is dominant.

He published his findings in 1865, but it wasn't until 1900, sixteen years after Mendel's death, that other biologists rediscovered Mendel's work. Over the years since, various scientists have tried to disprove Mendel's work, accusing him of falsifying information. Finally, in 2008, a book was published that settled the controversy—Mendel didn't deliberately falsify his results.

So, it took a 143 years after Mendel published his work for science to fully accept he was right. It's an example of how intractable scientific dogma can be.

Nikola Tesla

Tesla was a wild card, a brilliant eccentric who for years was best known because of his feud with Thomas Edison. Yet, more than 70 years after his death, he's now recognized as the inventor of alternating current, the harnessing of light, X-rays, radio, remote control, the electric motor, robotics, laser, wireless communication and even a device to harness cosmic rays to produce free energy.

Nikola Tesla arrived in New York in 1884 and was hired as an engineer at the Edison headquarters. He worked there for a year and at one point, Edison told Tesla he would pay $50,000 for an improved design for his DC (direct current) dynamos. After months of experimentation, Tesla presented a solution and asked for the money. Edison told him he didn't understand "American humor." Not surprisingly, Tesla quit soon afterward.

He tried to start his own light company, then dug ditches for two bucks a day, and finally found financial backers to fund his research into alternating current. In 1887 and 1888, he was granted more than 30 patents for his work and was invited to address the American Institute of Electrical Engineers. George Westinghouse was impressed with his lecture and subsequently hired Tesla, licensed the patents for his ACV motor and provided him his own lab.

In 1893 in Chicago, Tesla and Westinghouse lit the World's Columbian Exposition and partnered with General Electric to install AC (alternating current) generators at Niagara Falls, creating the first modern power station. Four years later, Tesla's New York lab burned and his notes and equipment were destroyed. He moved to Colorado Springs, then returned to New York in 1900 and was backed financially by J.P. Morgan. He started building a global communications network on Long Island, but funds ran dry and Morgan got fed up with Tesla's grandiose ideas.

Throughout this life, Tesla was persecuted by the energy power brokers of that era—Edison, Morgan and other heads of industry. During the last decades of his life, he lived alone in a hotel room, working on inventions as his physical and mental health decayed. On January 7, 1943, he died broke and alone in that room and on the same day, the US government moved into his apartment and confiscated all his scientific research. Some of this research has been released through the Freedom of Information Act.

These three men came up against the current scientific and religious dogma of their time, but as a result of their work, new paradigms were ushered into existence. In much the same way, scientists and researchers studying consciousness today are birthing a new paradigm about the nature of time and reality.

"I believe that we stand on the threshold of a new phase of science," writes biologist Rupert Sheldrake in *Dogs Who Know When Their Owners Are Coming Home.* "And precognition may be able to tell us something very important not only about the nature of life and mind, but also about the nature of time."

That said, mainstream science has made it extremely difficult to gain grant money to study precognition and other psychic abilities. As a result, very little laboratory research is taking place on the frontiers of consciousness. However, that hasn't stopped nonscientists from exploring realms beyond the borders of the everyday world. Today, popular workshops on the expansion of consciousness abound, ranging from meditation and shamanism to dream interpretation and out-of-body travel.

Mainstream scientists tend to reject studies of precognition that show positive results by labeling them "anomalies." As mentioned earlier, they also invoke the adage "Extraordinary claims require extraordinary evidence."

But there's also another reason for their unwillingness to accept precognition: It would overthrow the foundation of science that rejects the concept that the future can be known in the present. Other scientists, especially theoretical quantum physicists, say that quantum physics actually requires precognition to exist.

Ironically, when parapsychologists, such as Dean Radin, use statistics to show that precognition is real, skeptics are dismissive of statistical studies. Typical of this disdain is an article about Radin's research in the online *Skeptic's Dictionary*: "Nobody in his right mind will identify a statistically significant statistic as real evidence of precognition. To Radin and other psi researchers, I say: Just find one person who can reliably pick the winner at the race track or the state lottery, or give us fair warning of the next terrorist attack, and all skeptics will bow at your feet."

More likely they would point out all the times that the psychic was wrong, thus dismissing any hits as anomalies. Otherwise, they would be forced to change their beliefs about the nature of reality.

Tipping Point

But it seems that the tipping point is already happening. People today are far more willing to talk openly about their hunches and visions than they were 30 or 40 years ago. In the past, bookstores offered limited choices on books dealing with metaphysics. Stilted, jargon-filled tomes were bookended by skeptical rebuttals telling readers none of these things that interested them were real.

Then along came Shirley MacLaine's *Out on a Limb* and Oprah's book club. Suddenly, alternative "New Age" thought became commercially viable. These days, you can walk into your local Barnes & Noble and find New Age sections featuring a variety of titles on astrology, the paranormal and UFOs to popular science books that attempt to explain the weirdness. And then there's the Internet, where the right search terms yield innumerable sites that include many online workshops in the expansion of consciousness. Then there are the actual physical institutions that offer sources and courses about the nature of consciousness.

Notable institutions that explore consciousness include the Esalen Institute in Big Sur, California; the Institute of Noetic Sciences, founded by astronaut Edgar Mitchell; and the Monroe Institute, founded by engineer, author and consciousness explorer Robert Monroe.

The Monroe Institute

In the late 1950s, Robert Monroe, a radio broadcasting executive, was experimenting with sleep learning and began to experience strange sensations of paralysis and vibrations accompanied by a bright light that shone on him from an angle. It occurred nine times over a period of six weeks and resulted in his first out-of-body experience (OBE). In 1971, he wrote an account of his experiences, *Journeys Out of Body*, which was followed by two more books—*Far Journeys* in 1985 and *Ultimate Journey* in 1994. By then, Monroe had become a prominent researcher in altered states of consciousness and had established the Monroe Institute in Nellysford, Virginia.

In his book, *Ultimate Journey*, Monroe stated that during an OBE, "You can go anywhere in any time past, present, and future. You can go directly to any chosen place and observe what is there in detail and what is going on."

Nancy McMoneagle, Monroe's stepdaughter and director of the institute, agrees: "Bob's premise was that everyone goes out-of-body and often we simply don't remember it. So, sure, it's possible that someone has an OBE that later supplies a precognitive bit of information."

The institute hit the big time after *Omni* magazine ran an article about it in the October 1993 issue. The author of the piece, Murray Cox, recounted his experiences at the institute, where he took the Gateway Voyage, one of the many programs it offers in altered states of consciousness. Cox had an interesting take on Monroe himself: "Lying in my cell on the second day, I thought of Don Quixote whom Monroe reminds me of. Where Don saw giants, Sancho Panza, his sidekick, saw windmills. Gazing into a simple barber's basin, the Don saw the Shield of Mambrino and Sancho wondered, How can these things be? Monroe, I think, is a descendant of the Don, telling us there's more to reality than what we see or touch."

Ronald Russell wrote about Monroe's unusual journey in a 2007 book, *The Journey of Robert Monroe: From Out-of-Body Explorer to Consciousness Pioneer.* As McMoneagle says, the mission of the institute has always been to further the experience and exploration of consciousness, expanded awareness and discovery of self through technology, education, research and development. The institute's vision statement is the Global Awakening of Humanity, which is done by providing people with the tools to reach and explore expanded states of consciousness.

She notes that all programs "need to encourage curiosity, be fun, put the individual squarely in control of their own experience and how they want to constructively apply it to their own evolutionary process. In other words, there can't be any external locus of control, no religious or philosophical belief system or other dogma, and no program leaders can put themselves forward as a guru or authority over the individual."

Out-of-body experiences, then, may be one way to access the future. But what, exactly, happens during an OBE? As McMoneagle explained, during an OBE you may experience vibrations or sounds that herald a separation of consciousness from the body, a sense of falling, rolling or lifting from the physical body, and "a recognition of your personal identity in the nonphysical state—i.e., you're still you whether you're out of your body or not!" Even without input from your five senses, you *know* that you still exist beyond physical matter. During the OBE, your mental focus directs your experience.

What began because of Monroe's OBEs in the late 1950s has evolved into a smorgasbord of programs that expand consciousness and awareness about the true nature of reality and time.

The Nature of Reality

Bell's theorem (see Chapter 11), like Bohm's implicate order, like the holographic universe that Talbot wrote about, implies a seamless interconnection among all of us, more than seven billion souls on the planet. What affects one, affects all. We are like bees in a hive, birds in a flock, horses in a herd, dogs in a pack, linked as if by a single consciousness. We are the butterfly effect in chaos theory that says the flutter of a butterfly's wings on one side of the world may create a massive supertornado on the other side of the world. Or, put less poetically, small effects may eventually lead to much larger, unforeseen events.

Now more than ever, we live in an interconnected world—and it's not just technology in our daily world that connects us. Cultures worldwide have referenced an underlying reality where we are all connected.

The Hindu term *Brahman* refers to the fundamental connection of all things in the universe. The appearance of this universal oneness in the soul is called *Atman*. Zen Buddhism refers to *satori*, a sense of unity felt with the universe and an awareness of the compassionate intelligence that permeates the minutest details. According to Chinese philosophy, *chi* is the life force that permeates all things and empowers the universe.

These Eastern ideas parallel concepts of the noosphere, an idea created by Pierre Teilhard de Chardin, a French philosopher and ordained Jesuit priest. He was convinced of the existence of an invisible "ordering intelligence," a mental sphere that linked all of humanity. That's similar to Bohm's implicate or enfolded order, a kind of primal soup that births everything in the universe, even time, as we mentioned earlier.

In more modern terms, spiritual teachers talk about *Source*—the divinity within that unites us all.

The Time of Our Lives

Linear time only exists in our conscious mind. In the deeper reality, all time—past, present and future—unfolds simultaneously. When we live in the present moment, we recognize that the ultimate reality is an omniscient *now*. By working with our intuition and our awareness of synchronicity, we encounter premonitions and recognize precognition as an aspect of the expansive present. In essence, the present moment is a temporal hologram containing all time.

Epilogue

The beauty of sensing the future is that anyone can do it. All it takes is awareness, paying attention to the synchronicities you experience and creating an inner climate that is conducive to precognition. Once you experience it a couple of times, whether in your waking life or in dreams or other altered states, you may discover that it occurs more frequently.

If you keep track of these experiences, you'll be able to identify certain patterns that are unique to you. You'll know what signs and symbols to look for, how synchronicity is most likely to manifest itself for you in terms of sensing the future and you'll develop a deeper trust in your own abilities.

We would love to hear about your precognitive experiences. You can get in touch with us through the contact form at blog.synchrosecrets.com.

About the Authors

Trish MacGregor has been a professional astrologer and writer for more than thirty years. She's the author of several dozen astrology books and, for a decade, she and her husband, Rob, co-authored the Sydney Omarr series of astrology books. Her most recent astrology book is *The Biggest Book of Horoscopes Ever*. She has also written on dreams, the tarot and synchronicity.

As T.J. MacGregor, she is the author of 40 novels that have been translated into fifteen languages. She won an Edgar Allan Poe Award for her novel *Out of Sight*.

Trish lives in South Florida with her husband and daughter, Megan, along with a noble golden retriever and two cats. She can be contacted at: blog.synchrosecrets.com.

Rob MacGregor has written books on meditation, yoga, dream interpretation, developing psychic abilities and ghosts and haunting. His most recent books are *The Jewel in the Lotus: Meditation for Busy Minds* and *Bump in the Night: Ghosts, Spirits & Alien Encounters*. With Trish MacGregor, he has co-authored books on synchronicity, astrology and alien encounters.

He is also the author of 19 novels. His Will Lansa mystery series included *Prophecy Rock*, winner of the Edgar Allan Poe award, and *Hawk Moon*, a finalist for the same award. His adaptation of *Indiana Jones and the Last Crusade* was a *New York Times* bestseller. It was followed by six original Indiana Jones novels.

Index